FINDING INDIA

First published by Unicorn
an imprint of the Unicorn Publishing Group LLP, 2019
5 Newburgh Street
London W1F 7RG

www.unicornpublishing.org

10 9 8 7 6 5 4 3 2 1

ISBN 978-1-912690-54-1

Book design by Vivian@Bookscribe

Printed and bound in Turkey

FINDING INDIA

*A fifty-year magical,
medical odyssey*

MICHAEL FARTHING

UNICORN

CONTENTS

Finding India is dedicated to my family,
friends, colleagues and the many other contributors
who have joined me on this journey of discovery.

FOREWORD

by
Professor Dame Parveen J Kumar DBE, BSc, MD, DSc, DEd, FRCP, FRCPE, FRCPath, FRCPI
Professor of Medicine & Education
Barts and the London School of Medicine
Queen Mary University of London

Finding India is Michael Farthing's account of a fifty-year fascination with India. He weaves his personal experiences into the changing political and social Indian landscape, starting with his first overwhelming experience of India as a young man, to his more mature reflections later in life.

His first visit to India was in 1969, only 22 years after the end of British rule and India's establishment as an independent self-governing country. At the time he had just finished his third year as a medical student in London and it would be the last opportunity for a long vacation before continuing his studies. 'India appealed because it had a long history and an exotic culture', he writes. In the late nineteen-sixties many young westerners were attracted to visit India for various romantic reasons. For Michael, however, part of the appeal was to see 'the immense social, medical and healthcare challenges in a country with poor resources'.

Finding a suitable post as a medical student was a bit haphazard. He sent his CV to many organisations indicating that he had a good degree in pharmacology, had completed his basic pre-clinical studies and would be willing to do anything deemed helpful. He eventually received a reply from CCWM, the Congregational Council for World Mission, a successor organisation of the London Missionary Society and the Commonwealth Missionary Society. They invited him to join the team at the Church of South India Hospital in Jammalamadugu, Andhra Pradesh, South India, a place he had never heard of, but one which was to have a huge influence on his future career and thinking.

From the notes and letters he has always kept, he recorded a vivid picture of life and work in a mission hospital in a remote rural area.

The young Michael lived with a Scottish missionary family: a husband and wife, William and Margot Cutting, who were both doctors and their three children. Dr William Cutting had grown up in India where his father had also been a missionary doctor. He introduced Michael to medical practice, which included clinics he had set up in outlying districts. He and his wife were kind, supportive and inspirational.

Every day started with prayers in the hospital chapel before a long day of helping poor villagers who travelled miles by bullock cart to attend the hospital or visiting those in outlying clinics, who were unable to travel. Michael was welcomed by the team of Indian doctors who ran the hospital. Starting as a surgical assistant, he learned to perform some basic surgery and was also invited to re-organise the pharmacy, which he did most successfully. He admired what could be achieved with very basic resources; ideas that could be brought back to a high-resourced country like the UK.

In these early days in India, an enthused Michael visited other parts of southern India, including 'Ooty' or Ootacumund, in the Nilgiri Hills, 2300m above sea level where the British in Madras created a hill station to which they escaped from the summer heat. He writes about staying with families in Kerala, Bangalore and Madras, where he took a bus to visit the extraordinary Hindu temples at Mahabalipuram. Immersion in Indian life for three months also encouraged him to learn and absorb the ancient Hindu philosophy and culture. He wore Indian dress and bought a set of tabla, on which he practised late into the night.

As has happened to many visitors from the West, his experiences led to a profound change in the way he looked at the world. He admired the contentment and fulfilment that radiated from the villagers, even in their seemingly impoverished circumstances.

The lessons learned stayed with him and returning to his studies in London he decided to pursue research into intestinal infections, particularly those relevant to the resource-poor countries in the southern hemisphere. After graduating from University College Hospital Medical School in 1972 he held posts in Addenbrooke's Hospital, Cambridge and then went on to specialise in gastroenterology at St Bartholomew's Hospital (Barts), London, where I first met him.

The book is fascinating to read as Michael describes his personal experiences, but has used his usual academic rigour in research to pepper his comments with quotes from the experiences of other relevant literary authors.

A particularly delightful chapter in the book describes a period of six weeks in 1980 when he was invited to be resident doctor on the set of *Staying On*. This film was based on Paul Scott's Booker prize winning novel of the same title, which was a 'pilot' for the Granada TV serial, *The Jewel in the Crown*, on the last days of the Raj. The filming took place in Simla, a hill station in northern India in the foothills of the Himalayas, not far from where I myself had been educated in an old English boarding school. Michael describes daily life with the cast, including Celia Johnson and Trevor Howard. They stayed at Woodville Guesthouse, created out of the Summer Palace of the Maharaja of Jubbal.

When filming came to an end, Michael and his wife Alison stayed in Agra, where he writes about seeing the Taj Mahal at sunrise and sunset; here he also describes a memorable visit to New Delhi where they stayed with the Bhagwant Singh family, part of my own extended family, who were responsible for the creation of New Delhi, alongside Edwin Lutyens, in the early 20th century.

In the 1980s Michael was made a Wellcome Tropical Lecturer and held overseas posts as visiting lecturer and Assistant Professor in India, Boston and Costa Rica, before returning to Barts.

In 1990 he was appointed Professor of Gastroenterology at St Bartholomew's Hospital Medical College, and later Barts and the London School of Medicine and Dentistry, before going on to distinguished leadership posts at the University of Glasgow, St George's, University of London and then as Vice-Chancellor at the University of Sussex.

Since the Millennium he has visited India frequently, giving lectures in New Delhi, Mumbai and Kolkatta and continuing his medical research collaborations and exploration of the sub-continent, all described in this book. He also writes about the cultural links between Britain and India, in art, books, films and music and adds a historical note to each chapter, giving a synopsis of the political developments in India as they arose.

And yes, he did return to the hospital in Jammalamadugu in 2012 and visited an old friend. It was no longer the vital centre it had been, but India had moved on.

This book will be read with great pleasure by all those who love India and those who are interested in medicine in India. It will also attract many who would enjoy an account and introduction to India from an India enthusiast and a gifted writer.

PREFACE

I have never written a diary. Moreover, I had no pre-set ambition to assemble this collection of thoughts, memories, reflections, brief stories, ideas, experiences, journeys, friendships and steps in growing up, into a 'scrap book' of a narrative. However, when challenged as to why I had kept the letters, papers, bus and train tickets, shopping receipts, photographs, notes and a few brief chaotic accounts of events, and other fragments, then maybe I did have some vague plan. Suffice to say, I believe I always knew that the journey which began in 1969, just before the first manned moon landing, and which has continued for fifty years since, was never going to be a trivial life accident and, most likely, to be one that would have such a powerful and enduring effect on me. As I think now about completing the task, I realise that almost a lifetime has slipped through my fingers, this project being one of the threads that has held it together.

The process of pasting together these journeys, relationships and events into a cohesive whole has been challenging and exhilarating. The brain is a remarkable organ. Sometimes it has been possible to trigger the opening of otherwise dark residues of information just through the re-reading of a letter written several decades before but on other occasions doors remain closed and events refuse to come into daylight despite unremitting provocation. The delight in being able to recall a face in colour, in fine detail: a face that had not been physically in range for several decades and, at the same time, the deep frustration of reading my own sketchy account of an event or a weekend away with friends and having no memory of it whatsoever. The joy of being able to put a face to a name by bringing together a notebook entry and a photograph, and the relief of finding a detail in a letter that finally brings sense to a casual jotting, makes the process of discovery and revelation very different from sticking postage stamps in an album.

What is totally undeniable since I began to put together these personal observations and encounters in this vast region of the world, is that this ancient subcontinent of India has both changed beyond recognition and at the same time remained doggedly as it was more than a century ago, perhaps longer. There have been major advances, even in the time that I have been an 'India watcher', in the delivery of healthcare and education, in the development of science, information technology and culture, and a massive strengthening of the manufacturing base and the national economy overall. Being part of the new emerging and fastest growing economies is a great achievement and the envy of many in the West who witness collapsing markets and economic stasis. However, not all Indians have benefited from this progress, with many still living in abject poverty in the peri-urban slums around most major Indian cities and in some of the villages which still dominate life in the subcontinent. We should not forget, however, that since achieving independence from Britain in 1947, India continues to be the world's largest democratic state.

Finally, it would have been short-sighted and, indeed, reckless to have started this undertaking without recognising that many have been there before me. I mean of course foreigners, and especially the British; writing about India, recounting their experiences, lamenting its past glory, yearning for the freedom and escapism that a colonial, expatriate life offered 'up and coming' young men and women during the British Raj and the extraordinarily important series of novels, films and plays set in the country during a period that spans several centuries. In the words of the historical novelist, Hilary Mantel, 'novelists make history transparent'. In her 2017 Reith lectures she stressed the importance of bringing the dead to life in the novel, which is not always within the grasp of historians.

For some fine artists, India has provided an unparalleled inspiration for life-long creativity; of British painters, Howard Hodgkin is perhaps the most evident, with his India experience spanning more than fifty years and his India-inspired works constituting the largest body of work from a single region of the world. From 1965 until 2016, the year before he died, he would spend variable periods of time in India, up to several months at a time producing new work; he once said, 'I couldn't work without it.' Perhaps he captured this inspiration when he was interviewed in 1982 when he said, 'the way people live in India.... Everything is very visible somehow there. Life isn't covered up with masses of objects, masses of possessions.... All the functions of life are much more visible.' His India collection was the subject of a major new 2017 exhibition in the Hepworth gallery in Wakefield, Yorkshire.

Writers, film-makers and artists have used metaphors drawn from the Indian subcontinent to express emotions and find truths that might not have surfaced through more formal media. I have experienced and enjoyed many of these visual and literary works of art and other forms of creativity; I have used them as a way of charting and signposting my journey, physical and metaphysical, and telling stories which often describe people and places with greater honesty and with Hilary Mantel's assertion of the enhanced transparency of historical fiction.

APOLOGIA

There have been some critical accounts of the way in which India and its political masters have pursued development during the past sixty years. I read Ronald Segal's *The Crisis of India*, published in 1965, before starting out on my first visit. It made depressing reading then and remains a low point in India's recent, post-colonial history. Some of the facts around this time will emerge later but I was struck when I read the book again recently by Segal's remarks in the opening chapter, entitled 'A Visitor to India'. I quote, 'Much, if not most of what I write may be considered hostile and even hurtful to the Indian people. I do not mean it to be so. If there is that in Indian tradition, culture, and politics which I find repugnant, it is because I believe it to be hostile and hurtful to the Indians themselves, fortifying the ugly and cruel and destructive in their lives. Were I asked today by someone, "Do you like Indians?" I would only answer, "I like people – people are all I really believe in." His account is critical, and he did this previously in his important commentary, *Sanctions against South Africa*, for which he has perhaps more right to comment since he had lived a considerable part of his life in South Africa and it was his home country.

I would say, however, having made observations over fifty years rather than his visit that spanned a few months, that we should proceed with care before demanding radical changes in culture, religious or other beliefs and social structures of any nation state to those that might be closer to our own. We can give no assurances whatsoever that they could be implemented affordably, peacefully and with a measure of success that would allow a nation to move forward and transition into a new stable and viable entity.

Some years after I returned from my first visit, James Cameron's personal account of an Indian experience, *An Indian Summer* was published in 1974. It followed soon after he married for the third time, on this occasion to an Indian woman, Moni. In the Foreword, he writes in a similar vain to Segal; 'In this book I have said things which may sound critical, wounding, even angry. In expiation I can say that I have been as bitter about many societies, including my own. I do not mean to be hurtful to a warm and generous people who have never been other than kind to me; wherein I have seen things cruel and hostile it is because they are cruel and hostile to India itself. Only now, after 25 years of knowing India, can I make the presumption of claiming a small share both in its rare joys and its frequent sorrows.'

It is as if he had just read, assimilated and regurgitated Segal's sentiments. Both use the words, 'cruel', 'hurtful' and 'hostile'. Both viewed India during the first twenty-five years of its post-colonial period as journalists, and for Segal, in addition, as a political activist and son of the anti-apartheid movement in South Africa. Both were trying to see India as it was and where they thought it should be, and both were looking for a story, for an angle on a nation in difficulty. They did little in their accounts to reflect on the impact of direct British rule for more than a century, and a potent economic and political influence for at least two centuries before that. They did not consider the impact of two world wars in which the people of India had more than a passing engagement (more than a million Indians served in the military, 70,000 losing their lives) and the differing visions of Gandhi, Nehru and Jinnah for the future of this ancient, unwieldy civilisation, but newly independent nation, as it began to find itself again in the late 1940s.

I like J.G. Farrell's introduction to his 1971 *Indian Diary*, which he wrote when researching his Booker Prize winning novel, *The Siege of Krishnapur*, where he opens with the lines, 'The main feeling I have after my first twenty-four hours here in India is one of great security due, I think, to the lack of aggressiveness in the people.' These thoughts concur exactly my own early impressions. I will resist the temptation to fire gratuitous salvos at those individuals, faiths, politicians and political movements, local captains of industry and foreign powers that might at times have impeded change and progress but focus on the positive experiences at both a personal and wider social and intellectual level that have given me so much and that have allowed me to duck in and out of the penumbra of change.

George Orwell, in his essay, *Why I write* (1946) attests that 'there are four great motives for writing . . . Sheer egoism, aesthetic enthusiasm, historical impulse and political purpose.' I think he has missed one: pleasure, through reflection. My main aim in sharing *Finding India* is to bring to you some of the richness of the experience of people and places, of ideas and creativity, and place this honestly, alongside the bad fortune, failings and inadequacies of one of the world's great nations, which I have gathered over a lifetime.

EXTRACT FROM *PASSAGE TO INDIA*

Lo, soul, seest thou not God's purpose from the first?

The earth to be spann'd, connected by network,

The races, neighbours, to marry and be given in marriage,

The oceans to be cross'd, the distant brought near,

The lands to be welded together.

A worship new I sing,

You captains, voyagers, explorers, yours,

You engineers, you architects, machinists, yours,

You, not for trade or transportation only,

But in God's name, and for thy sake of soul.

Walt Whitman (1819-92)

First published in *Leaves of Grass* (1872 edition)

IN THE BEGINNING

Where from do all these worlds come? They come from space.
All beings arise from space, and into space they return:
Space is indeed their beginning, and space is their final end.

1.9.1 Chandogya Upanishad

From the beginning of time, humans have had an insatiable desire to try and make sense of the world and of their place in it. How was the universe created? Why do we do what we do? Why do we meet who we meet? Why do we fall in love? Why do we make the choices we make? And the perennial question facing us all – and that special challenge for the university undergraduate – what is the meaning of life?

So why did I get on a plane one day in June 1969 and take a flight from London Heathrow Airport to Bombay, stopping at Paris and Rome, with an overnight in Cairo and a further stop-over in blistering Doha before landing in monsoon rains at Bombay's Santa Cruz airport? We left on Saturday 28 June 1969 in the afternoon and arrived in the early hours of Monday morning. I never recorded my thoughts on the matter but I can only assume I was looking for something; an adventure, an exciting challenge, an experience that would change me, hopefully for the better, and possibly to begin to understand why the British had been so enchanted by that great nation for several centuries. Incidentally, I recently undertook a brief visit to Mumbai, essentially for a breakfast meeting, and completed the outward journey as a non-stop flight in about nine hours and the entire round trip in just over two days; less time than my first outward journey in 1969.

When I embarked on this first visit, I had just completed my third year at university. I was studying medicine in London and had taken a scientific interlude, a so-called 'intercalated degree' in pharmacology, before the move across Gower Street into the hospital for the three-year clinical part of the course. It was the last real summer vacation I would have; the 'normal' university terms would become history as the pattern of clinical study was more like real life, namely about forty-five weeks a year. There was the sense of *fin de siècle* or perhaps Henri Cartier Bresson's '*le moment critique*'!

The previous summer I had spent about six weeks in Poland at a General Hospital in Warsaw with Alan, a Jewish medical student friend from London. Eastern Europe was still closed off from the rest of the world in 1968. Most of our Polish hospital colleagues did not have passports and those that did were usually not permitted to leave the country accompanied by other members of their family, in case of course they considered not returning. We could not speak openly about politics, and anti-Semitism in the university was rife. Alan's relatives were university academics whose jobs were under threat, simply because they were Jews. We never spoke openly on their phone at home as they were certain that it was 'bugged'. The only places to talk freely were in the seclusion of the Łaziencki Park (although conversation stopped as we passed occupied park benches that were scattered along the many serpentine pathways that traverse the park) or in a sailing dinghy in the middle of Lake Zegrze outside the city. We did this on several occasions. We had travelled overland by train from London to Warsaw via Berlin; once through the well-lit West Berlin's Zoologischer Garten Bahnhof, we passed into 'blacked out' East Berlin. Here, heavily armed East German border guards entered the train to check our papers accompanied by a fleet of over excited, hungry dogs displaying teeth and tongues; German Shepherd's, I recall. I was frightened. Not something I had ever seen before during extensive travel with my parents in Western Europe.

Perhaps the most alarming interlude was on 21 August 1968 when Russian troops in tanks moved overnight into Prague (it felt like it was in 'the shop next door') to quell Alexander Dubček's enthusiasm for a more liberal Czechoslovakia. We were sitting in the surgeons' room in the hospital at around 8.00am, talking together as we did every morning, over coffee or black tea and sunflower seeds, discussing the order of the day, to be interrupted by an urgent news release on Polish radio announcing the Russian intervention. The Polish doctors were vitriolic in their attacks on the Kremlin and were fearful that Poland might be next. I was not especially concerned for my own safety but was bombarded by communications from my father who was in constant contact with the Foreign Office in London asking whether I should return to the UK immediately. The Czechs were put in their place and we returned to the UK safely at the formerly scheduled time. It would be another twenty-one years before the Berlin wall fell and Eastern Europe was finally liberated from more than fifty years under Soviet control.

The following day, in the early hours of the morning I was struck by a momentous diarrhoeal flux which kept me in the hostel bathroom for an embarrassing number of hours; toilets were limited in the soviet-style student hostel and I can only imagine I was branded by the locals as a 'toilet blocker'. In the same way that the derogatory term 'bed blocker' was used frequently in the '70s when I was a junior doctor, to describe an elderly patient who did not need to be in hospital but could not be moved out because social services had been unable to get its act together to secure an exit route. Plus ça change! At the time, I attributed the affliction to the sunflower seeds we had eaten in the surgeons' room during the crisis but having been a student of intestinal infection and acute diarrhoea for the past three to four decades, I now believe this was highly unlikely. I only dared to eat sunflower seeds again recently when I grew my own 'organic' sunflowers in the garden at home. Completely irrational!

The year before, I had spent both Easter and the entire summer vacation in France, in and around the delightful city of Grenoble. I had a French girlfriend to whom I was deeply attached and a growing – almost pathological – affiliation to French culture and a much slower developing facility with the French language. It had become an addiction. That summer I took a course in the University of Grenoble's medical faculty studying (in French) the use of radioisotopes in medicine, for which I received a *Diplôme*. The main, overriding reason to be there was to be able to while away the summer in an idyllic environment with a lovely woman. Sadly, for me at the time, it was not to work out but that is another story. As in Poland, I was with a student companion Tony, with whom I travelled at weekends to exotic destinations on the French Riviera, such as Cassis and La Ciotat, where we imagined we were the new generation of 'playboys' of the western world. We smoked Gitanes and Disque Bleu, travelled in a decaying, ginger brown and cream liveried Hillman Husky but were totally out-classed by a companion French medical student, also on the course, who raced to the south ahead of us in his new, lemon yellow Triumph Spitfire, accompanied by a devoted, willowy, 'Voguish model' female companion. By day we scuba-dived in the clear coastal waters that filled the space between the bases of steep rocky ravines, *les falaises*, which skirted that part of the Mediterranean and by night we slid from bar to bar before watching the tables at the casino in Cassis. Lunch was bread, tomatoes and cheese, and vin de table rouge.

So, the pressure was on. What adventure could compete with these experiences of the past two years? I guess it had to be further away, another continent and somewhere with greater risk, and possibly from something I would learn. I wanted my eyes opened wider and to gain a better understanding of the remoter corners of the world. Frankly, I am not sure why India was the place to be. British students were already travelling overland through Turkey, Afghanistan and Pakistan to Nepal where the main aim seemed to be to consume as much marijuana as possible during the summer vacation in a forgiving, non-hostile environment. This did not appeal. I had not been overwhelmed by its reported magical powers as an undergraduate in London and saw no reason why it should suddenly start working in Nepal. It was also clear that many travellers returned with a variety of ailments which involved the gastrointestinal tract such as Tropical sprue and which had the outward appearances of a severe dose of cancer, although it never was. The other diseases of the overland travellers were similarly unappealing. Earlier in the '60s the Beatles had been there on a voyage of discovery which coincided with a rise in the popularity of ashrams as places of spiritual retreat, usually accompanied by a change from European to Asian costume and plenty of sex. However, I am not sure my desire to see distant parts was any of these. I was emotionally too conservative.

India appealed because it seemed so far away, it had a long history and an exotic culture (about which at that time, I must admit, I knew very little) but the social, medical and healthcare challenges more generally were immense, and I judged it would be a good way to immerse myself in the practice of medicine before starting the clinical course in the autumn. Although I knew that the British had a long-standing relationship with India and of course I was familiar with the concept of 'the British Raj', I knew nothing of the detail of India's history during the past century. None of my family had ever visited the subcontinent and thus in its broadest sense it was truly a journey into the unknown.

I thought it would be easy to organise. The offer of three months unpaid full-time service in a voluntary hospital (I guess it would now be called the much derided 'internship') would seem to be an offer none could refuse. However, it was not so. I wrote many letters to a variety of organisations, but the answer was repeatedly, 'thanks but no thanks'. With the help of a clergyman friend of my father, I found my way to the Congregational Council for World Mission (CCWM), the successor organisation of the London Missionary Society and the Commonwealth Missionary Society, formed by a merger in 1966. I wrote on behalf of myself and another student colleague requesting a posting for the summer in a mission hospital anywhere in India. I was completely straight that I had not started my clinical training but that I had a good degree in pharmacology, as well as having completed the basic pre-clinical studies, and would be willing to do anything that they deemed helpful.

Much to my surprise and pleasure I received a response from a Rev. A.J. Todman on 13 March 1969:

Rev Todman letter: March 13, 1969. (Author's collection)

Dear Mr Farthing

I have great pleasure in letting you know that I have received a letter from the Medical Superintendent of the CSI Hospital, Jammalamadugu, S. India saying they would be very glad for both you and your friend to assist at their hospital during the long vacation. They welcome this suggestion of yours to go there and will look forward very much to having you with them. Dr Ratnaraj says that they would, of course, provide you with board and lodging and probably some pocket money. I do hope therefore that you will find it possible to go with your friend to Jammalamadugu.

He goes on to suggest that I write directly to the superintendent, Dr Ratnaraj and continues,

If you have any further questions you would like to ask please let me know. If you are coming this way in the near future, I could show you one or two transparencies of the hospital at Jammalamadugu which might give you some idea of the shape of the place.
With every good wish,
Yours sincerely,

A.J. Todman

I was ecstatic. I responded positively and asked about cheap travel to India and specifically whether there were any charter flights sponsored by the CCWM for their staff, and I must have mentioned whether travel by boat might be an alternative. He replied on 18 April that only CCWM personnel could have access to travel concessions but kindly suggested that I approach the Bible and Medical Missionary Fellowship to see whether they could help. His observations on sea travel are apposite:

With regard to sea passages, as you know all ships are having to go right round the Cape of Good Hope and the journey to India now takes five weeks. It would not therefore be worthwhile to go out by sea as all your leave would be taken up by travel.

The Arab-Israeli six days war ceased on 10 June 1967 following massive territorial gains by Israel, but in March 1969, almost synchronous with the flow of correspondence with the Rev. Todman, President Gamal Nasser of Egypt declared the peace agreement null and void. This intervention triggered the so-called 'war of attrition', which resulted in intense fighting around the Suez Canal and led to its effective closure to foreign shipping. This conflict was concluded by a new ceasefire agreement brokered by the Americans the following year in August 1970 with no substantial change in the territorial arrangements. The canal did not re-open, however, for international shipping until 5 June 1975. I suppose I should have kept a closer watch on Middle East conflict and its implications on travel to Asia.

As advised, I wrote to Dr Ratnaraj expressing enthusiasm about his kind offer but was rather taken aback, at least initially, by his prompt response on 25 April.

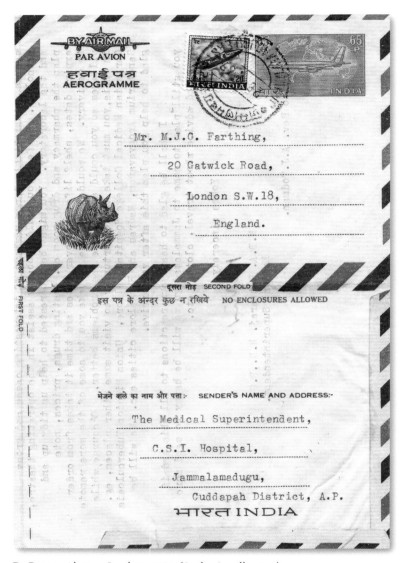

Dr Ratnaraj letter: April 25, 1969. (Author's collection)

Dear Mr Farthing

Thank you for your letter. It came as great surprise to us all that your companion is a girl, as there had been no indication of this from Mr Todman. I am sorry to disappoint you, but I am afraid that our social and domestic set-up is not geared to cope with young people of different sexes for a period of three months. You probably do not appreciate that in a rural Indian situation unmarried couples do not go around together, and this would either limit your activity or create misunderstandings and even problems among our own young people. We therefore feel that if you want to come with Miss Evans, it would be better if you arranged to go to a less rural place with a larger and more sophisticated institution like the Christian Medical College Hospital at Vellore. There, there are hostels for both men and women and a much wider companionship. It is still not acceptable for young unmarried couples to travel together in India. We would be happy to have you on your own or with another male companion.

As regards the opportunities here, there are so many patients that we do not have the time to teach formally. You would however be welcome on ward rounds and in the outpatients where you would certainly see an astonishingly large variety of interesting cases and gross pathology. We feel you could probably assist in the operating theatre, and the laboratory. You might be interested to help us tidy up and plan the pharmacy and drug room e.g. Listing drugs, prices, note expiry dates, shelf life, turnover rates and time it takes from order to delivery. We would also like to take you to some remote villages so you could appreciate the problems better. Of course, while in India, you must take the opportunity to visit some other places, e.g. Christian Medical College Hospital, Vellore, Union Mission Tuberculosis Sanatorium Arogyavaram, Madras and Bangalore cities etc. We will be glad to help you plan this after you arrive.

I shall be glad to hear your reactions to all this, and if you still plan to come to Jammalamadugu we will be happy to send more detailed advice about travel, clothes etc. Yours sincerely,

M.D.A Ratnaraj. M.B, B.S
Medical Superintendent

Copy to Rev. A.J. Todman

Clearly there had been a failure in communication at some point but there was no option but to follow one or other of the options outlined in his letter. Initially the social constraints he described came as a shock and my first thoughts were, 'What the hell am I letting myself in for?' Then there was a sense of exhilaration when I realised that this was a very, very different place from the one in which I lived and that I should go and find out more. I responded rapidly, indicating that I was keen to come and that my colleague would find another place to work in South India, which she promptly did. She found a sister hospital in Bangalore, about 270 km away, a distance which could be covered by bus in those days in about a day. The plan was that we would travel out to India together and then part company at the appropriate point on the railway line between Bombay and Madras.

Once the decision was made it was easy to see the benefits of what was on offer. An extraordinary place to be and to see, and from which to learn; and I would be alone. Alone, without a friend or a colleague. I realised that this might be a benefit. The last two summers I had been with a friend and in simple terms one was never alone and usually not lonely. However, travelling with another almost certainly impedes the meeting of others and reduces exposure to the unexpected. Great travel writers of the last fifty years or so generally all travelled alone, thrusting themselves into the new environment unprotected and unfettered.

And so, it was to be. Within a few days I started to receive useful information about the hospital, the climate and local environment and advice about travel. The first came on 11 May and was a long and I believe beautifully crafted letter from the nursing superintendent, Mollie Smith. Mollie, I was to learn later, was an English nursing sister missionary who had served in India, mainly at the CSI Campbell Hospital, Jammalamadugu for many years.

Jammalamadugu

11/5/69

Dear Michael

Hope you won't mind the familiarity, but we are mostly on Christian names terms out here and if you join us you will be also! Dr Ratnaraj was just going on holiday when your letter came and asked me to reply. I'm the Nursing Superintendent here, and you will probably stay with me at least part of your time! We are very happy that our letter did not put you off and look forward to meeting you early July. We will try and arrange something for Elizabeth also. Dr William Cutting (the other missionary here) is on holiday at present with his wife and family, and I have written to him to see what contacts he can make. I think our other CSI Hospital in Erode, further south, is quite a possibility. Anyway, we will let you know as soon as ever we can. Now business! If you can fly to Madras instead of Bombay the journey here is a bit easier, and we could probably arrange for someone to meet you and put you on the train. If this is difficult Bombay can be managed.

Yes, I advise you to get yourself vaccinated at once, and then early in June have TAB, and the middle of June cholera, inoculations. I think your own GP will do them, but if you have any difficulty contact the CCWM. (Vaccination is compulsory; TAB and cholera are optional but very necessary.)

'Vaccination' refers to smallpox. In 1967, just two years previously, the **World Health Organization** (WHO) estimated that fifteen million people contracted the disease and that two million died in that year. A vaccination certificate was essential to gain entry to India at the time and only ceased ten years later when the WHO announced the eradication of smallpox in 1979 following the highly successful global vaccination campaign. 'TAB' inoculation was for protection against two types of Typhoid, A and B.

Re clothes; cotton is the best! Drip dry is useful for ease of washing etc., and by July we shall have cooled down quite a bit, so terylene/cotton would be possible – but avoid nylon! You can wear shorts or long trousers, as you wish (I recommend at least <u>one</u> pair of trousers!) For travelling shorts are comfortable, and khaki is a good colour! For the hospital white is nicer but not essential. You'll need to change at least every day, but you can wash and dry things easily so three or four sets would be ok. If you wear trousers, a <u>slightly</u> wider leg than current fashion is useful – especially when sitting on the floor – but most Indian students are now imprisoned in drainpipes, so you would be in the fashion!!! Bush coats (short sleeved jackets) are cooler and more comfortable than shirts and are the usual fashion. Woven cotton underwear (vest and briefs) from Marks and Spencer's. Personally, I don't wear a vest, but men seem to! If you sweat a lot, it is useful and comfortable. You can get shorts, trousers, shirts, bush coats etc. all made here quite cheaply if you prefer to travel light with two sets and see what you want after arriving! Unless you hope to go to Kashmir you won't need anything warmer than one pullover! A lightweight mac might be wise – if we <u>do</u> get a monsoon you will be in time for it! A pair of sandals for the feet – you may take to the local variety when you get here. No one wears hats, but a pair of dark glasses is useful. Also, a <u>water bottle</u>!

I can't think of anything else, but perhaps this will stimulate questions from you! Ah yes, a pair of sheets and pillowslip and towel – we can help you out with such things in Jammi, but if you do any visiting you might need to take with you.

Looking forward to meeting you. We will let you know re Elizabeth.
Yours sincerely,

Mollie (Smith)

A letter, packed with useful information and full of good sense, warmth, charm and a wicked spark of humour, personal attributes which were revealed in greater depth during my time at the hospital. At the same time, there is a quaintness which gives it a flavour of those past times. I took much of the advice to heart, such as getting some clothes made locally on arrival, including trousers with a more generous cut, the local sandals (*chappals*) were a must, but gave the vest and bush shirt a miss. I did not take a raincoat, but the monsoon came to everyone's pleasure and relief and like everybody else I just got wet; although from time to time I do remember struggling the 300 metres or so across a sandy surfaced, waterlogged compound between the house and the hospital with an ancient, slightly limp umbrella left over from the British Raj, probably referred to as a 'gamp' (derived from Sarah Gamp, a nurse in Dickens's Martin Chuzzlewit), in those historic days! The protection offered was limited.

I think they were all embarrassed by having to decline taking the two of us but reluctant to work out how it could have been managed. It did not take long after arrival to work out why they were so concerned. However, the right outcome happened, and it was a better experience for both. William Cutting wrote again on 16 May, apologising for their reluctance to take us both but offering some alternative options for Elizabeth although by then the decision to go Bangalore had already been made. Within two weeks there was another delightful letter from Mollie with some more sound advice starting with a dress code for Elizabeth.

> *In case Elizabeth also wants advice on clothing the same general advice applies – cotton, drip dry, loose rather than tight, bright colours rather than pastel shades – and not too mini!!! Sleeveless frocks are now acceptable, especially in the towns, but legs are NOT much liked! Bangalore can be chilly (it is 3000 ft. above sea level) and so an extra cardigan and a good mackintosh are advisable.*

There followed some sound advice on anti-malarial prophylaxis, as both Jammy and Bangalore had mosquitos in abundance and the latter have '*outsize mosquitoes*'. Then came the shopping list!

> *William says will you bring for him DICHLOROPHEN, made by May and Baker – it's a treatment for tape worm. Don't know how much it costs, but about 12–20 doses. Also, we need some small clips for holding glass burettes to an i.v. stand (he said you'd have no trouble at all if I drew it! But I have my doubts!).*

Mollie interspersed the text with two charming sketches showing a clip attached to a stand and the other demonstrating how the clips then support a glass burette. I was in no doubt what was required with a combination of graphics and narrative.

> *They are just light springy metal, and you push the glass tube into them, and they hold it firmly – can buy them in Woolworth's or anywhere. If you get the idea, please bring three or four dozen. Thank you.*

With the foundations laid, Mollie then introduced Jammalamadugu and its environs. Today we would have gone straight on to the internet to find this information but back then the options were much more limited. The Rev. Todman offered 'one or two transparencies' to help with orientation (a kind offer which I did not take up). However, Jammy was very much off the map and I had little idea about the place I would soon be crossing the world to become part of. Mollie continued:

> *Jammy is hardly a town. Though I believe it calls itself one. But we aren't yet a municipality, and the population is only about 15,000. The hospital stands in a group of four large mission 'compounds' (fields) at one end of the village, about two minutes from the bus stand. We are 13 km from the railway (main Bombay–Madras line) and about ¾ mile from the Pennair River (which in monsoon times cuts us off from civilisation for one or two days at a time). There are low hills between us and the railway, and slightly higher ones eastward near Cuddapah (46*

km away). Soil is black cotton, our famous Cuddapah slab – hard granite like slabs 6-15 feet below the ground, which makes cultivation and trees and septic tanks and drains all equally difficult. Very dry and hot, sandy by the river, but quite a healthy place – and I think rather lovely in its own way. Grey stone walls and buildings which William says look like a cemetery, but I was born in Lancashire, so they look like home!! Language is Telegu. Hope the exams went well. Write soon re travel.

Yours sincerely

Mollie

Cuddapah slab is 'granite-like' as Mollie says, but is not granite; I discovered later, that it is a hard, black limestone. 'Black cotton', a soil found widely in the Deccan plateau is derived from the breakdown of basalt and other igneous rocks. The soil contains a high content of expansive clay which swells in the rainy seasons and forms deep cracks in drier seasons. It is an excellent soil for growing rice and cotton.

Within another few days there was a letter from William with recommendations about travel. We should use B.C. Buhariwala & Sons in Bombay as an agent to meet us and arrange the transfer from the airport to overnight accommodation in Bombay. They would organise rail tickets for the 'Madras Mail' (which connects Bombay to Madras) and put us safely on the train. This all sounded greatly reassuring. William goes on to describe the Red Shield Hostel and gave us the 'rough guide' to rail travel in India.

We will book rooms for you at the Red Shield Hostel in Bombay for the night of the 29th. This is run by the Salvation Army, and is not very luxurious, but it is quite a good area of Bombay, and you will meet a number of other Odd Bods who are in transit, and in general we have found it to serve the purpose.

We will book for you 3rd Class Sleepers on the Madras Mail Train that leaves Bombay on the 30th evening. This is a cheap way of travelling with economy and without serious discomfort. However, there is a very considerable demand for the tickets, some people queue for over 24 hours to get one, so it is better to get an agent to do the booking. We will ask Buhariwala to book Elizabeth to Guntakal, and you to Muddanuru.

From Guntakal we will have to make a further booking for Elizabeth for Bangalore. I think that we will ask one of our Indian Pastors there to do this, and also see that Elizabeth gets safely on the train. Mr Bussi Reddy is the Pastor and knows English well. Incidentally we will book Elizabeth as Elizabeth Smith, as I have forgotten her name, and Dr Ratnaraj has the letter with it somewhere in his office and we cannot lay our hands on it at this moment. (!) Elizabeth can get someone to meet her there, and we will meet you at Muddanuru station about 9.00pm and bring you the thirteen kilometres to Jammalamadugu that night.

William then provided more detail on the delights of rail travel.

3rd Class sleepers usually consist of wooden benches by day and three tiers of wooden bunks by night. You may need a simple sheet to put under and over yourself at night, and a foam or inflatable cushion-cum-pillow could add to your comfort with little extra weight, and these could be kept near the top of your suit cases. We generally eat Indian when travelling, but you could bring something with you. There is always coffee and fruit available at the stations, and a variety of Indian foods. You should ask your companions where the eating stops are and what they recommend. It would probably be wise to bring fairly large water containers for drinking water – they could be empty on the plane and filled at the Red Shield. Generally, we try to avoid drinking water at the stations unless we disinfect it with 'Halozone' (you can buy a small bottle of 'Halozone' tabs from most Boots stores, this disinfects water efficiently, but it has a fairly strong chlorine flavour – which you hardly notice if you are very thirsty).

William went on to briefly mention some tips on dress code, largely repeating Mollie's advice from a week or two before.

Do hope the exams go well and you are not too distracted. We look forward to having you here.

Sincerely, William

P.S. For ready cash – bring in a few notes. On unofficial exchange in Bombay you can get Rupees 22–25 instead of the official Rs.18. Taxis. Make sure the meters are on 'for hire' before you get in and pay a little extra for luggage.

So the plot was writ. There was still much to accomplish before the point of no return, the journey to Heathrow and embarkation on the United Arab Airlines (UAA) flight to Cairo and then onward to Bombay. Finals went well and we both got a First. I have no recollections whatsoever of the packing and other preparations, but I managed to get the Dichlorophen and the metal spring clips. I seem to remember I took a rather unattractive mid-blue cardboard suitcase which I expected to disintegrate at the slightest provocation, being familiar with a South London joke that was reverberating at the time. Why did all the immigrants from the Caribbean in the 1950s end up in Brixton? Because that's as far as you can get on a rainy day with a cardboard suitcase!

My overriding memory of the journey was the trepidation I felt about flying. Although I had travelled quite extensively through Europe with my parents as a child, it was always by train and boat. My father was totally phobic, pathologically fearful of air travel and sadly averse to any form of translocation away from home. Freud called it *Reiseangst* – profound travel anxiety. Mother had travelled as a young woman before the War and was convinced that seeing the world was a good thing to do. Father reluctantly succumbed to her perseverance. Thus, although I was accustomed to the concept of travel and modest adventure, the airplane was a new experience. Travel without my parents in the final year at school, and to France and Eastern Europe in my early university years, had been by car, train or boat; never by plane.

Taking off for the first time was horrific. I sat rigid in the seat, unable to look out of the window, my hands gripping the armrests like metal clamps and palms sweating profusely, waiting for the moment when the plane would stall and fall out of the sky. Every turn or dip of a wing was a fatal move, as was every bump from turbulence. However, we landed safely in Paris and the second take off for Rome was slightly less alarming. By Cairo I was almost a veteran. Two further take offs and landings made a professional out of me. I could almost have flown the plane myself; such is the arrogance of youth!

BOMBAY: FIRST IMPRESSIONS

Landing in the middle of the night at Bombay's Santa Cruz airport however was a very different affair, setting me back to below zero on the 10-point frequent flyer confidence scale. Anxiety levels began to increase when it became evident that the pilot was preparing for landing. UAA pilots, and by then I must have experienced two or three, seemed to have one feature in common; it appeared that they all began their aviation careers in the armed forces flying fighter jets. Instead of a smooth controlled turn, almost imperceptible, into final approach which I now know is the habit of senior pilots of British Airways and most other commercial airlines, they had a penchant for a brutally sharp banked turn, as if the manoeuvre had been performed with the flick of the wrist, and no sooner the turn had been achieved that same wrist flicked the plane back on to the required course to land. Manqué fighter pilots fully prepared for the next Arab-Israeli war! Sharp and snappy, but very bad indeed for the nerves of the inexperienced flyer.

However, the worst was yet to come. We were now racing towards planet earth at what felt to be an unreasonably high speed and an unnecessarily acute angle when I dared to look out of the window. The blackness was impenetrable. Then a few sparkling lights from roads or buildings began to appear and finally way ahead were the runway lights running away from us into the darkness. At this point the economy cabin began to fill with white, steamy smoke, billowing out from the region of the overhead lockers. More and more smoke, it just kept coming. Why was there no announcement? Surely the oxygen masks will drop at any moment?

Then there was a smell that I had not experienced before. A musty, dank, wood smoky smell; it penetrated throughout the cabin. My God, is the whole plane going to burst into flames? I found the courage to look again out of the window, expecting to at least see an engine on fire. However, nothing, just the darkness, the few sparkling lights; but now there was something new. Water! An endless expanse of water, as far as I could see. Was it the sea? There were no large lakes in the Bombay area that I was aware of. He must be making a landing on the sea. Oh my God! This is it! Smoke, fire and now water! Sure enough, he just kept going and as we descended, I realised that we were landing in rain, very heavy rain; we had hit the Bombay monsoon and the Santa Cruz main runway beneath us was indeed a lake. The plane finally hit the deck with a thud, water fountained up around the wheels and wings, and several rows of passengers behind me burst into applause; some cheered, some even sang what appeared to be a song of thanks. I assumed this was a special event because of the appalling conditions and the devilishly difficult landing; not at all, it was the local custom for many landings, especially for the internal domestic flights. There was no fire in the plane. The white, steamy smoke was water vapour, presumably related to the humid conditions outside the aircraft and the change in cabin pressure.

I should have added that the plane was a de Havilland Comet 4. Comets had been in the news some years earlier because of a questionable safety record. Several had fallen out of the sky due to structural problems related to metal fatigue; there was one memorable crash in India when observers reported seeing a 'wingless' Comet on fire racing to the ground. BOAC had handed on their fleet to other carriers by 1965 so it could well have been a 'used', ex-BOAC plane that had taken me to the Orient. The plane remained in service until 1981, largely under the control of the charter company Dan-Air (affectionately known at the time as 'Dan Dare' after the comic book hero), a forerunner of the budget airlines.

V.S. Naipaul also recalls a wet arrival in Bombay in the Foreword to *A Wounded Civilization*; 'The lights of Bombay airport showed that it had been raining; and the airplane as it taxied in, an hour or two after midnight, blew the monsoon puddles over the concrete.' He did not mention the smoky, rubbishy smell.

As we left the plane the smoky smell intensified; it was the odour of fires smouldering in the poor suburbs around the airport. This smell would become so familiar and evocative that it was almost reassuring to be aware of its presence. It became emblematic for future trips, the sign of arrival. Others have noted this distinctive feature. J.G. Farrell reports in the opening paragraphs of his *Indian Diary*; 'landing from the 'plane in Bombay I got a breath of that smoky, rubbishy smell that I remember from the poor parts of Morocco, Puerto Rico and Mexico, and from some parts of French bidonvilles. However, in Bombay it seemed to be all over the city, except perhaps in the magnificent Victorian-oriented Taj Mahal.'

'Bidonvilles' (literally translated as 'can towns') were the shanty towns which proliferated around the periphery of Paris and some other French cities in the 1960s and '70s. They were generally occupied by immigrants, usually the new arrivals. Like the slums of Bombay and other large Indian cities, that 'smoky, rubbishy smell' is one of the smells of poverty. Once experienced it is never forgotten and will not disappear until that poverty is eradicated.

The air outside the airplane was hot, motionless and laden with moisture. Humidity must have been close to 100 per cent. It was 1.00am at night. What would it be like in the morning?

After a tortuous journey through immigration, we suffered a deeply frustrating wait in the baggage hall. For many years after this trip I collected personal anecdotal data which convinced me that there was an inverse relationship between the level of development that a country had achieved and the transit time through immigration and the baggage collection facility; the less developed the country, the longer the transit. This held up for many years, but since 9/11 it is my impression that the situation has now completely reversed.

I prepared myself for the eventuality that the mid-blue cardboard suitcase might have disintegrated but not to see it at all was even more distressing. The khaki clad porters were only interested if you had a bag they could transport out of the baggage area for money. If you did not have a bag they were not interested. Unclaimed bags continued to circulate on the squealing baggage belt, but ours were nowhere to be seen. Then across the baggage hall I saw a disorderly pile of suitcases, holdalls and a random assortment of other bags and brown cardboard boxes, some spilling their contents on to the floor. There, nestling in this chaotic pyramidal discharge from the plane's baggage hold was my blue cardboard suitcase, still holding together and apparently still retaining its contents. The luggage had been helpfully removed from the baggage belt, but airport staff had failed to tell any of the passengers. It still happens today, even in advanced sophisticated airports. I grabbed one of the rusting, squeaky baggage trolleys and piled our luggage on to it. It had a mind of its own and only functioned if you pulled it backwards. The remaining hurdles of the health check (inspection of the vaccination certificate) and customs were by comparison covered without too much difficulty. I had to complete a Currency Declaration Form to be compliant with the Foreign Exchange Regulation Act, 1947. I declared £14 in notes and £60 as travellers' cheques. The form was stamped, signed and dated by a customs officer. At the bottom of the form was a *Nota Bene*:

(a) *Passengers are advised that the foreign currency and special rupee notes cannot be exchanged in India except on presentation of this form to a Bank or Money-changer.*

(b) *Visitors to India may please note that in case they do not wish to encash all the foreign currency/special rupee notes declared above they should retain this form with them for the production to the Customs at the time of their departure to enable them to take with them the unutilised balance.*

(c) *TRAVELLERS CHEQUES NEED NOT BE DECLARED*

It seems extraordinary in today's environment that monitoring of these relatively trivial amounts were being checked so closely. There is now no limit on the amount of foreign currency that can be brought into India, but a currency declaration is required on entry for amounts exceeding USD 10,000, the equivalent of about £6,250.

By the last week of September, I had amazingly only exchanged £5 in cash and £15 as travellers' cheques. I had survived on this and the small stipend provided by the hospital in local currency. The value of the pound sterling in 1969 translates to a current value of anything between £13 using Retail Price Index or £28 using Per Capita GDP. So, I travelled to India in 1969 with £74 which would equate to an equivalent today of between £962 and £2,072 to cover about a three-month period. When viewed in those terms I would guess it sounds quite reasonable.

A Buhariwala agent was waiting in the reception area bearing a sign carrying our names. It was a most welcome sight. We had arrived! Someone else could take responsibility for the next stage of the journey. He took our baggage trolley and it seemed to behave better immediately under the instructions of its new master with local knowledge. We waited at the kerbside outside the arrivals area. The air was warm, still and felt very wet. I was overcome with a massive sense of exhaustion and became rapidly aware that I was sweating at a rate never previously experienced. My shirt was drenched. My face was dripping. Within a few minutes a dark blue dilapidated eight-seater van pulled up beside us. Our bags were thrown roughly into the boot space behind the final row of seats while we were ushered into the tired, well-worn and deformed seats behind the driver. Our man from Buhariwala climbed into the van and sat behind us. He spoke modest English and was disinclined to engage. It was by now about 2.30am. He handed me a small brown envelope.

'This is for you, Sir. From the hospital. From a Dr. Cutting.'

It contained a small brown postcard from CSI Hospital, Jammalamadugu, dated 25 June 1969, just nearly three weeks earlier. The light in the van was poor; there was just sufficient from that in the street outside to be able to read the message.

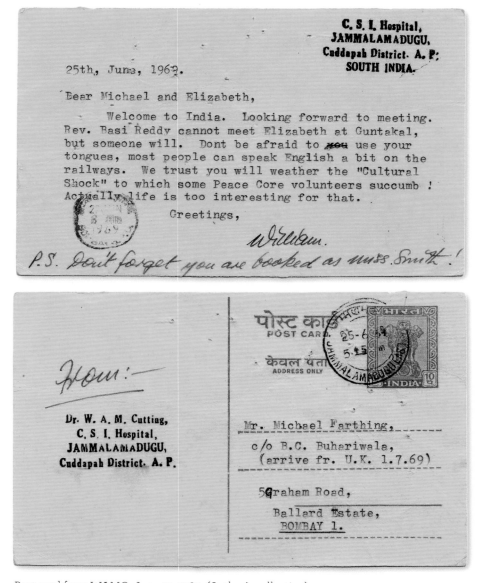

Post card from WAMC: June 25, 1969. (Author's collection)

Dear Michael and Elizabeth

Welcome to India. Looking forward to meeting. Rev. Basi Reddy cannot meet Elizabeth at Guntakal, but someone will. Don't be afraid to use your tongues, most people can speak English a bit on the railways. We trust you will weather the 'cultural shock' to which some Peace Corps volunteers succumb! Actually, life is too interesting for that.
Greetings,

William

P.S. Don't forget you are booked as Elizabeth Smith!

Good to know that we were still expected and that the detailed preparations before leaving England were working out, although we were slightly taken aback that we might be seen to be travelling as another 'Mr and Mrs Smith'.

We were too tired to talk and too tired and uncomfortable to sleep. So, I contented myself with the view from the window at my left shoulder, which provided a constant display of moving images such that I had never seen before. The van's noisy, ancient engine spluttered as we began to gather speed on leaving the airport precinct and joined the main highway in the direction of the city centre.

The journey through the outskirts of the city was unforgettable. Despite the late hour, life at the roadside continued apace and I assumed would do so until dawn. The city never sleeps. However, the roadside activity was not what I was accustomed to. Groups of men were sitting on the ground in their scant shirts and *dhotis*, some just in a *dhoti*, watching a fire, drinking tea, smoking a *beedi* (or *bidi*; tobacco wrapped in a tendu leaf) or a cheap cigarette, mending a broken rickshaw or just sleeping in the night air on a simple cot, some on the ground itself. Behind the 'night watch' were endless rows of primitive shacks – some single roomed homes, others fashioned into a simple workshop or café. Interspersed amongst this impoverished 'ribbon development' were the food vendors. Mainly fruits and vegetables and of course the ubiquitous street eateries whose owners, I subsequently learnt prepare *chaat*, samosas and, commonly in Maharashtra, 'pav-sample' – bread or other food with sambar. The entire scene was backed by lilting, evocative Indian music emanating from rasping speakers from another age and the all-pervasive smoky, rubbishy smell which was now stronger and accompanied by spirals of wispy rising smoke. Amongst these poor human street dwellers were their thin, undernourished animals. Black water buffalo, their shiny skin drawn tight over a protuberant skeleton, skulking in the shadows, and solitary dirty white cows, ambling along the roadside oblivious of other road users, idly seeking edible residues to fight the constant battle against hunger and to stay alive. A pile of rotting vegetable matter appears in a clearing between the shacks. Amongst the composting mass are two pigs 'truffling' for nutritious jewels to eat in the debris. Dogs sleep stretched out wherever they can find a space. The scene at that moment was not something I had ever seen before. The degradation of humans living so close to the ground, meddling with the unspeakable debris of existence, was totalling shocking. Was this the worst it could be or was there still more to come? Of course, there was worse to come but for the first night it was enough. I had never seen poverty exposed publicly before. I had never experienced street dwelling on this scale. I had not imagined that the sidewalks along a major thoroughfare would form the muddy, puddled living space for so many people and their animals. Was this not one of the major commercial centres of India? Was it not the home of the rapidly emerging Indian film industry that would soon be making more films each year than the rest of the world put together?

Sign outside Red Shield Hostel, Bombay, 1969.
(Author's collection)

At about 3.00am our blue people-carrier van came to a halt outside the Red Shield Salvation Army Hostel. This was to be our home for the night and most of the following day. A dim flicker from a bare light bulb produced a glow sufficient to outline an open street door, a small square vestibule and stone steps disappearing upwards into the gloom. A night watchman sat motionless behind the door and with a minimalist gesture signalled to us that we should ascend to the floor above. Buhariwala unloaded our bags into the doorway and arranged a rendezvous for 7.00pm the following evening. Their responsibilities would not be fully discharged until we were transported from the Red Shield to the mainline station and settled on the Madras Mail that departed at around 10.00pm.

The Red Shield was a simple place. The facilities were basic but after travelling for almost two days with the tiredness that inevitably follows, the immediate temporary surroundings were largely irrelevant. The temperature and humidity of the rooms remained high despite the late hour. The ancient ceiling fans lumbered noisily in their fixed orbits, pushing the warm damp air around the building, providing minimal relief. We climbed another two floors up the stone staircase and were shown into single sex, eight-bed dormitories. There was an unpleasant stale smell of humanity in the room allocated to me and the soft sounds that accompany sleep. In the darkness I was unable to determine how many of the beds were occupied. After placing the blue cardboard suitcase under my allocated bed, I lay on top of the firm mattress and parted company with my surroundings by rapidly entering the safe world of sleep.

It became clear at around 6.30am that my alimentary tract had not come through the journey unscathed. I awoke with nausea, abdominal cramps and rumblings, followed rapidly by a very serious signal that a visit to the bathroom was required. My first experience of the traditional Indian toilet was not without challenge. Two footrests separated by a black circular hole in a rather worn, stained white ceramic square was what was on offer. A smooth brass tap with a short length of flexible hose attached was the only other addition to the set up. I searched anxiously for toilet paper or a roll of tissue but was disappointed. I put two and two together and did it the Indian way. It was to be some days later after arrival in Jammalamadugu that I would learn the importance of delineating precisely between the role of the right hand for eating (in traditional Indian homes at that time the knife and fork were not used for eating, only the right hand) and the left hand for assisting cleansing of the perineum after defecation. This was indeed a different world, although many of us will recall that a similar toilet arrangement was common in France at the time and is still available in many of the *Aires* that pepper the margins of French auto-routes to this day. One is grateful however, for the addition of toilet tissue (usually provided) and a wash basin with warm water and liquid soap outside to complete the lavatorial ritual. My advice is to use the facilities for the disabled whenever possible, as the internal furnishings will be more familiar to the voyager Brit.

Fortunately, the bowel disturbance resolved within a few hours and by tea-time later that day, after a brief excursion on foot around some of the local sights in the vicinity, we indulged in the luxurious surroundings of the tea lounge of the famous Taj Palace Hotel. At the time, I believe the Taj Mahal Palace, Bombay was the most glamorous hotel in India. The hotel was commissioned by Jamsetji Tata (founder

Taj Mahal Palace Hotel, 2010. (Author's collection)

of the Tata Group and father of Ratan Tata, who succeeded him as head of the 'Tata Empire'); construction started in 1898 and was completed in 1903. Jamsetji Tata died the following year. The hotel was designed by Indian architects, Sitaram Khanderao Vaidya and D.N. Mirza, in the splendid mix of imperial and Mughal architectural motives, but completed by an English engineer, W.A. Chambers. It rapidly became the preferred watering hole of the rich: wealthy Indians, for whom it was an elite venue for weddings on a grand scale, and rich Europeans and Americans who want to taste the past splendours of the Orient. In 1947, it became a place of political significance, as a home for the Indian Freedom Movement and Sarojini Naidu, first woman President of the Indian National Congress, and Muhammad Ali Jinnah, the founder and future leader of Pakistan; both would use the hotel facilities to promote their cause.

This glorious history which gave the building its iconic status, became its downfall, as like the World Trade Center twin towers in New York City, it became a terrorist target in 2008 during the 26/11 attack on several public places in central Mumbai. The building was besieged for three days; about 200 people were taken hostage, but all were rescued without loss of life. Unlike the reconstruction of 'Ground Zero', which was argued about for almost a decade, the Taj Group of Hotels began reconstruction immediately and the hotel was open again for business, albeit in a somewhat compromised state, within months. I stayed in the hotel in 2010 when most of the major external structural work had been completed but the interior décor in the reception area was still on-going. By June 2011 when I visited again, the hotel was fully operational and restored to its former glory.

Today security is high. The hotel is surrounded by robust vehicle-proof barricades and taxis must drop their passengers on the street outside the fortifications. It is an unattractive option in the monsoon rain, which I encountered during one of my recent visits. Bellboys and porters handle it all with great cheer and a multitude of capacious golf umbrellas. Everyone entering the hotel is scanned by a metal detector and the comings and goings recorded by CCTV. An elite military response force is now based just behind the hotel in an adjoining street. Despite this appalling recent history, the hotel personnel are amongst the most courteous and helpful that I have encountered and give their fortress hotel a warmth and charm that fully compensates for the enhanced security.

Tea at the Taj was in 1969 – and remains so to this day – a treat. It is quintessentially English, with all the trappings of an English 'tea experience': the finest teas from India (Darjeeling, Assam, Nilgiri and many others), exotic coffee from India and other locations around the world, a selection of finely cut, white bread sandwiches with traditional fillings and an array of cakes and pastries that should carry a warning, 'this could damage your health'. I returned to the Taj Mahal Palace in 2012 and took the opportunity to re-run this experience in the beautiful Sea Lounge overlooking the Gateway of India and the Arabian Sea beyond. Like Raffles in Singapore and The Peninsular Hotel in Kowloon side, Hong Kong, many have taken the opportunity to recount their experiences. J.G. Farrell, on page 2 of his *Indian Diary* notes that there are 'people everywhere, one has never seen anything like it; the crowd on the roads and in the streets, only wealth gives you a little peace: you can withdraw to the Taj Mahal for tea or sit in the first class on a train'. He must have enjoyed people watching and continues: 'In the Tea Lounge of the Taj Mahal a group of young Indians talking very loud and possessively about Europe.' So perhaps the British Raj had not destroyed totally an interest in Europe in the new generation of Indians. I was also perversely reassured when towards the end of *Indian Diary*, I discovered that Farrell had experienced a similar abdominal disturbance in a Salvation Army facility in Calcutta towards the end of his tour. 'First day spent entirely in the Salvation Army Hostel with volcanic diarrhoea, the worst I can remember. The first twinges became apparent on the train from Benares, a journey passed comfortably enough on a hard wooden three-tier sleeper in third. An hour after arrival in Calcutta I was as weak as a kitten.' Unusual however for him to be hit by a diarrhoeal illness, three months after arrival as it normally occurs much earlier.

We were too exhausted to talk, so 'people watching' was the name of the game. In the window, sitting at a sizeable circular table, was a spirited, extended Bombay family enjoying colourful inter-generational exchange. An American couple, silver haired and beautifully dressed and groomed, talked animatedly about the day's adventures but taking coffee rather than traditional tea. They reminded me of my adopted American aunt and uncle, 'Dorothy and Norval from Boston and Maine', pre-war friends of my mother who had visited us in England on several occasions. On one visit in the mid-'50s they took us to Brighton for the day; when asked whether my brother and I would like to drink a Coca Cola (a 'Coke') we of course said yes but were completely amazed when a traditional Coca Cola branded orange coloured wooden crate arrived containing at least a dozen bottles. Our first experience of American post-war affluence. Dorothy and my mother would exchange letters very regularly every month or two (even during World War II), as was still the custom for people of that generation living far apart.

After tea, we left the hotel and walked across the Apollo Bunder to view the Gateway of India. The sun remained well above The Gateway, but the rippling Arabian Sea was beginning to pick up its golden light like creases across a giant mirror.

Howard Hodgkin, *Arriving*, 2013–2014, oil on wood. (© The Estate of Howard Hodgkin, Image courtesy Gagosian)

There are many images of this iconic entry point into India, but I especially like Howard Hodgson's abstract painting, *Arriving* (2013–14, oil on wood) which seems to catch the arch, the waves and the light and wraps them together as a welcome to Bombay, painted I guess in his small Mumbai studio. A warm breeze was gathering, which helped to freshen the sultry stagnant air that was hanging over the southern reaches of the city. There was no time for a full city tour but with some trepidation we flagged down a black and yellow local taxi. We asked for the 'Hanging Gardens', which we had worked out were about 8 kilometres away at the top of the Malabar Hill. We were relieved when the driver activated the meter, which was mounted precariously on the outside of the vehicle on the passenger side. Its loud mechanical ticking was curiously reassuring; we perhaps believed, naïvely, that at least we would not get ripped off on the fare. We followed the journey on our city map along Marine Drive, which circumnavigated the Back Bay. As we approached our destination and began to climb the hill towards the gardens, we caught brief glimpses of the circling vultures that 'service' the Towers of Silence or *dakhma*, the funeral site for Bombay Parsees, a tradition that has existed for some 3,000 years. This unusual burial site, used only by Bombay's 45,000 Zoroastrians, rests in 54 acres of forested parkland within the city, in the elite residential area, the Malabar Hill. Zarathustra declared that the dead body was impure both physically due to infection and decay, and spiritually because it had become invaded by evil spirits. Engagement of scavenger birds in the process would ensure that these elements would be removed. In recent years there has been a crisis because of the dwindling population of vultures, due to contamination of beef – which they were fed in between the arrival of dead bodies to retain them on site – by a noxious anti-inflammatory drug used in animal husbandry. While attempts have been made to re-establish the vulture community, other methods such as solar concentration are being used to dispose of the dead in the meantime.

Eventually we reached the Hanging Gardens, which were constructed in 1881 over the top of Bombay's municipal water reservoir. The gardens were fastidiously designed with endless hedges incorporating animal topiary. The views to the west across the Arabian Sea were spectacular and increasingly dramatic as the sun drifted towards the horizon.

We had asked our driver to wait during our brief tour of the gardens after which he delivered us back to the Apollo Bunder for a final look at The Gateway before returning to the Red Shield to collect our bags and make the final short step to Victoria Terminus.

We strolled around the stone paved area in front of the massive arch, built of yellow basalt in honour of King George V and Queen Mary's visit to India for the Delhi Durbar in 1911. We were approached repeatedly by street vendors with a range of goods, none of which were very appealing. We were offered the usual postcards, replicas of the Gateway and a variety of snacks of questionable provenance. I eventually parted with a few rupees in exchange for a folding pack of photographs of the key tourist attractions in Bombay. I thought this would solve the problem and the pestering would cease. However, it had the opposite effect and only encouraged other vendors to try and match the success of their colleague. There was only one thing to do and that was to escape. We walked briskly and determinedly away from the square in the direction of marine parade to watch the reddening sun on its final journey towards the ocean.

At that time, I had not heard the famous quote about the 'the Empire on which the sun never sets', although latterly it was often used to indicate the breadth of the British Empire. Its origin is thought to date back to the sixteenth century when it was used as a description of the Spanish Empire. So, as the sun was setting this night on Bombay, it must have been rising on the then remaining British islands in the Caribbean. Of course, in 1969 the Empire was gone but only by just over twenty years, well within my parents' memories, both of whom were alive, well and still working at the time. The Commonwealth remained, but in a condition, that can only be regarded as vestigial compared to the Empire at its peak at the turn of the twentieth century when it had penetrated all continents of the world.

BUHARIWALA AND THE MADRAS MAIL

At about 7.00pm we were collected from the Red Shield by Buhariwala and transported to Victoria Terminus, or Bombay VT as it was affectionately known, the largest and most important of India's railway stations and the headquarters of Indian Peninsula Railways.

The station is a massive Victorian Gothic construction in Indian red sandstone and limestone, adorned by details in Italian marble. It was designed and built by Frederick William Stevens in a celebratory style reminiscent of St Pancras station, which was created by another great British architect, Gilbert Gilbert

Victoria Terminus, Bombay, 1890s. (Wikimedia Commons/Samuel Bourne)

Scott. The building was opened in 1887 to celebrate Queen Victoria's Golden Jubilee. In line with many other politically driven 're-namings' in India during the latter part of the twentieth century, in 1996 VT became CST, Chhatrapati Shivaji Terminus in recognition of the legendary Maharata king and warrior, Shivaji.

The journey from the Red Shield was short and it was clear from the start that they were keen to see us on our way. As we disembarked the blue van and our luggage was stacked on a porter's barrow, I became aware that the station was a living organism. The main entrance hall was seething with men, women and children bearing a cornucopia of baggage and packages, all seeking their trains of the night. Many groups of travellers carpeted the stone floor between the marble columns of the ticket hall, creating an amorphous mass of humanity resigned to their fate of a wait and then a long journey through the night, and like us many would still be on the train well into the next day. Sometimes it was impossible to distinguish the bags and baggage from sleeping human forms concealed head-to-toe beneath sarees or *dhotis* or just loose bed sheets. Smooth, dusky humps like sand dunes in the twilight.

The Victorian grandeur of the dark, poorly lit railway terminus was now overpowered by the apparent abject poverty of many of the customers of Indian railways who thankfully can travel many hundreds of kilometres for a few rupees.

We followed the Buhariwala agent who stayed one step behind our porter; he pushed his barrow slowly but decisively towards Platform A, where the Madras Mail awaited us. We were booked in a Third-Class Sleeper. This decision had been made for us by William Cutting, through Buhariwala, whose primary concern was to minimise the cost of travel for two impoverished students. The classification of the travel opportunities on Indian railways was extensive and complex in 1969 and remains almost unaltered to this day, perhaps with the more recent addition of First-Class air-conditioned accommodation which was certainly not plentiful forty or more years ago. There are at least ten classes, ranging from the top: First-Class air conditioned with high-quality sleeping facilities, through Second- and Third-tier Sleeper, down to the lowest class known as 'Unreserved or General Class' (UR/Gen), which guarantees you a place in the carriage but that is all. No seat and certainly no sleeping place. This accounts for the frequent sight of passengers filling the walkways and corridors, with some clinging to the outside of the train as they speed through the Indian countryside. They have an UR/Gen ticket but there is no seat and no room left in the corridor or other public areas.

When the porter arrived at our appointed carriage, he began to unload the luggage speedily from his barrow, pushing our suitcases energetically through a carriage window. One by one they disappeared into a black abyss, an entry route apparently determined by the impenetrable accumulation of bodies and baggage on the carriage steps and in the corridor. I looked through the window to see where our bags were going and saw nothing but people. Passengers appeared to be piled three-deep like pilchards in a tin. I then realised that each of the three wooden tiers on either side of the compartment was already full of people. How would we claim our wooden tier and secure our berth? The idea that we could cope with a twenty-four-hour journey through India in those surroundings seemed utterly impossible. We made a rapid decision to try for an upgrade.

'How much would it cost to move to First Class? Is it possible at this late stage, so soon before the train departs?' I asked the agent.

He made an irritated, inaudible response and simultaneously sent the porter into the train to recover our bags; he then engaged in a pressured conversation with what seemed to be a responsible person in the Indian railway's hierarchy. Without any further discussion, we, with our luggage on a barrow, were hustled by our man from Buhariwala to the front end of the train and were shown into an empty compartment with two padded benches, above which there were two further cushioned benches, which I presumed were the sleepers. Piled at one end of each were a folded cotton sheet and a small pillow.

'This looks much better,' I said in a more optimistic tone, 'but what is the difference in price?'

'Buhariwala will buy new tickets and send account to Dr Cutting.' The guard issued us with a piece of paper indicating that we had been upgraded but no one asked to see our tickets again for the rest of the journey.

'But we should know the cost. How much will it be?'

By this time the agent was obviously getting impatient and bored with our company. The hour was late, and he wanted to be away.

'Sir, the train is leaving in two minutes. There is no time. Have a good journey. Don't forget, Miss Smith, you get off at Guntakal and Mr Farthing you stay on train until Muddanuru. You should take your breakfast at the station in Solapur. Safe journey.'

We were no longer in full control of our destiny. However, it was with some relief that we could sit quietly in a relatively cool and empty compartment of an otherwise seething train to recover from the evening's exertions and to be thankful that we were about to begin the 1,500-kilometre journey south to have, what would turn out to be, the opportunity of a lifetime. As the doors were slammed shut along the train and whistles blew it was obvious that there was no going back. With a final penetrating whistle from the steam engine itself, the massive metal serpent, the Madras Mail, began to move forward at just about 10.00pm, its wheels squealing and squirming against the metal rails pushing out of the station into the dark. The yellow lights in our compartment flickered with uncertainty, but stabilised as the train gathered speed. The evening air entered the carriage through a half-opened window in the compartment door, but it soon became evident that this was not without penalty. Whilst drawing in some freshness to the otherwise stale atmosphere, the breeze carried a multitude of tiny soot particles that were being discharged continuously from the engine's coal fire. The decision to close the window to all but an inch or so was uncontested.

For the first thirty or forty minutes, we watched the lights of Bombay dance in the distance as the Madras Mail cut its way through the southern reaches of the city when it finally entered the blackness of the progressively rural aspects of the state of Maharashtra. We agreed rapidly that this was the moment to retire to the sleeping bunks and within a few minutes, lulled by the rhythm of the train on its tracks, I fell into a deep sleep. Central India was lost to my dreams and sadly daylight did not come soon enough before the early morning pause at Solapur for breakfast.

I was hungry. I cannot remember when we last ate, possibly in the tea room in the Taj Palace, but I

Chai wallah mixing and cooling tea, 1969. (Author's collection)

remember the smell of frying eggs in oil, of the all purveying aromas of masala and steamy boiled rice and the high-pitched calls of 'chai, chai ... chai, chai' from the drinks vendors who ran up and down the platform with an undying enthusiasm to make a sale.

The chai wallahs demonstrated unbelievable skill in pouring a fully assembled cup of tea (tea, condensed milk, sugar and sometimes a secret ingredient such as garam masala or ginger) from the curvaceous spout of an aluminium tea kettle or another vessel into a small glass or metal cup separated by at least a metre. The kettle was held high in one hand and the glass held low, almost to the ground, in the other. A theatrical process, I understand, to ensure complete mixing of the preassembled ingredients combined with a cooling effect, making the tea ready to drink. There were other vendors racing up and down the platform with plantains, oranges and a limited number of other fruits. Still more were offering local cigarettes, *bidis* and *pan* (grated betel nut, slaked lime and spices), a popular option to chew after a meal. The remnants were spat out when the goodness had been extracted and left the tell-tale dark red stains on the platform and walkways. Others pushed carts containing a selection of traditional sugar-laden sticky sweets. I took a fried egg, buttered toast, tea and an orange. Eventually the train let out a rasping, steamy whistle, signalling to the vendors that it was time to scuttle from the train back on to the platform. The train slowly picked up pace and we were on our way south once again. We were forced to close the window as the flow of black particulate material from the engine had started again.

We spent the rest of the day on that train watching the landscape change as a constant series of moving pictures framed by the window in the compartment door. Sadly, my memory of these twelve or so hours is imperfect. In an odd sort of way, I do not think I concentrated deeply on the progress of the journey but was overwhelmed by the extraordinary scale of the country. The vast expanses of open plains, of endless scattered villages planted amongst groups of trees and other scrubby vegetation, of lonely ploughmen with their bullocks or buffalo pulling a wooden ploughshare directed by a human hand, of verdant green paddy fields fed water by the incessant cyclical movement of a donkey pump and groups of women in coloured cotton sarees bending towards the ground and tending their crops.

From time to time rocky outcrops would appear on the horizon as the railroad cut its way through the varied terrain of central and south India. There were more stops, more 'station food and drink wallahs' and more chai. We drank the water from our water bottles but constantly felt the thirst associated with the hot arid climate. There was never enough water and by now it was too warm to really break the thirst. Nevertheless, it was a profound relief to escape the troublesome humid heat of Bombay. The day passed calmly and was curiously relaxing. The dry heat brought tranquillity to our mood and the moving, ever-changing horizon was constantly entertaining.

We took short sleeps, talked intermittently about the adventures ahead and became somewhat unnerved as Elizabeth's departure point began to approach. At any moment in time we were never quite sure how much progress we had made, as we were missing a map. So, every time we approached a station we were desperate to check the name. Eventually Guntakal appeared on the name board of the platform and as the train came to a halt we moved Elizabeth's bags off the train on to the platform. We said our goodbyes and promised to write as soon as we were each settled in our respective new homes. I returned to the compartment and felt curiously alone. I leaned out of the open window to check that Elizabeth had been met, but as the train moved out of the station I lost sight of her as she disappeared into a fog of smoke and steam before confirming that there had been a successful rendezvous.

Somehow it was easier when there had been the two of us. I now had to scan the station names alone and with the failing light it became more difficult. Was it one or two hours to go? The sunset was breathtaking; partly the colours, the vibrant reds, pinks and oranges, but mostly it was the vast scale of it. The endless horizon running around the train for 360 degrees was alight, burning like a bushfire that straddled a nation.

Howard Hodgkin, *Bombay Sunset*, 1972–1973, oil on wood. (© The Estate of Howard Hodgkin)

Some years later I discovered that Howard Hodgkin had captured this coloured light show in abstraction with precision and deep emotion in his paintings *Bombay Sunset* (1972–3, oil on wood) and *Indian Sky* (1988–9, oil on wood), both now in private collections. However, as quickly as it had come, it went. The darkest of nights descended. There was no light pollution in rural India. The occasional twinkling cluster of lights in a small town would shine out like a distant constellation far across the universe. Perspective was lost in the darkness. Was the cluster 10 kilometres away or were they tiny stars 10 million kilometres away?

We reached Muddanuru at about 10.00pm. I checked the station name just one more time before stepping off the train with my blue suitcase, which thankfully had survived the assaults of travel. I stood on the platform and looked up and down, searching for someone who might be a credible host to my visit. I could see an exit sign 50 metres down the platform and began to walk towards it. Within the next few seconds the platform was empty of arriving travellers, just two men standing together beneath the exit sign. They turned towards each other and then began to walk towards me. It was with a great sense of relief that I had arrived in the right place.

'Welcome to India,' said William warmly, repeating word perfect the line in his card delivered by Buhariwala. 'Thanks for your card which we got immediately on arrival. We're tougher than those Peace Corps volunteers. It was good to know that the arrangements were all going to work.'

'Welcome to Jammalamadugu and Campbell Hospital,' said Dr Ratnaraj in a soft, warm tone. 'You will find it all a bit shocking, but you'll adjust. It's very hot just now.'

It most certainly was. It was well past sunset, and the sky was ink black but studded with sharp white diamonds set in their stunning constellations. There was a breeze of very warm, almost suffocating, air. It was hot, too hot for the moment but as Dr Ratnaraj correctly said, 'you will adjust', and I did. However, it was hot. Hot and dry. The hottest time of the year, in one of the hottest regions of the subcontinent.

We finished our preliminary introductions with a simple shaking of hands and continued with a few predictable brief exchanges about the journey and the efficiency of the arrangements that had been made at a distance. Dr Ratnaraj, the Hospital Superintendent, led me to his car which was waiting immediately outside the station. He was at first impression a gentle man of few words. Dr Cutting projected warmth and friendliness and helped me get my bags into the boot of the new-looking red Fiat, later to be re-launched as the Premier Padmini. Dr Ratnaraj drove the 20 km to Jammalamadugu at a gentle pace. I could see very little through the impenetrable darkness other than to realise that I would be staying in a simple rural setting for the next three months. There was a dim light over the front of the hospital building and across the compound William identified his grey stone house where I would be staying.

I said my thanks and farewells to Dr Ratnaraj and followed William along a sandy track towards the yellow lights of his house. I met his wife Margot briefly and was offered a local delicacy, a sweet lime drink, and then I was shown my room, the bed with its mosquito net and the traditional Indian bathroom, en suite, with a spacious splash area supported only by a tap, a faded pink plastic bucket and a dipping cup.

William walked back to the bedroom door but before leaving said, almost as an aside,

'Check the bathroom for snakes and scorpions before you take a bath in the morning. Use the underside of your shoe to dispatch any scorpions. Don't try and deal with a snake yourself. Let me know and I'll call one of the boys.'

'Yes, of course.' I was too tired to take in the enormity of his throwaway line.

'Goodnight and sleep well. You've earned it!' He left without further ado, just leaving me with the sound of his *chappals* gently coursing and clipping across the shiny stone floor.

Within a few minutes I heard what was to become the familiar tapping sound of typewriter keys coming from an adjacent room. I was to discover rapidly that it was his custom to write daily after both lunch and dinner; medical papers, reports of the hospital's progress in improving local healthcare – particularly of children, and letters to maintain contact with the outside world, especially to family and friends and colleagues from the world of medicine.

It was indeed the moment to retire, and I did so with a great sense of relief that finally the first part of this adventure was approaching completion, but another was surely about to begin. Five or six years after this memorable journey, I read *The Great Railway Bazaar* by Paul Theroux, his first travel book published in 1975, now widely regarded as a travel classic. He travels by multiple trains, following an elliptical path, taking first a southerly route through Europe, Central Asia and India to arrive in Tokyo, to then return by the northerly circuit on the Trans-Siberian Railway, finally arriving in Moscow and then on to Warsaw, Berlin and London. He indulged himself in several train journeys in India and Pakistan. He took the Khyber railway from Afghanistan to Peshawar in Pakistan, then on the Khyber Mail to Lahore and finally to Amritsar by taxi, home of the Sikhs' most holy place, the Golden Temple. Then on to Delhi by the Frontier Mail, to Jaipur and Agra, to Simla on the Kalka Mail followed by southerly diversions to Madras on The Grand Trunk Express and finally on the Howrah Mail to Calcutta. His inspiration was railway travel. On the first page of his story he quotes the English playwright and novelist Michael Frayn, who rephrased Marshall McLuhan's 'the medium is the message', to 'the journey is the goal'. I enjoyed the book, particularly his accounts of places I had by then also seen, but was in no doubt whatsoever that for me the journey was not the goal, it was much more than that and I hope that eventually you will see why.

❧

During the twenty-two years that followed Independence, before I made this first visit in 1969, there were many important historic developments. Most of these were driven by the politics of the day and the varying fortunes of the Indian economy. To deal with the challenge of governing such a large country after so many years of British rule, The Constituent Assembly (non-elected), led by Jawaharlal Nehru (who had been a major player in the independence and partition negotiations with the British), was established in 1946 and ran for almost three years, acting as the *de facto* Indian Parliament. During this period the Constitution of the new nation was written. India prepared for its first general election, opting for a Parliamentary system involving two houses, the Rajya Sabha (upper house) and the Lok Sabha (lower house). The party that wins the majority of seats in a general election has the opportunity to form the central government.

Almost immediately after Independence, India engaged in military conflict with Pakistani tribesmen supported by the Pakistani army, who had invaded Jammu and Kashmir; this had been formally designated as part of India about two to three months after Independence and partition but was not ratified by the State's Constituent Assembly until 1954. The year after Independence, Indian troops (euphemistically described at the time as 'police action') entered the still independent princely state of Hyderabad and effectively took control. In 1951, Prime Minister Nehru launched his first five-year plan based on centralised economic planning with strong central government control. Next year India held its first General Election (the First Lok Sabha, 1952–7); anyone aged twenty-one or older was entitled to take part in the process but of the 173 million voters at the time, many were poor and illiterate and living in rural areas. This was a huge undertaking so soon after acquiring self-rule. Nevertheless, Nehru ran a massive election campaign, travelling far and wide across the nation, resulting in the Indian National Congress Party gaining 45 per cent of the vote, thus returning him to power. In 1956, he presented a second five-year plan, this time focusing on rapid industrialisation. In 1959, the Dalai Lama escaped from Tibet and took up residency in India; this may have been a contributing trigger for war between India and China in 1962.

The 1960s were critical years in India's post-Independence politics. Domestic squabbles continued over the supremacy of the Indian languages; in 1960, following demonstrations by militants, Bombay State partitioned into Maharashtra and Gujarat to produce two new language-based states. In 1961 Goa was taken back from the Portuguese following an invasion by the Indian army. Pondicherry was *de facto* taken from French control in 1954 but did not formally become part of the union until 1962 when the treaty was finally ratified by the French government.

Jawaharlal Nehru was re-elected at the Second and Third Lok Sabhas (1957–62 and 1962–7) but died in 1964, just five years after his daughter Indira Gandhi had been elected President of the Indian National Congress Party. She was elected as a Member of Parliament following her father's death and was appointed by the new Prime Minister, Lal Bahadur Shastri, to be head of the Information and Broadcasting Ministry. 1965 saw the second Indo-Pakistani war; Indira Gandhi played a deft hand by taking a holiday in Srinagar, which was in the middle of the war zone, with Pakistani insurgents on the doorstep of her hotel. This act of defiance attracted the international media and may have supported her appointment as Prime Minister the following year in 1966 after Shastri's death.

The Fourth Lok Sabha (1967–70) again brought success to the Gandhi dynasty but with a diminished share of the vote. Indira Gandhi's first term was packed with major events; she reshuffled the Government, removing some of the old dinosaurs, set in motion laws to remove the Privy Purse from the princely states (she failed to get sufficient votes in 1969 but was eventually successful when proposed again in 1971), she nationalised many of the major Banks and some of the top oil companies, and oversaw the division of the Punjab into three linguistically-based new states, Haryana, Himachal Pradesh and Punjab. In 1969, India announced the creation of the Indian Space Research Organisation, ISRO (the same year that the Americans successfully placed men on the moon). India was surely on the move.

OVER THE MOON

*There is a light that shines beyond all things on earth, beyond us all,
beyond the heavens, beyond the highest, the very highest heavens.
This is the light that shines in our heart.*

3.13.7 Chandogya Upanishad

One late summer night, 21 July 1969, soon after my coming to Jammy and following a day of monsoon rains, was the moment when we became friends. Still warm, perhaps too warm for me as a recent arrival, but mitigated by a pleasant *garlee* (breeze or light wind) which slid around our shoulders. Sam (Dr Sammana Arthur Samuel) and I sat on the flat roof of his house, leaning back against a low parapet. We did not speak much, I recall; we were just getting to know each other. He was older than me but only by three or four years. He had trained at a relatively new, medical school not far away in Kurnool, an unremarkable town in Andhra Pradesh. We would visit his alma mater at some point later in this adventure. He was a diminutive, shy person. No more than 1.75 metres tall, certainly shorter than me but I can only claim to be average height for a European, and he was slim, very slim. My recollection in those days was that all Indians were very slim, not a trace of subcutaneous fat on any of them.

Food supply was usually adequate but never plentiful. Rice, the basic staple for South Indians was grown in abundance in the region, but like most village people – and at that time over 80 per cent of all Indians lived in villages – they were hard working, mostly toiling long days in the paddy fields without the luxury of modern farming machinery. The bullock and hand plough were as good as it gets. Occasionally one might even see a ploughing implement being dragged across a field by two coolies, with another pushing the ploughshare down into the ground to create a furrow. There was no opportunity for the accumulation of body fat deposits from energy foods that were surplus to requirements; every calorie was burnt in the pursuit of the next harvest. The only exception was the stars of the cinema; the rounded sometimes voluptuous men and women whose nasal voices and shiny, curvaceous bodies, always of course well covered and concealed, were fuelling the emergent Indian film industry. For them, the Botticellian form was a sign of wealth and thus success.

Sam was always well groomed. I remember him best in hospital 'whites'; white cotton trousers and white short-sleeved shirt starched and creased, all fresh from the *dhobi*. Sometimes the white trousers were exchanged for a more formal grey. His greased black hair never appeared to grow, consistently the same length. I guess the style was a typical post-war 'short back and sides', greased with the Indian equivalent of

Sam, 1969. (Author's collection)

Brylcreem (although it could have been Brylcreem itself, as North America, Europe and India were the prime markets at the time) and lightly perfumed with a spicy, jasmine fragrance that I find impossible to recall precisely. I think he went to the barber in our local bazaar every Saturday afternoon when we had completed the morning rounds and clinic. A weekly cut would have been the only way he could have maintained that impeccably neat, unchanging appearance. Finally, a neatly trimmed, diminutive black moustache almost certainly attacked by the barber at his weekly session; this was very much the fashion of the day.

Now we are looking up into a star-filled sky and watching the most generous full moon I have ever seen. There is no light pollution, as we now refer to the ancillary lighting provided by the modern metropolis, for there are no street or external lights in Jammalamadugu, only the dimmest electric lights, usually bare bulbs in houses which seem to flutter in intensity with the breeze and frequently fail altogether during the regular power outages. We were straining to see the surface markings on the moon as an unidentified commentator on *Voice of America* talked us through the last moments as *Eagle*, the lunar module containing Neil Armstrong and Buzz Aldrin, landed on the moon; that same moon that we were looking at from the flat roof of Sam's house in Jammalamadugu, Andhra Pradesh, South India.

The Apollo 11 mission had begun just a few days earlier on 16 July, with three astronauts on board, the third being the commander of the command module Michael Collins, leaving the Kennedy Space Centre at Cape Canaveral, Florida powered by the immense Saturn V rocket. The paradox is profound. The Americans had used state of the art rocket technology and computing power to blast men out of the earth's atmosphere and place them safely on to our moon, while we witness every day the truncated, impoverished lives of honest village people who happened by chance, to be born in this hot dry region of South India. What I learnt, however, that being a relatively wealthy and feted US astronaut does not necessarily make you happier or more fulfilled than a poor farmer in a loving family, living a simple life in village India in the 1960s. Except that the latter would lose some of his children before they reach school age, would suffer common diseases which would be inadequately treated, and few would enjoy education beyond the most basic.

We listened again to the *Voice of America* issuing from Sam's small rectangular, red plastic transistor radio that was positioned for optimal reception of the international signal on the flat roof. We sat together in silence propped up against the low parapet and listened to those now world-famous words: 'That's one small step for a man, one giant leap for mankind.' Words that would continue to reverberate around the world for decades to come.

Sam had no money for luxuries. It was a period when doctors in the mission hospital were paid at least 30 per cent less than their equivalent colleagues in the government hospital across the road. I wondered how he could have afforded the radio. I speculated some years later that it might have been one of the radios that Mrs Gandhi's son, Sanjay, had given away in their thousands to multiparous women as an incentive to undergo a sterilisation procedure, but then realised that those particular incentives were not introduced until the mid-1970s. India was the first developing nation to create a national population control policy from 1952, encouraged and incentivised by the international providers of food aid such as the US. The hospital had a busy programme in those days. Even I, the newest recruit, was taught to perform the sterilisation procedure of tubal ligation and after a few weeks I was deemed competent to undertake my own list under local anaesthetic.

The moon shone like a massive silver plate above us with the familiar surface shadowy irregularities, so easily seen with the naked eye, never more apparent. We heard again the voices of Buzz Aldrin and Neil Armstrong describe their moon antics like walking in zero gravity and placing the 'Stars and Stripes' on the moon surface with almost childlike delight.

'And we'll step off the ladder. That's one small step for a man, one giant leap for mankind.'

'Columbia, Columbia this is Houston AOS over....'

The paradox of the 'haves' and 'have nots' was never more sharply focused. Sam sat patiently with me, but I could see that his interest was waning. The relevance of this epoch-making journey for the US and the industrialised world could not be remotely shared with those struggling to eke out an existence in village India.

As the early hours of the morning arrived, the temperature decreased and the light breeze stiffened. It was the place to be. It reminded me of a midsummer's night that I spent outside in a deckchair in the garden of a Dutch friend who lived near Hoorn, a small nested community on the southern perimeter of the IJsselmeer. Just lying back, lazily looking at the stars, and from time to time amused by a streaking bright comet dashing home across the night sky.

I looked across the hospital compound and found my bearings using the dim yellow house lights to identify the other doctors' residences scattered apparently randomly across the sandy, bare landscape. House lights often flickered, not like a candle in the wind but due to the unstable nature of the mains power supply. Outages were part of everyday life.

The Ratnaraj house was still awake, as judged by the burning light on the ground floor; it was situated a short distance away along an unmade path. Dr Ratnaraj was a general surgeon and the hospital superintendent for fifteen or more years. It was he who had expressed some incredulity when he discovered that my travelling companion to India was a woman and not my wife, consistent with his somewhat conservative and socially compliant nature. He was a quiet, soft-spoken, private person and after this first week or so of my time in Jammy, I cannot say that I knew him well. He was a man who had undertaken post-graduate surgical training in the UK and knew the ways of contemporary Britain, but his heart and mind were loyal to rural Andhra. Despite this difficult start, he was kind to me, very kind. He was a slim man of medium height, generally seen in hospital 'whites' and always well turned out. His smooth facial skin, largely free of wrinkles, gave him a youthful appearance for a man in his mid-fifties. His hair arrangements followed a similar style to Sam's.

I rarely saw him off duty but on the few occasions that I did he always wore European dress. It was customary for men in that region to slip back into traditional *dhoti* or *lunghi* and shirt in the evening for coolness and comfort as many, even the professional classes, would still dine sitting on the floor.

Within a few days of my arrival, I think he had made up his mind that he would engage with me in a practical way. He was totally disinterested in my endeavours to re-jig the pharmacy so that drugs might be arranged systematically to be easily located for dispensing or audit, or with my ideas to construct a new business model for the pricing and selling of drugs; I rather fancied the 'Robin Hood' system and did eventually introduce something along those lines. However, he offered me something that was to have a profound influence on my development as a clinician: he invited me to assist him in the operating theatre.

It was soon apparent early in my stay that it was in the operating room, standing for hours over an open abdomen with the smell of bowels and ether in the air, that he was most content. He loved the process of cutting, the control of bleeding, the removing, the repairing; indeed, he adored all surgical interventions however large or small. He was a surgeon first and foremost and it was in surgical practice that he did his best work. He taught me many things and I think came to rely on me in a modest way, more than I could ever have imagined. More of that anon.

Flavia and Ratnama, Campbell Hospital, 1969. (Author's collection)

Ratnama, his wife was different. She was somewhat shorter and rounder and always wore a saree; at work in the hospital it was partly covered with a traditional doctor's long white coat. Her round face was to some extent concealed by a pair of dark, heavy-framed spectacles, too large for a woman of her proportions but nevertheless, à la mode. She liked jewellery and always wore gold ear studs often embedded with colourful gems, several gold bangles and a gold necklace. I do not think these items could have been bought with their salaries from the hospital. She was talkative and engaging but retained the polite reserve expected of a top man's wife in 1960s India. Wives at the time never addressed their husbands by name (it was thought to be unlucky, disrespectful or superstitious) and in public would still walk a few metres behind them. There was certainly never any outward display of affection. However, from early on in my stay I began to think that she was the power behind the throne. She dealt with the difficult relationships in the Hospital. If there was bad news she would deliver it. If a staff member had to be fired she would do it. She was his eyes and ears and the mother of their treasured sons, Vijay Kumar who was a medical student at CMC Vellore, and Michael who was still considering his future, which included medicine or engineering. However, the couple was an entity. A partnership to be reckoned with. Respected professionals who provided leadership to a team of devoted clinicians and hospital support staff in a challenging situation. Yes, a couple to be reckoned with and respected.

She also took to me in her own way. Her mission was to show me as many interesting clinical cases as she could. And she did, night and day. Whenever there was something interesting in the gynae theatre or on the labour ward or in outpatients, she would send one of the porters, dressed in hospital khaki shirt and shorts, to find me. She would write a very brief note on a scrap of paper describing the case, fold it in half to preserve confidentiality and then instruct the porter to find me with all speed. At night, the porters would come across the sandy path to the Cutting house armed with a smoking, yellow flamed hurricane lamp; they would wake me and then wait while I dressed, to escort me back over to the hospital. Ratnama's cases introduced me to all the common operative gynaecological procedures, complicated deliveries and Caesarean sections and other emergencies in women. I would never have seen cases in such abundance if I had remained in London. It was she who taught me the art of tubal sterilisation under local anaesthetic.

'Come we should go. We need to sleep if we are to work tomorrow.'

Sam was beginning to lose his patience with me.

'Let's wait just a few more minutes and make sure the mission is going as predicted. It's such a beautiful evening.' I was not keen to retire, having become entranced by the unbelievable achievements of Apollo 11 and the technological tour de force that allowed us to witness their adventure in real time in an Indian village.

Sam looked up to the sky as if asking for help. He could not avoid catching another glimpse of the moon and paused just briefly to connect again with the enormity of the event we were witnessing, albeit at a distance.

'Just a couple more minutes?' I asked plaintively.

The *Voice of America* droned on in a celebratory tone, clearly revelling in the momentous achievement. The space race was deemed important in demonstrating superiority during the Cold War, remembering that the Russians had beaten the Americans in getting the first man into outer space in 1961 followed by the first woman in 1963.

Half listening to the commentary, my eyes drifted again across the compound, straining in the darkness to find the other houses.

Right next to Sam's house lived Yardley and Flavia. Yardley! What an extraordinary name. Yardley's perfume; an East End perfume factory which quite by chance was, at that moment, being sold for a small fortune to British American Tobacco. Its owner, T. Lyddon Gardner who had a home in Hove (later to become part of the city of Brighton and Hove, Sussex) was to pass some of the proceeds to the newly created University of Sussex to build an arts centre, which opened in the same year, 1969, as the Gardner Arts Centre. Nearly forty years later I would find my way there as the University's seventh Vice-Chancellor.

Yardley (it was 'Yardley Bob' to be totally accurate), like Dr Ratnaraj, was a general surgeon. He was in his late thirties to early forties, but incredibly self-confident, at times over confident; surgically competent but I would say of a modest intellect. He was tall, somewhat rotund and tended to wear his clothes rather on the tight side, revealing his generous fleshy curves. He clearly had not been to the 'Mollie Smith School' of easy living in India. I fantasised that he modelled himself on the contemporary heroes of India's booming film industry. What distinguished him from the other members of the medical staff was his hair. The hairstyle, that is. Black, brilliantined hair, neatly cropped at the back and sides but wound on the top into a glorious quiff. It reminded me of a popular piece of confectionery of the day, the 'Walnut Whip'; a pyramidal coil of milk chocolate, filled with sweet white goo and topped with a walnut. It was originally made in 1910 by Duncan's of Edinburgh and revived in the 1970s by Rowntree, now part of the Nestlé empire. Again, I think he aspired to mimic the famous male movie stars of the day in all aspects of grooming and sartorial splendour.

Yardley was less interested in me and spoke most negatively about my interventions in the pharmacy. He never wanted to discuss the intricacies of a clinical case but on one memorable day he did show me how to drain a sizeable amoebic abscess by 'blindly' plunging a large bore needle straight into the liver with a flourish that reminded me of a matador thrusting his sword to finish off the bull. Or perhaps a competitive fencer, standing back with his rapier elegantly poised, ready to lunge it forward into his opponent's breast. Luckily the patient survived the procedure and went on to make a spectacular recovery following a course of antibiotics.

Yardley Bob was married to a polite, shy, calm young woman whose name I do not think I ever knew. She seemed compulsively overawed by her surgeon companion some years her senior. I only met her on one occasion and my memory of her is deeply defective. She was studying medicine at the Christian Medical College, Vellore, but was struggling. Although it was never made explicit in everyday conversation, I was made aware soon after my arrival that she had had many attempts at all of her exams at every step along the way, but it was still widely expected that she would join her husband in Jammy in the fullness of time. However, some months after I returned to the UK I received a letter from William wondering 'whether she would ever pass her finals'.

Mollie and a midwife, Campbell Hospital, 1969. (Author's collection)

Mollie, of course, also lived on the compound. She lived alone and although she had suggested in one of her early letters that I might spend some time in her house, it never happened. She was a solid member of the community, head nurse, in charge of the School of Nursing and a leader of the clinical community in every sense of the word. I found her somewhat austere and never developed a particularly close relationship with her. She was a blunt Lancashire woman. She worked all hours and did not seem to have much of a life outside her job. I judged it was difficult to be a single woman in such a conservative society at that time. I think she was, like many of the hospital staff, a true believer and genuinely sustained by the central part that the chapel played in the day-to-day life of the hospital. There were moments when I thought she might be better placed as a career nun, although for her personally there may have been little difference between her current vocation and the formal taking of vows. At one point during my stay she did share with me that there was a moment in her life she did receive a proposal for marriage; but I think that is about as far as it went.

Sam was desperate to sleep and suddenly stood up and made it quite clear that he was moving towards the staircase that would take us back to the ground level and allow him to go to bed.

'Come, it is time to say goodnight.'

Most of the house lights in the compound had now been extinguished and the absence of any auxiliary lighting meant the trip back to the Cutting house was not without hazard. I did not have a torch and there was a distinct risk of stepping on a snake or a scorpion.

The Cuttings' house, Campbell Hospital, 1969. (Author's collection)

Sam and his sister, Mary, Campbell Hospital,
1969. (Author's collection)

'Let me walk you back to your quarters.'

Sam picked up the radio and moved off in a decisive way, which was not always his custom. Mostly he walked slowly, as if deep in thought and considering carefully his next action.

We walked past the home of the Reddys, the final husband and wife team at the hospital, again a general surgeon, Purushotham and his gynaecologist wife Flavia. She also took me under her wing from time to time, particularly when there was a difficult or unusual case on the go. The lights of their house were out and there was a sense of calm as the compound finally went to sleep. Sam left me at the door of my new home after shaking hands and wishing each other pleasant dreams.

Sam became a very good friend during the ensuing weeks. I was closest to him in age and his superiority of knowledge, and relatively advanced position on the career development pathway, gave him a safe position as guide and mentor.

He soon introduced me to Mary, his sister of a similar age but a couple of years his senior, who was a nurse in the hospital. She was a shy woman, as were all the nurses, schooled to be reserved in their social interactions with men, particularly the unmarried variety. She was always immaculately dressed in her crisp, unblemished nurses' uniform. White blouse, pristine white starched saree and a white starched nurse's cap with a thick blue stripe around the periphery; all that could be seen of her were slim brown arms and her beautiful brown baby-face almost identical to Sam's. She was always warm and friendly but deeply shy.

SUSEELA

Sam was keen that I met his family and on one occasion took me to his home in the neighbouring town of Proddatur. His parents were reserved, not very talkative but very generous. He also took me on a weekend visit to his medical school in Kurnool, an unremarkable town, some five hours north by bus from Jammy. We left on the 3.15pm bus one Friday afternoon about five weeks into my stay, arrived at about 9.00pm and stayed overnight in the Kurnool Medical College men's hostel. We met some of his former colleagues; Krishnamurthy entertained us to coffee in his room the morning after arrival and took us for a typical South Indian breakfast of *idli* ('flying saucer' shaped, fermented rice cake) and *dosa* (a rice pancake cooked on a griddle to be either soft or crispy) lubricated by a fiery sambar. Although I had become increasingly accomplished over the weeks in eating with my right hand, *idlis* presented a special challenge, particularly in persuading the highly mobile samba (spicy liquid sauce) to remain associated with the *idli* and not to run down the arm and drip from the elbow before the concoction had reached the mouth. I recall travelling on an early morning express train from Madras to Bangalore in a carriage full of breakfasting travellers. Food was brought on to the train in Madras by local self-employed vendors who passed from coach to coach selling their wares to the travellers, then hustled off the train by the guard before it departed. One gentleman who opted for *idlis* gave up trying to eat elegantly and was happy to retrieve the drips of samba from the tip of his elbow with a highly exercised, almost prehensile tongue.

Krishnamurthy was surprisingly outspoken about the corruption in some of the private medical schools of the day, indicating that many students paid a bribe to get in and irrespective of their performance during the course, paid again to get their degree. Kurnool Medical College was a state medical school created in 1956, affiliated to the Sri Venkateswara University in Tirupati, just after the creation of the new state of Andhra Pradesh; I do not think he was referring to any practices locally.

We visited the various departments which were not of any great interest but we had a very traditional delicious South Indian vegetarian lunch at the Hindustan Hotel in town and then went to the movies, where we saw *Those Magnificent Men In Their Flying Machines*.

> *Those magnificent men in their flying machines,*
> *They go up up, Tiddley up, up,*
> *They go down, Tiddley down, down.*

The musical ditty was apparently conceived by the wife of Elmo Fox, the then-managing director of Twentieth Century Fox.

On the way back to the Medical College we visited the local bazaar; a collection of small shops and stalls with everything that one might need to survive day to day in India. It was at about this time that I consciously wanted to be absorbed into the local culture. White faces were very uncommon in the area at the time and while I was always treated with incredible kindness and respect I felt somewhat out of place. Almost all – perhaps all – women wore the typical saree, usually cotton but occasionally silk for weddings or other special events. Most men would also follow a traditional line in dress wearing a classic cotton shirt worn over a loosely tied *dhoti*. Only professionals such as doctors and lawyers would wear European attire during the day but would commonly revert to more comfortable looser clothing when at home in the evening.

So, I bought a *dhoti* (or *pancha* as it was known locally); a rather beautiful fine white cotton length of cloth with a red delicately stitched border, long enough to be wound around the waist and pulled up between one's legs to be finally tucked in at the waist. I already had one or two traditional *khadi* shirts made by the tailor in Jammy. I also bought some joss sticks, which took an important place on my desk and accompanied the reading and writing that took place in the evenings. It was part of my physical and spiritual transformation into Indian ways. We returned to the medical school campus and I was somewhat surprised when Sam suggested that we should make a nocturnal visit to the women's hostel. It was about 7.00pm and already dark.

'I want to introduce you to Suseela.' Sam spoke in a quiet, somewhat embarrassed tone.

'Of course! Who is she? Is she a cousin or another relative?'

'No. Well not exactly. Come!'

He took my hand as was the custom and we walked purposefully cross the campus without further conversation.

As we arrived at the front door of the Women's Hostel it became clear that the said Suseela was already waiting for her visitors at the top of the steps. She was a petite, dark-haired beauty of an extraordinarily shy demeanour. She smiled at Sam, but they did not exchange words and there was no physical contact.

'This is Suseela. She is in a class a couple of years behind me. She will sit her finals next year.'

She smiled but without transmitting much emotion. She looked frankly embarrassed at being exposed in this way to a foreigner. I did not know quite what to do next but took the traditional route of saying something.

'How nice to meet you. We have had such fun in Kurnool. Sam and his friends have been so kind.'

She just smiled and gently rolled her head from side to side, the traditional gesture acknowledging agreement or acquiescence. I felt out of place and assumed they wanted to spend time alone. However, the conventions of the day did not permit such an occasion. I walked away, casually turning back to see them exchanging a few brief words without a smile; *trés serieux*! Within about thirty seconds Sam had left her alone standing on the steps and ran towards me again catching my hand as we quickened our pace back towards the men's hostel. I wondered just who Suseela was, but assumed she was becoming an important part of Sam's life.

On Sunday morning, I rose at about 7.00am, took a bath (the traditional cup and bucket variety) and was taken to church by Sam and the family at 9.00am. Afterwards, the Pastor served us refreshments at his house. For lunch we returned to the Hindustan Hotel located just behind the old bus-stand, which had a tiny, tacky frontage squeezed between two open fronted shops; *Rabhu Electricals* on the left and *Gurudev Novelties* on the right, from which their contents and clients spilled out chaotically into the street. It was hot in the dining room, but the food was good and incredibly inexpensive. Today, Kurnool boasts the Hotel New Hindustan, which has a smart air-conditioned dining room which probably seats about one hundred people and serves many varieties of biriyanis as their speciality dish.

The day sped by and before long we were saying our farewells and climbing into the bus which would take us home. I wondered whether I would ever hear of or see Suseela again as we lurched our way through the darkness on the bumpy road back to Jammy. I can tell you now that I did, but it was not for another forty years and then in rather sad circumstances.

This first week of induction had been perhaps the greatest change in daily living that I had ever experienced. There were moments when I felt isolated and alone but mostly there was little time for misery. The days started early and we worked till late; the dry heat had a calming effect that induced a welcomed tiredness at the end of the day, ensuring undisturbed sleep.

That night I wasted no time in getting out of my clothes and sliding under the mosquito net into my traditional cot. And what would tomorrow bring, I asked myself as I let go of this world and drifted into another?

To the historian, the late 1960s are reminiscent of the late 1940s, likewise a time of crisis and conflict, of resentment along lines of class, religion, ethnicity and region, of a centre that seemed barely to hold. I wonder if these parallels occurred to the Indians who lived through these times, to people in authority in particular, and to the Prime Minister most of all.

Ramachandra Guha, from *India after Gandhi,* 2007

Indira Gandhi had two sons, Rajiv in 1944 and Sanjay just two years later. They were destined to become part of one of the most powerful political dynasties in India. They were educated at the famous Doon School in Dehradun, in the foothills of the Himalayas. Rajiv went on to study at the University of Cambridge where he met his future wife Sonia but showed little interest in politics and went on to train as a commercial airline pilot, serving with the domestic carrier, Indian Airlines. Sanjay did not attend university, although he did take an apprenticeship with Rolls-Royce in the UK for three years, possibly led there because of his passion for sports cars. He was a career politician, close to his mother and like his brother also obtained a pilot's licence.

Sanjay would go on to play a prominent role in the Indian government during the 1970s, often heavily criticised for his heavy-handed approach to power but always in support of his mother. He died prematurely before the end of the decade, whereas Rajiv would enter politics and become the sixth and youngest Prime Minister of India following the assassination of his mother in 1984. He served for five years but eventually was killed in an attack by a suicide bomber whilst campaigning for re-election near Madras in 1991.

Indira Gandhi won the Fourth Lok Sabha (1967–70) but the vote share to the Congress party was decreased; nevertheless, she became Prime Minister for a second term. Battles within the Congress party raged and following her expulsion from the Congress for 'indiscipline', moves were made to split the party into two (Congress 'O' for 'old' and Congress 'R' for reform). Forcing through the nationalisation of the banks and stripping the maharajas of the privy purse was beginning to reveal an aggressive, dictatorial side to her leadership which she explained by insisting that it was to 'ensure a better life to the vast majority of our people'. However, her agricultural strategy was beginning to work with sensational increases in crop yields.

The 1970s and '80s would prove to be extremely difficult years for this politically driven and powerful family.

3

THE HOSPITAL IN THE VILLAGE BY THE SWAMP

There is a bridge between time and eternity; and this bridge is Atman, the spirit of man. Neither day nor night cross that bridge, nor old age, nor death nor sorrow.

3.13.7 Chandogya Upanishad

After a week at the hospital I had established a routine. I was fully adjusted to the new time zone (four and a half hours ahead of the UK) and now waking early enough to sit at the desk in my bedroom to make a few notes about the previous day's activities, write letters home to parents and to a girlfriend who I think was less than happy about the protracted separation (not helped by the by the bald fact that my travelling

The Campbell Hospital, 1969. (Author's collection)

companion was another woman). I did not write a formal diary but collected odds and ends, photos, souvenirs and fragments of prose that have helped me assemble this retrospective. The sad aspect was the lack of a view. The room without a view! The desk was set in front of a window, but it was a window at the back of a veranda which was shrouded by heavy vegetation so that the view was limited to about a metre.

'Jammalamadugu' means, in Telegu (the language of Andhra Pradesh), 'bushes or vegetation growing in stagnant water' or a swamp. I never really discovered 'the swamp' but the Pennair River was not far away and during the rainy season it would burst its banks and cut the town off from the outside world, sometimes for many days at a time.

The Pennair River, 1969. (Author's collection)

During this period there certainly were submerged sections in the Jammalamadugu hinterland which would be easy to designate as swamp. The hospital was in a remote area of Andhra Pradesh far from a major city. The State capital was Hyderabad, some 400 km away, which meant a minimum of six or seven hours by road. The nearest town was Proddatur, 25 km away, which was a busy bustling conurbation where you could buy most things.

However, Jammy had very little. There was a bus-stand from which you could take a bus to many places but travelling by road in a public vehicle was hard. The buses were old, rusty and dusty; diesel monsters without glazed windows, just bars to stop you jumping out, and a granite-hard suspension. I think they were built before the modern clutch had been invented. You felt every bump or cavity in the poorly constructed dirt roads. They stopped frequently, so progress was slow. When all the seats were taken, people stood in the aisles. When the aisles were full, they climbed on to the roof, and when the roof was full, they clung on to the external fabric of the bus. At the time, there did not seem to be any enforceable regulations about the permitted number of passengers that could be carried by a public bus.

Jammy had a bazaar that sold basic fruit and vegetables. There were colourful spices displayed in abundance, various sorts of butchers depending on whether you were Muslim or Hindu, there were a few roadside coffee shops – sort of 'holes in the wall' – a barber and various places you could go to get things mended. There was a roadside 'hospital' for auto rickshaws, a place to rejuvenate a bicycle and a range of other vendors selling pots and pans and other household items.

India in the 1960s – and still today – repairs broken objects. It makes unserviceable machines work. It cannibalises the parts from dead engines and puts them into salvageable, tired engines. It takes tyres that have lost their tread and turns them into sandals. India invented recycling before it became the politically correct obsession of the West.

Bicycle repairs. (Author's collection)

THE THIEF OF BAGHDAD

Importantly there was an outdoor 'picture house'. Cinema would be too strong a word. A screen would be erected in a suitable open space, seats assembled in rows at the back but most of the audience would opt for the cheapest seats at the front, sitting on mats on the ground. It was, in today's parlance, a pop-up movie theatre. Of course, the film could only start when the sun had set. Sam took me there several times, but I found it hard going. The films were either in Hindi (emanating from Bombay, Bollywood) or they were local movies produced in Andhra Pradesh in Telegu (Tollywood) or they were Hindi or Tamil movies dubbed in Telegu. Either way it did not mean a lot to me. However, it did give one the flavour of what small town and village India was consuming in the 1960s. The stories were all traditional myths and legends, Gods would appear when required, the actors were of a variety which sported considerable undulant coverings of adipose tissue, heavy make-up, outrageous costumes and hair-dos to die for; at least for those living in the late '60s village India. These were not real people. The actors themselves seemed to be mythical creatures and were of course blazing the trail for the Bollywood explosion of the 1970s and '80s when modern social drama overtook the romantic musicals of the later post-war period. Pundits would say that the 'Golden Age' of the Hindi movie industry was from the late 1940s to the early '60s and after that money, rather than creativity, drove the industry.

The film I remember best was *The Thief of Baghdad*, a Hindi movie without English subtitles that had just been released in India in early 1969. It was the end of my first month in Jammy on 30 July. I had just completed an evening Caesarean section with Ratnama and was then whisked off by Sam and the Reddys to the local cinema at about 9.00pm. The evening air was cool and refreshing, and it was a pleasure to sit out under the stars and be forced into a crazy world of fantasy and action. The film was not a sophisticated product, despite have a leading director of the day at its helm, Shriram Bohra and being crammed full of the stars including Dara Singh as Mehmood (the main protagonist who seeks revenge following the murder of his father by a treacherous warlord), Helen as Yasmin (Mehmood's sister) and Nishi as Shehzadi Rukhsana, who becomes Mehmood's object of love. The plot is both simple and complex; either way I had lost it along the way and was glad when we finally got back home soon after midnight.

Throughout this period of Indian cinema, screen lovers could barely touch each other (in line with the wider social mores of the day) and by 1969 it was widely believed that there had never been an overt kiss in an Indian popular film. The first modern screen kiss is generally accepted to have occurred between Shashi Kapoor and Zeenat Aman in the film *Satyam Shivam Sundaram* (Love Sublime), in 1978. Chief Minister and movie actor M.G. Ramachandran said that this scene was an insult to Indian cinema and it started a major row about film censorship. Despite this and perhaps, not surprisingly, the movie did well at the box office. However, further research reveals that there had been an earlier kiss between the famous actress of the day, Devika Rani and Himansu Rai in the film *Karma*, back in 1933. This event seems to have escaped reputational ruin for either party and survived the censorship process on the basis that they were real life husband and wife. Anything goes, providing you are married!

What was perhaps even more important than the moving images and the dreamy narratives was the music. The popular music of the day was movie music. The songs from the movies were blasted through primitive, raucous sound systems in the bazaars to the point of distortion, at weddings and at celebrations like Diwali; these songs could bring people to tears as they reflected on the story that the music depicted. Many could sing the songs by heart.

Asha Bhosle was the 'back singer' in the *Thief of Baghdad*. Back singers pre-recorded the songs for a film to which the actors would then mime the words. She had a haunting, penetrating voice that could draw tears from a concentration camp guard. The high-pitched vibrato rang like a human sitar through the film. It was impossible to separate this voice and its melodic utterances from the heart of the narrative. For more than five decades Asha was at the centre of popular Indian cinema. She worked with many of the leading Bollywood directors and particularly composers, such as O.P. Nayyar (1950s and '60s), Rahul Dev Burman (1970s) and Khayyamand (1980s and '80s); her name became synonymous with a film's success.

Her sister, Lata Mangeshkar was also a very successful and much in demand 'back singer' who was part of the dynasty which dominated Indian film music for more than fifty years. They would often work side by side in a movie. Asha's life was far from straightforward with divorce and her daughter's suicide contributing to her grief. In the end, she seems to have lived out in her own life some of the tragedies of her screen heroes. Although musical theatre was popular in Europe and America in the 1960s, it did not dominate the popular music scene. There were other important things going on such as The Beatles, The Rolling Stones, Bob Dylan and The Beach Boys.

The people who lived around Jammy constituted primarily a farming community and an important part of the rice-growing industry of South India. Wheat in the north and rice in the south; and it is still very much the same today. Although, as I drove from Chennai (previously Madras) to Jammalamadugu recently, I noted that rice fields were giving way to other commercial developments, especially in Chennai's penumbra. The rapidly growing digital technology industry was insidiously replacing agriculture as a dominant commercial enterprise.

Most people were poor, earning at best a few rupees a day, barely enough to provide rice, dahl and another vegetable for their family. Men and women worked together in the paddy fields with infants slung across their mother's back or abdomen. This was subsistence living. Personal possessions were minimal, usually consisting of just the clothes they stood up in. Women might have a few bangles and toe rings, a stud in their nose or ear – usually a marriage gift – but that was all. Marriages were virtually all arranged

Ploughing a paddy, 1969. (Author's collection)

between parents living in the same village and were often consanguineous, mostly fixed while the child was still below the age of ten years. Literacy in the state was patchy but generally low, much lower, for instance, than its neighbouring state, Kerala, which even then was approaching 90 per cent; one of the upsides of 'democratic communism'. In Andhra at the time it was common for children to be working in the fields or helping their mother at home by the age of twelve years.

Life ticked on just fine at this very basic level until something went wrong to disturb the equilibrium. In fact, one of my overwhelming early impressions during that first week in village India was that poverty was not all bad. That probably sounds terrible but there was an extraordinary contentment, maybe resignation, but I think fulfilment that radiated from local village people that stayed with me for many years after I returned to life at home. At times, I felt a tinge of envy that life could be enjoyed and celebrated with such simplicity, as well as a sense of guilt at times that we had it so good and did nothing but complain about the terms and conditions of work, the government and most of all the weather.

A common social disruptor was illness or accident. Illness or an injury that precluded further work could bankrupt a family in months. If the coolie father became seriously ill, the first port of call would likely be the local 'registered medical practitioner', the RMP. It is perhaps surprising that these individuals had not undergone formal medical training. They were 'registered' and were permitted to 'practice', but their practices were imprecise, sometimes unethical and at times dangerous. A good example of the day was the frequent use of ineffective injections. Vitamin B_{12} was a popular remedy at the time and was used widely as a placebo. It was also a rather dramatic potion to administer because of its pink colour; patients were genuinely impressed. RMPs would sometimes hold the loaded syringe aloft to ensure that the patient had a good look at what was going to pumped into the deltoid muscle of the shoulder. It was used as a tonic or 'pick me up' which, when given by injection, had an enhanced placebo effect. There are a limited number of indications when it is entirely appropriate for B_{12} to be given in this way (such as pernicious anaemia, which is due to an inability of the intestine to absorb B_{12} because of lack of 'intrinsic factor', a protein secreted by the stomach which is essential for its absorption) but mostly it is not required. The good thing is that it usually does no harm, except of course when the RMP of the 1960s repeatedly used the same needle to inject a series of patients and cross-infected individuals with an infectious disease, such as one of the chronic hepatitis viruses.

RMPs charged their patients handsomely and when the money ran out there were only a limited number of options left. Local government hospitals often had a bad reputation, and this was certainly the case in Jammy at the time. For those living in the environs of Campbell Hospital there was another option, for poor patients who were often treated at low or no charge. Nevertheless, the loss of a key worker in the family could lead to ruin. Children might be led towards a life as beggars (sometimes after inflicted mutilation of a limb), possibly leaving the family to live as a slum dweller in a larger town, or for girls a life of prostitution. This was rough injustice and reminded me of the extraordinary safety net that the NHS and social services in the UK provide for its citizens faced with a similar life-changing event. It is easy to be cynical about something we have absorbed into our collective consciousness and services we love to hate. Beware of what you wish for!

I was halted by a knock at my bedroom door.

'Michael, breakfast will be ready in ten minutes. We must visit the children's ward before what will be a long outpatient clinic.'

William spoke quietly through the gap between the locally made, hardwood double-doors that separated my room from the dining room; they were just apart and I assumed that they had never quite fitted together or, to be generous, perhaps had drifted apart over the years following the marked seasonal changes in temperature and humidity.

'I'm awake. Don't worry I'll be there. Thanks for the call.'

I had to bathe and dress before breakfast with the family. My bathroom adjoined the bedroom, 'en suite' in today's vernacular, but was simple and followed the traditional Indian model. Half doors (resembling those of a saloon bar in the 'Wild West'), so that modesty was preserved, ventilation was facilitated but that full seclusion was never achieved. There was nothing that resembled a European bath or shower. Bathing took place in a low walled enclosure in the corner of the bathroom. It contained a single cold tap on the wall, a bucket and a small dipping cup both made from a rather unattractive shade of pink plastic and a drain hole in the floor. There was a large antiquated electric water heater on the wall above the bathing area which fed a second tap (presumably hot) closer to ground level but it looked such an ancient beast that I never dared turn it on. In truth, the air temperature never went low enough, even in the early morning, to make cool water washing anything but a pleasure. Bathing was accomplished quite simply by filling the bucket with water from the cold-water tap and then repeatedly dousing oneself with water using the dipping cup. Once the body was wet, a light soaping was then in order, followed by a 'wash off' using the dipping cup.

The dress code was easy and followed the same pattern, day in day out. White or pale coloured short-sleeved shirt, pale cotton trousers (not too tight) and local dark leather traditional Indian *chappals* (a design which was copied to create the now ubiquitous 'flip-flops') for Indians and English alike. I became very attached to my *chappals*; they returned with me to England at the end of the trip and I wore them for years until they finally disintegrated. They became 'transitional objects' in the true Winnicottian sense.

I slid quietly through the ill-fitting bedroom doors to find the family already attacking their breakfast. Breakfast, like many things in Jammy, did not change much from day to day. It would start with 'porridge' – not porridge oats as we would be so familiar with in the UK, but a gluey, granular preparation made from sweet sorghum (a cereal grain) or ragi, a type of millet (it bore some resemblance to semolina) usually topped with a coarsely ground, unrefined dark cane sugar preparation called jaggery. It was said to be better than regular sugar because of its iron content. Boiled cow or buffalo milk could also be added to taste. This was followed by an egg fried in ghee on toast and traditional English (Indian) tea.

Margot Cutting sat at the head of the table and directed operations remotely in the kitchen. The Cuttings had a delightful, rather elderly, bearded male cook, who was supported by a female helper and a boy. The kitchen ran very smoothly but as the regime flowed with great regularity and consistency from day to day, the service team was faced with few surprises. Margot had trained in medicine in Edinburgh with William but on coming to India as medical missionaries she had been fully occupied raising their three children, Alastair, Catriona and the most recent arrival, Kenneth, now in his third year of life. Kenneth had been born in Jammy under the supervision of Ratnama; a normal delivery without complications I understand. A major concern for a mother (and her medical advisers) when delivering a baby in rural circumstances, is the possibility of fatal haemorrhage around the time of delivery. Margot took the precaution of putting a few pints of her own blood in the fridge during the run-up to the birth so that she could be sure of the availability of a compatible and infection-free transfusion. When I arrived, Margot was seriously pregnant, about twenty-eight weeks, I recall, with her fourth child.

By the time I arrived in Jammy, Alastair, then nine years of age, was away at Lushington Boys' School in Ootacamund ('Ooty' as it was affectionately known), a hill station in a beautiful location in the Nilgiri hills; a place much favoured by the British as a way of escaping the summer heat of the plains. I had the chance to visit towards the end of my time at Jammy, when I accompanied Alastair back to school for the beginning of the autumn term. Catriona, then about five years, was taught at home by Margot. Kenneth, a two-year-old, just played, ate and slept. I remember them all as lively, contented and well-adjusted children. They were certainly the products of their parents. All of them had a fine, pale, freckled complexion with various shades of red/flaxen hair. Indubitable Celts! They were a charming cohesive family totally committed to their mission in India; they never complained about the many challenges that they faced every day.

SICK CHILDREN

'Time for work,' William announced with gentle precision.

'Yes, you should be off. Both of you.' Margot stood up at her place at the table and signalled towards the door; as if we did not know where it was.

William got up from his chair at the other end of the table, gave Margot a light kiss on the cheek and waited for me to join him at the front door of the bungalow. It was 7.25am. Before starting work at the hospital, it was customary for all staff to gather in the chapel for a short service. Two hymns and a prayer and we were fortified for the day. We sat cross-legged on rugs on the floor. The musical accompaniment was a hand-pumped portable harmonium. These instruments were introduced into India by missionaries in the mid-nineteenth century and remain popular to this day. Sometimes there was percussion support in the form of the traditional paired Indian drums, the tabla.

The children's ward was limited in space but hugely in demand. Beds and cots were crammed together with barely enough space for staff to move between them. Mothers generally stayed with their children day and night and took an active role in their day-to-day care. The preferred place at night was to sleep on the floor under their child's bed. The facilities were rudimentary and the diagnostic and therapeutic options limited. However, the care was excellent, largely due to the vast clinical experience of the doctors and nurses. William was the paediatrician in charge and Sam was his trainee. Together they did everything. William's ambition for Sam, already a qualified doctor, was to undertake post-graduate training in paediatrics at the Christian Medical College Hospital in Vellore, a small town in Tamil Nadu about 280 km away. William always knew that he would not stay in Jammy for his entire career and was keen to ensure that there was a succession plan in place.

'Sam, everything seems in good order. I don't think that infant with presumed TBM (tuberculous meningitis) is not going to make it. But go ahead with the intrathecal streptomycin anyway.'

William moved along the ward towards the next cot.

'Yes, I agree. Nothing much to lose.' Sam looked rather downcast at the thought of losing his patient. We moved to the next bed.

'This babe still looks very dry. I don't think the oral rehydration is working. Could you put up a scalp vein drip … in fact why don't you show our young doctor how to do it? About time he learnt to do something useful!' He let free a wry smile. He was joking, of course.

I was soon introduced to some of the practical clinical procedures, such as placing scalp vein needles to allow intravenous fluid replacement of dehydrated infants and lumbar punctures to sample cerebrospinal fluid. I remember being quite shocked when I learnt that there were no disposable needles and syringes in the hospital. Everything was recycled after cleaning and heat/pressure sterilisation. The main problem with the needles was that they were always blunt and were difficult to sharpen effectively. This made

A bullock cart, 1969. (Author's collection)

placement for a novice even more challenging. The glass syringes were similarly difficult to operate, as with repeated use and advancing age the plunger failed to move smoothly in the barrel and the gradation markings on the barrel became increasingly indistinct with repeated cleaning and sterilisation.

Bacterial and viral meningitis was common; tuberculous meningitis was not infrequent. For the latter, we were still giving anti-TB drugs directly into the spinal canal, something that was discarded as being unnecessary a few years later. The main killer diseases of children in Jammy, and indeed in most of India, were infections and under-nutrition. We saw everything. Malaria was rife and killed many young children every year in the area, particularly the *P. falciparum* variety and its attendant complication, cerebral malaria. It was usually treatable with quinine but typically patients presented late, often too late during the illness, beyond the point when treatment would be effective. Many patients would travel for several days in a bullock cart to get to the hospital, a journey already delayed by an unhelpful engagement with an RMP or another traditional practitioner.

Most of the infants admitted to the ward wore charms on string bracelets or necklaces, clear evidence that they had been to a traditional healer. Scarification was also used widely at the time by local healers with recognisable patterns to prevent or treat specific diseases. These totally ineffective interventions further impoverished poor families and, even worse, added to the delay in the instigation of effective treatment. Once these children crossed the hospital threshold the charms were removed, symbolically enforcing the fact that they were now under the care of a different belief system.

I became fascinated by the diversity of design of these 'protective' medicinal charms and decided to rescue the objects before they were consigned to the waste bin. Some were simple dyed cotton bands around the wrist, others were suspended around the neck by a cotton string; the latter varied in form from small brass plaques containing inscriptions in Sanskrit while others consisted of mini cotton sacks, dyed with vegetable dyes containing uncooked rice grains. I understood at the time that these charms were not used randomly but had specific disease- or symptom-related indications. Scarification took a variety of forms; one memorable creation was a 'noughts and crosses' pattern which usually extended across the infant's abdomen. My recollection is that this was to protect the infant from neonatal tetanus. William's father, Dr Cecil Cutting, a medical

Health charms, 1969. (Author's collection, photograph by Electric Egg)

missionary for many years in Chikballarpur in the Nandi Hills (Mysore State originally; now in Karnataka), was also fascinated by these charms or *mantrums*, and writes at some length about the phenomenon in his book *Hot Surgery*, an account of his experiences published in 1962.

There were many other superstitious practices, including the mother's desire to sleep with an iron implement under her pillow to ward off evil influences. One example I recall was a small iron hand-sickle, which the mother had surreptitiously brought into the hospital. These practices were disliked and strongly discouraged by the hospital staff; justified by the notion that they had no informed basis or efficacy, but perhaps even more important because they were regarded as being pagan practices and therefore against the teachings of Christ. I think my interest in these health tokens raised suspicions in some of the staff that I might be a sympathiser.

At least half of the children in the ward that morning had a combination of severe under-nutrition, either marasmus (profound wasting due to calorie deprivation) or kwashiorkor (wasting plus oedema and abdominal swelling due to ascites) and acute gastroenteritis.

Classically, the downward cycle in health started towards the end of the first year of life when the infant was being weaned from breast milk, which had protected it from the harmful bacteria that it was at risk of encountering through contaminated food, water and other elements of the environment. One of the great steps forward in understanding the relationship between repeated infections, malnutrition and growth retardation was made at around this time by an American physician, Nevin Scrimshaw and his Costa Rican collaborator, Leonardo Mata. They showed in a longitudinal study that ran over several years that under-nutrition in an isolated mountain village, Santa María Cauqué in Costa Rica, occurred in infants and children in the absence of famine or less severe food shortages but coincided with frequent, recurrent respiratory and intestinal infections and other systemic infections such as measles. The challenge was to seek new strategies for reducing infection while ensuring that infants and young children were adequately nourished. It was one of the 'new arguments' for aggressively reinstating breast-feeding in the developing world at this time and dissuading mothers from moving towards the trend in the West of using infant formula and bottles. William was actively engaged in introducing new practices to improve childhood nutrition both in hospital practice in children with advanced malnutrition but perhaps, more importantly, in teaching mothers in the villages to use ways to prevent it happening and to be able to spot the early signs so

Marasmus, 1969.
(Author's collection)

Kwashiorkor, 1969.
(Author's collection)

that intervention would be more likely to succeed. He had picked up very early on the findings of Scrimshaw and Gordon, namely the lethal interaction between infection and under-nutrition; it was not just shortage in the supply of food.

Just over a decade later I had the privilege to work with Leonardo Mata in the University of Costa Rica, San José. He was a truly inspirational man with a voracious appetite both for work and beautiful young women! He had a special blend of strengths; a strongly scientific mind and a deep belief in the scientific method, a respect for the ethical aspects of human experimentation and a sense of being part of that simple impoverished mountain community that he and his team lived with and observed over a ten-year period.

There was one case on the ward that seemed to me like something from the last century; a six-week-old baby with neonatal tetanus. In the West, tetanus was a largely unseen disease due to the widespread use of tetanus toxoid vaccine and the availability of anti-toxin. However, in village India, the disease was not uncommon because of the traditional practice of placing a cow dung poultice on the umbilical cord stump soon after delivery and severing of the umbilical cord. Cow faeces are a rich source of the bacterium *Clostridium tetani*, the causative organism. The baby was in a tragic state with uncontrollable spasms most apparent in the face with the typical 'false smile' known as *risus sardonicus*. Despite muscle relaxants and anti-toxin, the baby died after a short period as we had no facilities to offer long-term mechanical ventilation of an infant.

Rheumatic fever was still common in older children, as were its consequences, mainly damage to the heart valves. As a medical student, I found it extraordinary to be able to listen to the whole range of common heart murmurs in the hospital at any one time. Thankfully, polio was on the wane due to the increasing use of oral vaccination and I never saw a case of smallpox, which by 1969 was virtually eliminated from the subcontinent, although not officially eradicated from the world until about ten years later in 1980.

Sam and I followed William around the ward, stopping by each bed to check the patient's 'observations' (blood pressure, pulse rate and temperature) and, when necessary, to change the intravenous fluid regime or to modify the prescription chart. The ward sister would listen attentively as William passed on instructions in Telegu. He would stop to speak to anxious mothers who seemed to have no idea whatsoever as to what was going on, but desperately concerned that their precious child should survive. Sadly, death was not an uncommon outcome on the ward. Sam would stop off intermittently to re-site an intravenous cannula that had blocked or become dislodged. The ward round complete, we then moved swiftly on to the children's outpatient clinic.

The outpatient clinic usually began soon after 9.00am and would continue until 1.00pm or later; it finished when the last patient had been seen. There was no appointment system at the time. Children and their parents just arrived at the hospital, booked in at the reception desk and then waited with utmost patience, either standing in the outpatient corridor or sitting on the ground around the front entrance to the hospital, until they were seen by a doctor. I do not recall anyone complaining about waiting to be seen. Many had travelled hours or days to the hospital and were just grateful to get access to a doctor. Sam sat in one small office and William in another across the corridor. Each patient was seen for no more than three or four minutes and between the two of them I would guess that they saw between 150 and 200 patients in a morning. I sat with William most of the time, but Sam would call me across the corridor if something unusual cropped up. He would also use William as a resource when he was stuck over the diagnosis of a sick child.

There was no time to do anything very much. The parents were usually asked to give a one- or two-sentence account of the problem while standing by the physician's desk; a moment of observation including a clinical assessment for anaemia, then a stethoscope would be run over the chest and a hand placed gently on the abdomen. The clinic nurse would take the temperature if there was a clinical concern about fever; a child with serious pneumonia or malaria would be admitted. Most patients would feel uncomfortable about leaving the clinic without a prescription. The list of affordable medicines was not extensive, most were harmless, so the treatment options were limited. Antibiotics were available and were offered for serious infections. Anaemia was common and usually due to hookworm infestation which could be treated with anti-worm drugs and iron tablets.

We could make a confirmatory test for anaemia easily while the child was in the clinic using a rather primitive colorimetric method of assessing haemoglobin. A drop of blood was mixed with hydrochloric acid, which converted the haemoglobin to acid haematin. The mixture was diluted until it seemed by eye to match a coloured glass standard. The lab could also check for the presence of malaria parasites in the blood but that was about all. What was remarkable was that the extensive clinical experience of the medical staff enabled the diagnosis to be made correctly in most cases. We always tell medical students when they are struggling to assess the diagnostic options, that common things are common.

That morning I saw a child with vitamin A deficiency diagnosed not by a blood test but by the detection of a classic clinical sign of deficiency, Bitot's spots. These spots can be seen on the conjunctiva and are due to the build-up of keratin debris. They were first described in 1863 by the French physician, Charles Bitot. I saw a deformed tibia due to osteomyelitis and a bizarre abscess in a child just below the scapula. At the time, it did not stand out as something peculiar but, as I think now, I just wonder whether it could have been a so-called 'cold abscess' as a complication of pulmonary TB?

It was now about 12.45pm and I decided to walk out into the corridor to check how many more patients there were still to see. I could see the end of the line, which was good, but my eyes were attracted towards a slim young girl of about twelve years who was making the most extraordinary movements of an arm and a leg down one side of her body. It was quite alarming, and I immediately returned to the consulting room to ask William what should be done. He was completing a consultation with a prescription for some cough linctus and then walked with me to see the girl.

'Sydenham's chorea!' He said without a moment's hesitation.

'I'm sorry. What did you say?' I responded quickly.

'Sydenham's chorea. Saint Vitus' dance. A well-recognised complication of rheumatic fever.'

'Will she have a murmur?' I said, anticipating the challenge of sorting out which of the heart valves had been involved.

'Probably not. She may have, of course, but often the heart is spared in Sydenham's.'

'Is it urgent? Do we need to do something immediately to stop the involuntary movements?' I was feeling overwhelmed by the sometimes violent and clearly distressing uncontrollable movements of her arms and legs.

'No. Nothing. We'll just reassure the girl and her parents that this will all subside in a few weeks, and we'll see her again in the clinic in two weeks, so you can check that I am right.' He smiled. 'We'll give her an injection of long-acting penicillin which will clear any residual beta haemolytic streptococci and get her to continue on a high dose oral regime for a further week.'

William spoke briefly to the family while still in the waiting area, in front of an interested but increasingly alarmed group of other patients and well-wishers, and sent them on their way.

'Before they leave, can you arrange for them to have a prescription for penicillin which they can pick up from the hospital pharmacy? And have a listen to the heart before they leave and see what you can find.'

I could not hear a murmur and before I had completed my examination and arranged for the prescription, William and Sam had finished the clinic.

'Come on it's time for lunch.'

We walked back to William's bungalow in the intense midday sun. It was hot. Very hot. Must have been over 30°C. But I was acclimatising and found the hot and dry environment surprisingly relaxing. Nobody rushed anywhere. Everything was taken at a measured comfortable pace. Enforced tranquilisation!

Lunch was on the table and the family had already eaten on the account of our late arrival.

'Heavy morning?' asked Margot in her soft Edinburgh accent.

'Not especially. Just the usual. But plenty for our young aspiring doctor to see!'

He looked back at me smiling and gave a reassuring wink.

We both disappeared off to our respective bathrooms to 'wash our hands' but were back at the table in no time. I remember it as a rather gloomy dark room with little natural light. The house was built of grey/black Cuddapah stone like the rest of the hospital and the residential quarters. Thick walls to keep the house cool during the blisteringly hot summers. And it worked. Even though summer night-time temperatures remained relatively high, perhaps not falling much below 30°C, the house was pleasant always. The dining table was rectangular and covered in an unattractive plastic tablecloth. There was nowhere comfortable to sit, which perhaps reflected the lifestyle of work, eat and sleep. Relaxation and recreation were never built into the daily routine.

Lunch was always 'Indian lunch'. Simple basic curry and rice and spicy pickle, usually lime. Today it was chicken curry. Tomorrow most likely it will be mutton curry and the day after that hard-boiled egg curry. I was always struck by the preponderance of bone in the meat curries. Sometimes it would be vegetarian curry for which South of India was well known. Lunch for me was the best meal of the day. I came to adore the Indian cuisine and have done so ever since. All drinking water was boiled and then chilled in the ancient refrigerator. Deserts were limited but some fruits were available. I arrived at the end of the mango season and became addicted to its potent aromatic flavours. I swear it was the mangos that induced a sleeping state within minutes of completing lunch. I have mentioned the deeply unattractive plastic tablecloth. Practical but nevertheless unattractive; it had a faux lace texture which meant that it was impossible to get properly clean, and I was always conscious of an unpleasant stickiness when one's arms or hands encountered its surface. The other remarkable feature of the table's furnishings was the covers that shrouded the sugar bowl, milk jug, chutney jars, jam pot, etc, etc. They were made of a coarse cotton lace with a ring of coloured beads attached around the periphery to add weight to the cover to prevent it becoming dislodged. Flies were abundant and needed to be excluded from tasty foods. These lace covers were widely used across India and can still be seen in use in homes today.

Everyone took a rest in the afternoon while waiting for the midday temperature to subside. Everyone, that is except William. I can still hear the click, click, clickety-click of his ancient, 'stand up and beg' black Underwood typewriter as he caught up with all the tasks that sat heavily on his desk. He was an assiduous letter writer; I guess his way of keeping in regular contact with the outside world. The telephone functioned poorly in South India in those days, with calls needing to be booked with the exchange many hours before, with no guarantee whatsoever that the connection would be made. Even if contact was achieved, the background crackling and the coming and going of the signal almost negated completely the joy of a conversation. The fax had not been invented; telegrams were still available but were expensive and only to be used in emergencies. William wrote reports of the work of the hospital and despite the difficult circumstances managed to write papers for medical journals, describing his work in childhood nutrition. He continued to write to me regularly after I left Jammy, sending news of the family and the hospital. One day I received a letter in red typescript. I was concerned that something terrible had happened. Nothing terrible at all; only that the black reel of inked tape had run out and he was relying solely on the red. Supplies often took weeks or months to arrive in Jammy and were deemed to be a costly, expensive luxury.

MOTHERS AND BABIES

I would generally take a brief sleep after catching up with my personal correspondence, always written in longhand. Forty-five minutes was usually enough to recharge the batteries and give one the energy to start the second half of the day's work. Just as I was getting my clothes back on there was a knock on the main front door and I could hear one of the porters asking for me. Then there was a knock on my ill-fitting bedroom doors, a smiling face and a brown hand offering me a folded pink piece of paper, a chit (derived from the Hindi word *cittha*, meaning 'a note'). It was to be the first of many. Almost certainly a message from Ratnama or Flavia.

> *Dear Michael,*
> *There is one Eclampsia (one of the toxaemias of pregnancy). Please come and see in the*
> *maternity ward. You don't get many eclampsias in the UK and you may not get another*
> *chance to see.*
> > *R. Ratnaraj*

I thanked the porter, put on my *chappals* and followed him across to the maternity ward where Ratnama and Flavia were anxiously looking at the woman's charts displaying two key and alarming observations.

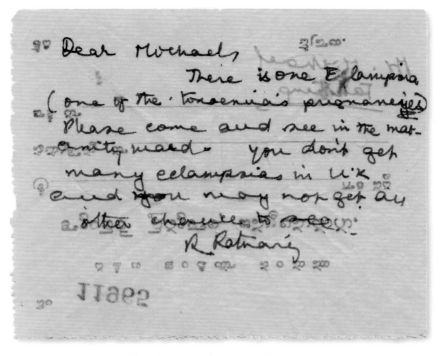

Chit, July 1969. (Author's collection)

Her blood pressure was very high and rising and she had large amounts of protein in her urine. It was not difficult to see that this was a very ill young woman and someone who might not survive.

'She is very young, probably only 16 or 17 years [age in rural South India at the time was never known precisely]. They are usually young and almost invariably the first pregnancy.'

I noticed that her mouth was dry and twitching and she was very drowsy, almost unconscious. As far as they knew she had not had a convulsion yet, but the twitching was not a good sign, I thought.

'What will you do?' I inquired with concern.

'Try and get her blood pressure down. We use I.V. [intravenous] hydralazine. I have asked Willy to bring some from the pharmacy. She's dry so we'll give a little fluid cautiously and we need to check how the foetus is doing.'

She palpated the woman's abdomen to assess the stage of pregnancy.

'She's about thirty weeks. I can't see the baby surviving this.'

The ward sister passed her a foetal stethoscope. She placed the instrument over the side of the abdomen where she had located the baby's back.

'Very difficult to be sure but I don't think I can hear the foetal heart.'

Flavia intervened.

'Shall I try?'

'Yes, of course. Please do.' Flavia took the stethoscope and moved it round different sites on the abdomen, but eventually stopped and shook her head.

'There may be something but if there is it's very weak and very fast. Clearly there is foetal distress.'

Ratnama then made the critical decision that enabled a plan to be formulated.

'We'll give her the hydralazine gently and then prepare her for an emergency section under spinal. The spinal will also help lower her blood pressure, but we'll need to be careful we don't overdo it.'

Delivery of the foetus at this stage, even in its state of immaturity would give the mother the best chance of survival but would be unlikely to produce a viable infant. The facilities to support premature babies in this rural setting were largely non-existent and transfer to a more sophisticated set-up was simply not feasible. Nevertheless, the choice in favour of the mother was made and the decision taken.

Hydralazine was given by I.V. infusion and the blood pressure monitored by the nursing staff every fifteen minutes. It had a good effect and there was a modest decrease in the pressure. The young woman was barely conscious, and the outcome looked to me to be grave. She was transferred to the simple operating theatre where Ratnama and Flavia were already scrubbing up in preparation. It was a plain room, with a stone floor and flaking, painted walls. Ventilation was provided by an open window and the two operating tables and other equipment were basic. There was an anaesthetic machine which could deliver an oxygen-halothane/nitrous oxide anaesthetic, but I never saw it used. There was also an ether-oxygen machine (the EMO machine) which was used for open abdominal surgery and other surgical procedures which were not amenable to the discrete regional anaesthesia offered by a spinal anaesthetic.

The patient was now on the operating table and Flavia had scrubbed and gowned and was placing the local anaesthetic into the spinal canal. All the surgeons were skilled at this procedure, as it was the favoured way of achieving anaesthesia for many operative procedures because of the relatively primitive arrangements for giving a general anaesthetic, compounded by the lack of a trained anaesthetist on the hospital staff.

Once it was clear that regional anaesthesia had been achieved, with Ratnama in the lead and Flavia assisting, they proceeded rapidly to deliver the foetus through a midline abdominal incision (not the more cosmetic 'bikini line', Pfannenstiel incision) because of speed. I watched from the sidelines and was impressed by their team work and technical skills. Within literally a few minutes the baby was out and the cord clamped. A senior nurse was taking care of the semi-conscious patient at the head end of the table. The baby was very small, was blue, limp and inactive and made no respiratory efforts. There was no cry. The two surgeons looked at each other and signalled with their eyes over the tops of their white cotton gauze masks that there was nothing further to do. No attempts were made to resuscitate the infant and it was just wrapped in a white cotton sheet and taken out of the theatre. It was officially recorded as a stillbirth. Whether it was dead on delivery, I am not sure but either way it had no future for the reasons I mentioned earlier.

The young mother's blood pressure remained better controlled but her level of consciousness was unaltered. They delivered the placenta, closed the uterus and then the abdomen with great speed and she was returned to the women's surgical ward for close monitoring. Their speed and skill had ensured that blood loss had been kept at an absolute minimum such that transfusion had not been required.

Ratnama continued to provide leadership in this dire situation.

'The baby was dead *in utero*, so there was nothing more to do. I will speak to the family and tell them the bad news. Flavia, will you keep an eye on her during the next few hours? Keep her gently hydrated and keep going with the hydralazine. Be gentle though. Let's see if she can pull through.'

Ratnama left and Flavia followed the porters who were delivering the girl back to the ward on a trolley. It was obvious that no one felt good about the situation, but they had seen similar obstetric disasters before and had to remain calm and professional whatever their personal feelings were about the case.

That was the end of surgery for the day. I walked across the quadrangle in the centre of the main hospital building and began to assess the magnitude of my next major challenge, the reorganisation of the pharmacy store and the development of a rational scheme for the payment for prescription drugs. Dr Ratnaraj had spotted that I had just completed a degree in pharmacology and assumed that this would be an excellent preparation for the job in hand. Not so, but nevertheless I did know how to list and arrange drugs by their class of action and had some sense of their role in modern therapeutics.

Before I arrived at the pharmacy I was stopped by a young man; he was deeply distressed, weeping visibly and speaking to me with great pressure in Telegu. He was quite well groomed and dressed and when he saw that I did not understand his protestations he tried again in fractured English.

'Sir, please Sir, you must help. Please. I cannot go back to village without child. You must have one child. There must be many.'

I was lost. What was this all about?

'My wife, Sir! You have just seen her. Our baby is dead. Please find another for us. There must be many here. We cannot leave without baby. Any baby!'

Of course, he was the father of the stillborn infant of the woman with eclampsia. No baby and maybe no wife.

'I am sorry. There are no babies. Everyone is accounted for. Stay with your wife tonight. She will need you.'

'Doctor, I cannot go back home. You must see; I am desperate man.'

'Stay with your wife. She will need you. We will see you again in the morning.'

It would be a long night for them. I had no words that would give him relief from his loss or his loneliness that day.

I was disturbed by the encounter. I felt the intensity of his distress and could do nothing to relieve it. Was this the pattern for the future? Would I become a breaker of bad news, without being able to offer any relief?

SWEEPERS

I picked up my feet and continued the short journey to the dispensary with a sense of sadness and impotency. The first challenge was to meet the pharmacy team and gain their confidence. It was just two people – Devapryam, the boss and Willy, his helper. This was not a dynamic duo. And it was clear from the outset that the pharmacy was in chaos. There was no rational approach to drug storage so that no one, other than themselves, could ever find a drug; the arrangements in the pharmacy store were random.

There was no system for keeping an eye on drug expiry dates, no transparent and consistent pricing system and the environment in which drugs were stored and dispensed was just plain dirty.

We sat down together, and I gave them some of my initial observations.

They looked rather downhearted after hearing my words, but we resolved together to make things better. So, we started to clean the storeroom, remove the discarded cardboard boxes, empty bottles and other detritus, and then Deva summoned a sweeper to remove the thick layer of dust that coated the floor, the shelves and other surfaces. There were several large glass carboys that must have contained an important fluid at some point, but we agreed that they were now without function and should go. Willy was very reluctant to see anything leave through the door (he thought that everything could be useful given time) but I insisted on the basis that it would free up valuable space and facilitate the next stage of our work, namely the orderly arrangement of drugs on the newly cleaned shelves. I could see that they both were becoming uncomfortable about my willingness to engage with the physical tasks on hand and finally exclaimed with great alarm when I took the rather primitive sweeping implement (a traditional hand broom made, I think, from grass reeds bound tightly at one end with twine to make a handle) into my own hands to bring added vigour to what seemed to me to be an inexorably slow process. I had of course broken the cardinal rule; I had crossed the caste divide. Sweepers, sometimes called 'the untouchables', were a low caste, perhaps the lowest; born to sweep and only they shall sweep. Traditionally they also perform the most objectionable of duties such as sweeping floors and clearing the latrines of excrement. I soon realised my mistake and rapidly put the hand-held swishing brush back on the floor for the sweeper to return to his God-given duty.

The pharmacy team, 1969.
(Author's collection)

Caste was not a feature of life in India that often crossed my path. Christians, especially Christian missionaries, did not recognise caste and regarded everyone as equals; this was certainly evident in the hospital. I suppose the incident with the Dalit sweeper was more about his job and job description, his role, rather than anything that was determined by an accident of birth. Mahatma Gandhi abhorred the caste system and called repeatedly for its abolition. Successive Indian governments had attempted to remove it and sought out interventions for affirmative action to help the lower, so-called scheduled castes to achieve improved social mobility. Indeed, there are notable examples where Dalits have reached high positions in politics or business but at this time in history these were the exceptions rather than the rule. The main issue for Hindus is that the castes derive directly from the body parts of the supreme creator of the universe, Brahma, God himself. Thus, the system is right at the core of the earliest constructs of Hinduism and so difficult to simply dispose of by social reform or legislation. India is the only Hindu country in the world, and despite the accepting nature of the religion with respect to the beliefs of others, there has been a rise of modern conservative elements which have demanded a return to more traditional ways.

Our work in the pharmacy store continued but by this time it was a dustbowl. We all vacated the room and left it for half an hour, waiting patiently for the dust to settle. The boys looked exhausted and the sweeper had retired to a safe distance across the veranda to find new sweeping powers. I decided that we had made an excellent start and would call it a day. Tomorrow we would draw up an inventory of the drugs in the store room and on the shelves of the dispensary, and work out a rational way of displaying them on the available shelves such that anyone could find their way to a drug without having to enter Willy's maze and join the magical mystery tour to which only he had the key.

I thanked 'the team' profusely and said that we would assemble the following afternoon to continue the good work. I informed them that I would be seeing the superintendent later in the day and would report on the excellent progress we had made. They politely acknowledged my sentiments, but it was not difficult to detect some disquiet. I was creating turbulence in their formerly undisturbed lives. They had for two or possibly three decades been left to their own devices and now someone, someone from outside, was creating waves. However, they took it with grace and were curiously deferential.

The sun was beginning to leave our skies and cool air was gracing the hospital compound. A day to remember. Life in rural South India had an unscheduled brutality; a stark, uncompromising brutality against which it was impossible to mitigate. A brutality that was of routine nature, an 'everyday' sort; it was deeply embedded in everyone's lives. Sadness and loss were normal, to be expected and almost missed if they failed to appear.

I walked back across the compound in the twilight, seeing once again the dim lights of the doctors' houses come to life as they prepared to eat before retiring after another day. For me at this stage every day was different; something new to learn, a new procedure to master and yet another disease to challenge us in these relatively primitive circumstances. For the doctors, my teachers, every day must have seemed much the same but they were committed to the service of their patients and to their Christian mission which was central to their very existence. Despite my own non-conformist religious up-bringing I had not seen this kind of selfless devotion to the pursuit of duty in doing God's work. My admiration was unquestioned although it did not reach the point of a 'second coming' such that I was drawn back into the Church. Nevertheless, I joined in with most of their activities, as a mark of respect for them and what they did, rather than a sign of any inner belief that I might hold.

William had not returned to the house by the time I had arrived but I made my presence known and decided to take a bath as usual before dinner. I threw my shirt and trousers on to the bed, removed my right *chappal* and made my way to the bathroom door with my right hand bearing the *chappal* aloft. I gently pushed open the swing door and with my left hand threw the switch to turn on the bathroom light. There, immobile just in front of the bathing area was my quarry: a black scorpion. I walked quietly up behind it and dispatched the creature with a decisive blow from the under surface of the *chappal*. I had learnt the law; dispatch the scorpions yourself before bathing but if you find a snake, call for help. Over the weeks, I kept my 'kills' and took some home in a small cardboard box. I suppose I was rather proud of my new adeptness in ridding the bathroom of what in England would be regarded as a dangerous and potentially lethal pest. Most of the scorpions I tackled were black; little did my comrades back home know that it is the sandy coloured variety that is most potent, the black being more of a nuisance than a killer. Fortunately, I never found a snake in my bathroom, but others did. They were always handled by our local experts and on one occasion proudly paraded in the hospital compound.

The only other creatures that disrupted life in the hospital environs were the non-sacred wild pigs for whom, other than humans, there was no natural predator. From time to time population control was required.

Dinner was a relatively brief affair. Catriona and Kenneth were usually in bed by the time we ate, and William was always keen to get to his typewriter to keep up with his correspondence, reports, medical papers and other professional writing. Pregnant Margot was interested to catch up on the activities of the day but was also pleased to retire to the peace of her bed. Dinner was always Western cuisine; to be honest it was simple English, unless there was a special celebration. Food sources were limited and so were the skills of our cook, although he always said he especially liked to cook for us in the evening. This I guessed was partly out of deference to us and our native English/Scottish fare but if the truth were known I would imagine that it was quicker and easier; it must have been bliss not to spend hours grinding spices for the garam masala. I found the evening meal of English food dull and without taste by comparison.

I was beginning to take on the mantle of an Indian. I liked their food. I admired their lifestyle, was interested in their religions, and increasingly drawn towards the simplicity of day-to-day living in rural India. I was embarrassed by our consumerism and our commercialism back in England. I was adjusting

A snake, Campbell Hospital, 1969. (Author's collection)

to the relative isolation of the Indian village and no longer craving the external stimulation of television, newspapers, films, theatre, opera, popular music, fashion, Oxford Street and Carnaby Street shopping, restaurants and all the other paraphernalia of London life in the late 1960s. I was experiencing a transformation. I had departed. I was working in another dimension. I was thinking about other worlds and I felt good about it. Lonely at times but still, on balance, I felt good about it.

As I gaze back over several decades of a lovely life, I still feel good about it. It was a transformational experience and an investment in life. The love for that country and its people and the benefit I reaped has never left me. Subsequently, I found other national affections but this was the first and remains the foremost.

Some days I would make myself available for night call. Although Campbell Hospital did not have a fully functioning accident and emergency department, its staff were available at all hours, if required. One evening when I was sitting at my desk there was a gentle knock at the door and one of our porters passed me a small chit with his right hand while in the left he held aloft a hurricane lamp emitting an orange glow, looking a little like Robin Starveling, one of the so-called 'rude mechanicals' who plays moonshine in Shakespeare's, *A Midsummer Night's Dream*! A theatrical device to demonstrate the passage of time. I opened the folded square of paper, which had my name on the outside, and inside it read:

A wild pig, Campbell Hospital, 1969. (Author's collection)

> *Dear Michael*
> *There is a Caesarean at 8:30pm. Please come.*
> *Thanks*
> *R. Ratnaraj*

On another occasion, I was on night duty with William and performed a 'cut-down' to gain venous access in a dehydrated infant with marasmus. That same evening, I sutured a facial laceration, the cause of which remained obscure although I suspected it was the result of an assault.

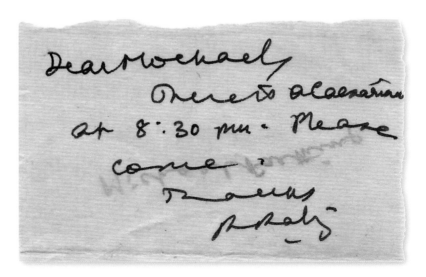

Caesarean chit, 1969. (Author's collection)

During the two or three years I had spent as a student before coming to India I had started to write. Just scribblings; nothing more, nothing less. However, on an evening like this I would return to my desk, while William was clattering away on his typewriter, and throw a few chaotic words by hand on to paper. The words came from nowhere. They said nothing of great import but must have come from a part of the brain that was turning over in response to where I was physically and metaphysically. In a way, it would be an embarrassment to reveal them but what the hell. Juvenile emissions of this nature are intuitively abhorrent, but I delight in reading the adolescent writings of our great poets and writers (if only to see the meaning of the word 'progression') and to learn about their journey through the worlds of creativity.

Many evenings would close in this way. I would linger at my desk, thinking about the two worlds that I now inhabited, wondering whether I would ever be able to reconcile the abyss that seem so massive between them. Finally, the scribbling's ceased and I flipped the switch of my desk lamp and crawled again beneath the mosquito net that framed my simple traditional Indian cot. Sleep always descended at great speed and was never interrupted until the morning sun started its work across the hospital compound.

The next day began in the same way that days at Campbell Hospital usually began. I took breakfast with the family, following which there was a brief service in the hospital chapel, a round with William on the children's ward and then back to the pharmacy, now that the dust had settled. Willy and Deva arrived at the pharmacy ahead of me after the morning service. It was a sign of solidarity and an acceptance that there was a job to be done. They rapidly made me aware that they had made some preparations and had ideas as to how we should reorganise the shelves of drugs in a more orderly fashion. I was delighted. It was evident that anything would be better than the status quo and I was delighted to let them take the lead. I had never seen them move so fast. Shelves were cleared, boxes were stacked in piles on the floor, and step-by-step medicines were reassembled in a logical order back on the stone shelves. They were ecstatic that they had invented a system. Miraculously, it was now possible to find a drug by class and alphabetical order. It was their system not my system and they could explain it to anybody.

There was only one final task to complete before the pharmacy could be launched into the twentieth century. We had to decide on a fair system for drug pricing. I suggested the 'Robin Hood' system; take from the rich and give to the poor! They liked it immediately. So, we agreed a pricing system that enabled the poor to buy drugs well below cost price but expected the rich to pay a charge well above cost price. Those in the middle just paid the going rate. They loved it. The challenge, however, was to distinguish between the rich and the poor. I certainly could not do it because the rich would always dress down when they came to the hospital and the poor would wear their best clothes and put on any jewellery they owned. Ratnama was the person who could see through the superficialities, so if there was ever any doubt as to which patients should pay for their drugs, Ratnama was the final arbiter.

So, after just a couple of weeks my job in the pharmacy was done. Willy and Deva had found a new lease of life and I was released to gain more experience in the operating theatre and the village clinics. Ratnama and Flavia continued to call me to see interesting cases, day and night. Wherever I was in the hospital the delicate handwritten notes would find me by way of one of the obedient hospital porters.

Friday 18 July
Michael
Please come to the maternity ward
R Ratnaraj

Friday 25 July
Michael
Please come to WOP to see one Procedentia
R Ratnaraj

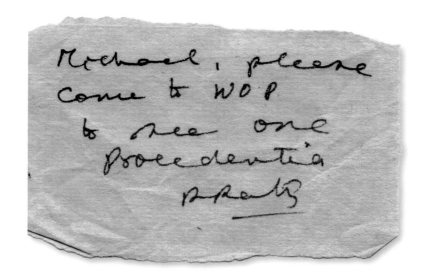

Later in my stay Flavia also found opportunities to teach me something about her own discipline of obstetrics and gynaecology. She was junior to Ratnama and more reserved. Women, even those with a professional qualification, would avoid being alone with another man, I guess as a sign of respect for their husband. For unmarried women, it was just totally unacceptable in those days and I believe could ruin a woman's reputation for life. My first note from Flavia came in early September.

Monday 8 September
I have posted one Fothergill's at 10.30am.
Will you assist?
Thanks   FP

A few days later she sent me another note and a package. We had got to know each other better and I think I must have been talking to her about my travel plans in South India before returning to the UK later in September.

Dear Michael
I am herewith sending you some Chilli Powder (Mixed).
If you want to do take home
You can take all of it.
Flavia P

These plastic bags are not very good
If you have better ones
Send these back
FP

An important part of the work of the doctors at Campbell Hospital was the outreach practice. William had been, I believe, a major instigator of the village clinics encouraged in part by the appalling delays that were evident in patients getting to hospital for care. Poor patients from the surrounding villages might travel a day or more by bullock cart just to gain access to the hospital. Ill patients would often deteriorate badly during transit and some did not arrive alive. William strongly endorsed the principle that in general the management of a disease is easier and likely to be more successful the earlier it is diagnosed and treated.

BREATHLESS IN MYALOOR

Five years earlier, William had started a twice-weekly clinic in a village called Myaloor, 18 km away from Jammy, and another in Kannelur about six months before I arrived. Patients would assemble outside a small dispensary and wait calmly for their turn to see the doctor. The building, like most in the area, was made of black Cuddapah stone. Patients sat on the steps of the veranda or lent against the square stone pillars that supported the red pan-tiled roof.

I went on many occasions with either Sam or William. We could perform a few limited tests and other diagnostic procedures; carry out simple therapeutic interventions such as abscess drainage and dental extractions, and acute medical treatments for infections and heart failure. The first patient I ever treated for acute asthma was in Myaloor, during one of our regular village clinics. He was unshaven and was wearing the traditional white cotton *dhoti* and white *khadi* cotton shirt, both carrying a speckling of the red dust from the fields. He was a frail, elderly man who by his appearance had spent all his life working on the land.

He had been seated on a chair by one the nurses and was clasping the table in front of him with both hands. I learnt later that by doing this manoeuvre, breathless people fix their clavicles and allow the accessory respiratory muscles to work more efficiently. His chest was so tight that air was scarcely passing between his lips and the forceful inspirations were causing the skin and muscle covering the intercostal space to retract. We had no oxygen, which in a better-equipped setting would have been routine, no inhalers or bronchodilators but we did have adrenaline. I drew up a dilute solution into a glass syringe through a repeatedly used and inevitably blunt needle and then asked one of our nursing sisters to explain to him that I was going to give him the medicine by injecting it under his skin. I wiped the area to be injected with a cotton wool swap dipped in an iodine-alcohol solution and I pushed the needle with some difficulty through the brown parchment-like skin which covered his left forearm. I looked across our impoverished make-do consulting room, waiting for further advice from William.

He was examining a child's chest, and before speaking removed the stethoscope from one of his ears. If you do not do that it is difficult to hear what you are saying.

'Good. Have you checked that you are sub-cutaneous and not in a blood vessel?'

'I've pulled back and there is no blood coming into the syringe.'

'Good. Then you're ready to go. You just need to give it very slowly. Keep a finger on his pulse to check that you're not pushing up his heart rate too much and, of course, monitor his breathing. It should begin to get easier over the next fifteen to twenty minutes.'

I tried to look reassuringly into the old man's eyes. He was distressed but remained calm, apparently completely confident that he would get better. Slowly over the next twenty to thirty minutes his breathing began to improve and there was a modest increase in his pulse rate, indicating that the adrenaline was getting into the right place. Air started to move more freely through his pursed lips and the in-drawing between his ribs became less evident. He could relax his grip on the edge of the table and I think I saw a smile in his eyes. I emptied the syringe into his arm and pulled out the needle, placing the syringe with needle still attached into an awaiting white enamel kidney bowl.

I left the old man to continue his recovery and went over to William, who by now was with another patient.

'What should I do now?'

'We'll let him go home and see him again in the clinic next week.'

'Should we give him a short course of prednisone or some antibiotics?'

'There's no sign of infection, so no antibiotics, but a short five-day course of prednisone is a good idea and may delay a recurrence.'

I led him over to the makeshift pharmacy; it was just a large box of drugs on a table in the corner of an adjoining room and found a bottle of prednisone. The pharmacy assistant who accompanied us on the visits to village clinics counted out five days' pills and instructed him how to take them, gradually decreasing the dose over a period of the treatment. He was asked to return to the clinic the following week.

The line of patients waiting to be seen gradually diminished and eventually the clinic nurses closed the dispensary box containing the modest array of medicaments and we began the journey back to Jammy along the dry, rutted, unmade road along which we had come. For these villagers, this was as good as it gets. We were no more than 'bare-foot doctors'. We had more knowledge and experience to make a clinical diagnosis but very limited access to the routine lab tests which would be regarded as standard in the UK and almost no effective drugs other than a few antibiotics, basic anti-TB and anti-malarial drugs, iron tablets and a few vitamins often given as placebos. The gap between what a patient would expect at the teaching hospital in Gower Street, London and here, off the beaten track in rural India, was immense. Our patients were undemanding and always profusely grateful. While I knew that what they were getting was sub-standard I also knew that they did not have the same expectations of survival that someone of the same age in London would have. An accident of birth; nothing more, nothing less.

SIMPLY SURGERY

With the pharmacy project complete, and my other activities – such as rounding on the children's ward and observing gynaecological surgery and Caesarean sections – now well established, I needed something else to justify my time at the hospital. The superintendent, Dr Ratnaraj, knowing that my work in the pharmacy was done, invited me one morning to assist him with a gastrectomy. I had never seen a gastrectomy and had no idea why we were going to do one. However, enlightenment was close at hand.

We stood together side-by-side in our bare feet (as was the custom) at the antiquated scrub sink which was more like an animal's drinking trough with a couple of taps above it than the more sophisticated arrangements that I subsequently became familiar with when I returned to study surgery in London. I watched how Dr Ratnaraj meticulously scrubbed his fingernails and then the fronts and backs of his hands with the small nailbrush which had been loaded with soap. Our hands and arms dried quickly in

Theatre scrub, Campbell Hospital, 1969. (Author's collection)

the warm air and we then proceeded to gown- and glove-up. The surgeons' latex gloves were washed and sterilised time and time again until they lost their flexibility and began to fall apart. One of the theatre nurses would help with closing the ties at the back of our green gowns and in securing the white gauze facemasks which were also washed and recycled on a regular basis.

Before his mask had been secured, he looked across at me and said:

'Help the nurse give the chloroform induction before we start the patient on the EMO machine.'

'So, you still use chloroform,' I said with some trepidation.

'Yes of course. We have nothing else.' I had seen the large five-litre brown glass bottles in the pharmacy during the clean-up operation and had looked up the complications.

'But isn't it rather dangerous. I thought that it was very toxic to the liver in some patients.'

'That may be so, but *we've* never had a problem.' He waited for the theatre nurse to pull the patient's hospital gown up to his chest, clear of his abdomen, so he could begin to cleanse the skin prior to surgery.

By this time the patient was lying on his back on the operating table, apparently calm and relaxed having received a sedative on the ward. One of the theatre attendants was holding his head and another handed me what looked like a metal tea strainer containing several squares of white surgical gauze. A moderate size brown ribbed glass bottle was handed to me and using a glass dropper with a rubber bulb on the top, I loaded chloroform onto the gauze. The environment around the patient's head became suffused with the familiar overpowering sweet smell of this distinctive volatile liquid. I wondered who would be unconscious first, me or the patient.

The patient started to move about on the table, but his restlessness was physically restrained by the two theatre orderlies who stepped quickly forward from their sentinel positions either side of the open theatre door.

'More chloroform,' the superintendent said brusquely.

In less thirty seconds the patient was calm, breathing steadily and rapidly entering the world of surgical anaesthesia.

The theatre nurse picked up the black rubber facemask from the anaesthetic trolley, asked me to remove the chloroform gauze and slickly placed the mask over the patient's nose and mouth, fixing it firmly in place with a black rubber strap which ran behind the patient's head and back onto the mask. The patient began to breathe slowly and deeply as he inhaled the ether-air mixture from the EMO (Ether-Macintosh-Oxford) machine. Ether was first used on any scale in the provision of anaesthesia for surgery in the mid-nineteenth century. Dr John Snow (better known for his discovery of the mode of transmission of cholera in London in 1855) was one of the early protagonists of both ether and chloroform. According to his own case records, he administered chloroform to Queen Victoria, at the request of Prince Albert, to reduce the pain of labour during her eighth (Prince Leopold, 1853) and ninth (Princess Beatrice, 1857) pregnancies, without complications. One month after the birth of Prince Leopold there was a critical jibe in a leading medical journal, *The Lancet*, about the use of chloroform in obstetrics. Queen Victoria wrote in her journal, however, 'Dr Snow gave that blessed chloroform and the effect was soothing, quieting and delightful beyond measure.'

The EMO machine was launched in 1941 but was superseded by halothane and intermittent positive pressure ventilation by the late 1950s in many industrialised countries in the Western world. However, in low-income countries it continued to be used for many years. The main advantage of ether is that it is cheap, safe and can be delivered by relatively inexperienced practitioners.

'Are we ready to go?' Dr Ratnaraj said in an urgent whisper, seemingly not wanting to wake the patient up but anxious to get on with the procedure.

During the induction phase of anaesthesia, he had painted the abdomen with the yellow iodine-alcohol solution, applied green cotton drapes to isolate the abdominal field and looking intently at the abdominal field, held out his right hand to receive a scalpel with which he would make the skin incision. It was a para-median incision running vertically and traversing what appeared to be most of the abdomen. With speed and incredible skill, he arrested any bleeding points using surgical clips and fine cotton ties, and within what seemed to be a few minutes methodically went through all the layers of the abdominal wall and entered the peritoneal cavity. In more affluent parts of the world it would have been standard practice to arrest bleeding points at the edge of the incision by diathermy haemostasis, but Jammy did not have a diathermy machine and its use was precluded as ether and chloroform (both volatile, flammable liquids) were being used as the anaesthetic agents.

'There,' he said, 'feel that!' He caressed the stomach in his left hand while palpating the first part of the duodenum – the duodenal bulb – between the thumb and forefinger of his right hand.

'Massive chronic DU – duodenal ulcer. And see how narrow the duodenum is at that point. There is severe scarring following years of chronic ulceration.'

I could feel the thickened duodenal wall.

'That's why he has been vomiting as well as suffering pain. And see how dilated the stomach is. A clear sign of pyloric obstruction.'

Without raising his eyes from the surgical field or further comment, he stretched out his right hand towards the scrub nurse who without a word picked up a scalpel from the tray of instruments and placed it into his open hand. He made an incision through all layers along the anterior surface of the scarred area of the duodenum, placed two surgical clips at the centre of each margin of the incision and handed them both to me indicating that I should pull them apart and allow him then to close the duodenum by suturing in the opposite direction thereby increasing its calibre.

'This is a pyloroplasty. This is the simplest way to allow the stomach to empty again providing of course the sutured incision does not leak. We now need to reduce gastric acid secretion so that the ulcer doesn't come back.'

He reached up to the top of the stomach and identified the right and left vagus nerves running along each side of the oesophagus. These nerves are responsible for promoting a large part of gastric acid secretion. They are the conduit, for example, by which the stomachs of Pavlov's dogs would start secreting acid at the sight of food. He mobilised the nerves for a centimetre or two, resected a short segment from each side and then began to close the abdomen.

I learnt during future abdominal operations that this was not as straightforward as it might sound. Operations of this nature in the industrialised world would have used a very different anaesthetic procedure, which would have included a muscle relaxant such as one of the synthetic derivatives (for example, tubocurarine) of curare, the lethal drug placed on arrow tips and used by traditional hunters particularly in South America. However, if you are going to paralyse a patient you must intubate the trachea (using an endotracheal tube) and ventilate the patient using a mechanical ventilator; anaesthesia would be achieved not by ether/air but by a more modern anaesthetic agent, at that time it would have been halothane. The benefit of the muscle relaxant is that the abdominal muscles remain soft and pliable, making it easier to replace the abdominal contents after surgery. In this case, we had not displaced the bowel to any great extent, so it was not a problem, but on other occasions in Jammy it certainly was.

The procedure so far had taken no more than about twenty minutes. Dr Ratnaraj's success as a surgeon working in sub-optimal conditions was his speed, cleanliness and his insistence on working in a bloodless field. My recollection was that most of his patients did well after surgery and wound infections were uncommon.

He rapidly closed the peritoneum with a continuous catgut suture, showed me how to close the muscle layer and then removed his gloves and said:

'There! You finish off!' He took off his mask and gown and left the operating theatre without waiting for a response.

I was stunned. However, the scrub nurse remained calm and just handed me the forceps, holding the curved surgical needle loaded with catgut suture material and guided me through the closure of the remaining muscle layer. She then assisted me in producing a neat closure of the skin by a series of interrupted cotton thread sutures.

By the time I had completed the procedure, my heart had stopped racing and I looked down at my handiwork with a sense of pride. I had 'done something useful' and was delighted to have begun to master the basic surgical technique of suturing.

Before I had completed tying the final skin suture I was aware that the patient was already beginning to wake up. One of the theatre nurses had removed the anaesthetic mask and turned off the EMO machine and was supporting the patient's jaw on both sides to ensure that the airway was clear. Another nurse sucked out the secretions from the back of the patient's throat; ether is well recognised to stimulate mucus secretion and indeed it is one of the downsides of its use.

Later in the day Dr Ratnaraj sent a written message by one of the porters inviting me to join him on the ward to review the patient and discuss his post-operative care.

I arrived to find Dr Ratnaraj standing at the end of the patient's bed with the ward sister. He was examining the patient's chart. He became aware of my arrival but without altering his gaze he said quietly:

'Pulse and blood pressure are fine. He seems to be doing well but it's early days. We'll give him I.V. fluids for a couple of days. I try to avoid placing a nasogastric tube but if there are any signs of gastric dilatation we'll pass one.'

'Yes. I see.'

He placed his stethoscope quickly over his chest.

'Sounds clear now. Come back and check him in the morning. Make sure he's passing urine and that his fluid balance is OK; and check the wound and make sure his lungs are clear.'

'Yes. Yes of course.'

'Oh … and your skin closure was excellent. See you in the morning.'

At that time, duodenal ulcers were thought to be due to stress, poor diet and aggravated by smoking tobacco and alcohol; with no medical cure at hand surgery was common especially for persistent complications such as bleeding, pyloric obstruction, peroration and uncontrollable pain. Within just thirteen years the cause of the disease had been identified; it is due to an infection with the bacterium, *Helicobacter pylori,* which can be cured with antibiotics.

By the time I had reached the Cutting's bungalow a porter with a paraffin lamp had followed me across the compound and arrived at the house with the operating schedule for the next day. A hand-written message was added at the bottom of the typed list of operations.

> *Please join me in theatre at 8.00am after morning chapel.*
> *Ratnaraj.*

This would be the pattern of events for much of the rest of my stay in Campbell Hospital. Dr Ratnaraj, during the ensuing weeks would teach me how to perform many of the routine operative procedures that were within the domain of the general surgeon. We did appendicectomies, hernia repairs, bowel resections, cholecystectomies and cancer operations in the bowel and stomach. Gradually he would let me do more and more, and latterly always let me open the abdomen as well as close at the end of the procedure.

From time to time Dr Ratnaraj would become rather irritable in theatre and on occasions leave prematurely. I came to learn that he did not like working with the other surgeons and I think was glad that I remained respectfully calm when he had these odd changes of mood. On one occasion, we were halfway through a mastectomy; he had removed the lump and some axillary lymph nodes, when he threw several instruments across the theatre and left without comment. I had never closed a major mastectomy incision before but with the aid of the scrub nurse we got the skin edges together without excessive tension and did a reasonably good job at getting an acceptable cosmetic result. As the patient was beginning to recover from the anaesthetic, Dr Ratnaraj came back into the operating theatre and looked at the closure.

He looked at me with a gentle, minimal smile.

'Thank you.'

He was a kind, retiring man who expressed very little emotion. Beneath that superficial austerity, which for some was their only experience of him, was a passionate devoted surgeon, careful and caring, who lived for the service of others. His unpredictable, sometimes irascible behaviour was difficult for those working alongside him and during these days was unexplained and seemed out of character. I was grateful for the time he spent teaching me and for the extraordinary opportunities that had unfolded during my time at his hospital.

Ratnama and Flavia soon realised that I was becoming 'useful' and taught me how to perform a 'tubal ligation' under local anaesthesia. In the 1960s and '70s it was believed that this was the most cost-effective way of reducing the birth rate and thereby controlling the size of the rapidly growing Indian population.

It was government policy and in the 1970s was championed by the Prime Minister's son, Sanjay Gandhi; at the same time, it proved to be good business for the hospital. I learnt that every documented tubal ligation resulted in a standard payment to the hospital; this helped to finance other hospital activities, including the opportunity to treat many of the low-income patients without charge.

Ratnama took me through a few of these sterilisation procedures and then would book a list for me to do on my own several mornings each week. I never really grasped the criteria for tubal ligation, but most women would have had at least five or six children before being persuaded that this was the right thing to do. There were incentives in place for the patient at the time, but it was not until the 1970s that Mr Gandhi introduced the offer of a transistor radio or a bicycle for those willing to participate in the sterilisation programme. There is no doubt, however, that during my time at the hospital, tubal ligation was felt to be the most effective means of contributing to the national drive of population control. The number of procedures performed was regularly reported by the hospital and it was regarded as one of the key performance indicators, alongside attendances at the outpatient department, hospital admissions and the number of surgical procedures performed annually.

To be frank, I never really liked the procedure, not just because of the ethical issues which I do not think I had really thought through at the time, although I am sure this was a factor, but mainly because we performed the operation under local anaesthetic and it was extremely difficult to perform without causing the patient some short-lived but significant discomfort. That aside it was quite a simple procedure. After infiltration of the skin, muscle layer and peritoneum with local anaesthetic, the surgeon makes a small abdominal incision, the Fallopian tube on one side is located by hooking it up with a gloved finger; it is then pulled up very gently through the incision and picked up with soft forceps. A short segment is resected, a cotton tie placed around each of the open ends and the tube then replaced carefully back into the abdomen. It was traction on the tube that caused the pain, so every effort was made to minimise this part of the process. The same approach was then applied to the other side. It was extremely uncommon to see any complications of the surgery and recovery was rapid. Patients would leave hospital the following – or on some occasions the same – day. Multiparous women who were delivered by Caesarean section often underwent tubal ligation at the end of the procedure. I was never quite sure whether they had been consented for this additional intervention. How would they ever know? 'The ligated' would not have another pregnancy, which for many would come as a great relief. For other women, it may have led to questions being asked about their value as a child producer. A now barren woman would have known what that would have meant in village India in the 1960s.

As these memories find their way on to the printed page and I consider my complicity with a major national population control initiative, I am profoundly shocked. At the time, I think I felt that I was being useful, contributing to the day-to-day work of the hospital, and enjoying the technical challenge. However, I am now faced with the harrowing thought that I was taking responsibility for a questionable procedure that I, myself, had not obtained the consent of the patient. In truth, I have no idea what the women had agreed to and whether written informed consent was obtained in every instant.

On a limited number of occasions, I assisted the other two male surgeons, Drs Reddy and Yardley Bob in theatre. However, there was one memorable occasion when I got a call from Yardley to go to Men's Out-Patients. I found him standing over a recumbent patient in one of the examination rooms.

'Ah there you are. Come, palpate this abdomen!' His voice boomed across and along the out-patient corridor, very much in the style of Sir Lancelot Sprat of *Doctor in the House*, which had graced British cinema screens some fifteen years earlier in 1954. I suppose I felt like the vulnerable, young medical student Simon Sparrow (a role which is thought to have launched Dirk Bogarde's career as a film actor) who was the butt of Sir Lancelot's attacks.

The patient looked absolutely petrified and Yardley made no attempt whatsoever to quell his fears. In fact, he was amplifying the patient's anxiety state by waving a large empty glass syringe and needle above his head like a ringmaster in a circus.

'Come quickly. Feel the liver. If you're not quick, it will have gone!'

He released a short almost menacing laugh accompanied by a rather unpleasant hissing noise through his nose. The patient squirmed without realising what he had said.

I tried to reassure the patient by approaching slowly and seeking his permission to palpate the abdomen but only by visual signals. I gently and somewhat timidly passed my hand over the four quadrants of the abdomen, as Dr Ratnaraj had taught me.

'What do you find?' He blasted forth.

'I am not sure.'

'Well look first. Remember, eyes first…. What do you see?'

'I think there is some asymmetry. The right upper quadrant appears swollen.'

'Yes. Yes. And what is the swelling due to? What is its consistency?'

'It is quite soft.'

'Yes … and? Here let me show you.'

He gently moved me aside and demonstrated that the swelling was fluctuant indicating the presence of fluid.

'This is 99.9 per cent certain to be an amoebic abscess of the liver. Nurse! Skin prep!'

He wiped the skin quickly over the swelling with the iodine-soaked gauze and without waiting for it to dry, he plunged the large bore needle through the abdominal wall into the swelling. He then pulled back on the syringe and dark red, thick fluid slowly began filling the barrel.

'There I told you. Anchovy sauce! Classic appearance of the contents of an amoebic abscess!'

This was the first and only time I saw 'anchovy sauce' draining from the liver, the textbook appearance of the issue from an amoebic abscess.

My clinical experience in the hospital continued to grow, as by now I was not only assisting the hospital superintendent in theatre but also increasingly engaged in gynaecological procedures and obstetrics. With two months behind me, I think I was now regarded as a credible surgical assistant. In the last few weeks I helped with appendicectomies, hysterectomies, Caesarean sections, diagnostic laparotomies (usually inoperable cancer) and a variety of gastric surgical procedures. I was also active on the Children's Ward and was now competent at lumbar punctures and placing intravenous infusion lines. I attended a series of normal deliveries and on one occasion was shown how to perform a low forceps delivery. As life in the hospital became busier for me, I could see the moment was rapidly approaching when I would leave Jammalamadugu for a final exploration of South India with Elizabeth, beginning in Bangalore.

Saying farewell was difficult, as I had adjusted well to life in Jammalamadugu but fully realised that I must return home and continue my studies. I had a farewell dinner at the home of the boss, Dr Ratnaraj, when I thanked him profusely for the opportunity he had given me and to the generosity both he and the other medical staff in the hospital had shown me, particularly with respect to the teaching of clinical medicine and surgery. There was another dinner at Mollie's home, which was also a delightful event. We organised a farewell dinner for the senior staff and other special friends at the home of William Cutting. The cook was asked to acquire five chickens, which of course he competently did, but somehow managed to let them escape into the compound before they found their way into the pot. Happily, we organised some porters to pursue the birds and bring them back to the kitchen. The dinner was a very moving event with exchange of gifts and garlands and at an appropriate moment, I said a few words of thanks and farewell.

SWAN SONG BY THE PENNAIR RIVER

Sam returned from Vellore having completed a short course in child health. We took the hospital vehicle after work to the Pennair River. He was tired, and we did not talk much. There was a most stunning technicolour sunset, accompanied by a solo male voice singing a plaintive song in Telegu. The man was not visible from where we were sitting; a group of young boys played together on a sand bank just off the shore and seemed, like us, to be totally entranced by the song which weaved its way around us, coming and going as the evening breeze picked it up and then dropped it again. It was as if someone had set this up as a 'Swan Song'.

I could tell that Sam was feeling sad that I would be leaving the following day; he found it difficult to find the words to say just that. We promised to write to each other and I encouraged him to continue with his ambition to take on further postgraduate study in paediatrics at CMC Vellore and then return to Campbell Hospital as William's successor. He gave a minimalist South Indian head roll, indicating that he would, or probably would.

That evening I left Jammalamadugu for Cuddapah, where I spent a final night in Andhra Pradesh with the Rev. Joe Pratt and his wife Peggy. He was the last of my missionary 'minders'; the chaplain of Christ Church, Cuddapah. The following morning at around 6.00am I boarded the bus for Bangalore; it took about eight and a half hours to cover the 250 km, whereas today the travel time is usually five to six hours. At the bus-stand I took an auto rickshaw, essentially a motorbike (which sounds like a sewing machine) with two rear wheels across which is straddled a bench seat, the entire assembly being shrouded in a lightweight roofing structure which gives some protection from the elements, except for cross-cutting, horizontal monsoon rain. On arrival at the Church of South India Hospital, Bangalore I was greeted by Elizabeth, our first meeting since we had parted company at Guntakal railway station eight – nine weeks ago, that brief stopping point for the Madras Mail on its journey from Bombay to Madras. We embraced warmly. As I think about this now, it was the first time in more than two months that I had had any physical

Boys at the Pennair River – 'Swan Song', 1969. (Author's collection)

contact with a woman other than professional contact in a clinical setting. Said like that it seems quite shocking, but it was about the customs of the day and was the reason why Elizabeth and I ended up in different hospitals. It seemed an age since we had started this adventure together and were now looking forward to exploring the delights of Kerala.

In 1971 Indira Gandhi called an early election, the Fifth Lok Sabha, when she won a landslide victory with her new Congress (R) party, also referred to the Congress (I) party, for 'Indira' although this terminology was subsequently ousted. On this occasion the electorate had risen to 275 million, more than 100 million greater than in the first election of 1952. Mrs Gandhi, now elected for the third time, had a mandate to push through the 'progressive policies' that she insisted had been held up by her former 'reactionary' government. Khushwant Singh, writer and journalist, made wise comments in 1971 in the *Illustrated Weekly of India* after the election: 'Indira Gandhi has successfully magnified her figure as the one and only leader of national dimensions ... however, if power is voluntarily surrendered by a predominant section of the people to one person and at the same time opposition is reduced to insignificance, the temptation to ride roughshod over legitimate criticism can become irresistible. The danger of Indira Gandhi being given unbridled power shall always be present.'

In 1971, she decided that India needed to produce a 'People's car'. It must be affordable, efficient and indigenous. Who better to head up the project and be Maruti Motors's first managing director, than her devoted son, Sanjay? He lacked a college degree and an engineering or management background but had undertaken a brief internship at Rolls-Royce in the UK. The car was apparently to be propelled by a Triumph motorcycle engine. Maruti went nowhere and the company was finally liquidated in 1977, but re-launched as a joint venture with Suzuki of Japan in 1981 and is still flourishing.

Just before the Fifth Lok Sabha, Pakistan held its first election, which had been called by General Khan, President and Chief Martial Law Administrator. Zulfiqar Bhutto's Pakistan People's Party, based in West Pakistan, won the day but this unsettled East Pakistan's population, feeling they were being ruled by an elite in the West. Although they shared a religion, the East Pakistani's resented the belittlement of their native language Bengali and felt they were exploited by acting as the food producer for the West. However, it was the insistence that the national language should be Urdu that led to revolution. Civilian unrest promoted military action by West Pakistan, resulting in a massive loss of life. It has been described as genocide. The oppressed in East Pakistan had only one safe place to go and that was West Bengal, in India. This drew Indira Gandhi's government into war with Pakistan with a massive offensive on the Western front. Bangladesh declared independence on the 26 March 1971 and West Pakistan eventually surrendered to an Indian defeat later that year.

Internally, Mrs Gandhi was seen to have kept calm and pursued a difficult international dispute to a worthy conclusion, at least as far as Bangladesh and India were concerned. From being a primarily a 'domestic' Prime Minister, she had entered the international arena during the conflict, meeting President Nixon and Henry Kissinger in the USA and travelling to the Soviet Union for high-level talks.

TEMPLES, TIGER COUNTRY AND TEA

4

Who sends the mind to wander afar? Who first drives life to start on its journey?
Who impels us to utter these words? Who is the spirit behind the eye and the ear?

Kena Upanishad

Jammy provided a rich source of experiences for understanding village life in India, but it had its limitations. It was a tiny community with few facilities and everyone at the hospital was keen that I should broaden my exposure to South India. I felt that there was a powerful wish for me to see more, to understand their country better, their languages and customs. While I had thrown myself into the work of the hospital and had gained the most incredible clinical experience, I would say greater than many, if not all my peers in London, the opportunity to engage with the world outside Campbell Hospital was also welcomed.

THE BARBERS OF TIRUMALA AND LORD VENKATESWARA

A memorable adventure began on Saturday 4 August. It was a road trip to Tirupati, a moderate sized city about 35 km from the holy place of Tirumala where the ancient religious site of the temple had been established more than 1,500 hundred years ago. *Tiru* in Telegu means Holy or sacred and *Mala* means hills; thus the 'holy hills'.

It was to be a family adventure and included Margot, Catriona and Kenneth and would span a long weekend. We left Jammy at about 7.00am with William driving the rather dilapidated four-wheel drive, white, long wheel-based vehicle with the hardest suspension I had ever experienced. Many of the roads at that time were rudimentary without a prepared surface and so the annual cycle of heavy monsoon rains followed by baking heat created concrete-hard rutted tracks that no vehicle could negotiate to produce an acceptable outcome for those inside. Unlike the soporific effect of the rhythmic clickety-click of the Madras Mail, which frequently led to a welcome nap, the irregular bumpy churn that resulted from Andhra's rural roads led to a constant sensation of disquiet, even mild distress. It was like riding on rocks.

As the sun started to appear during that memorable Saturday morning and the outside temperature began to rise, it was a close call as to whether to have the car windows open to mitigate against turning the vehicle into a baking oven or to keep them closed to exclude the clouds of dust that plumed away from the tyres as they wrestled with the unforgiving rutted road surface. My notes about the travel interlude describe it as a: 'pleasant ride – hot – got sunburnt on one side'.

William and Margot sat in the front and I shared the back seat with Kenneth and Catriona. Conversation was difficult and frequently drowned out by the noisy drone of the tired, clattering diesel engine that laboured relentlessly in front. There was at least five hours of travel ahead of us and the easiest option was to beckon the gentle hand of Morpheus to spirit one away to the world of sleep. Although the total road journey was only about 400 km it was rarely possible to cruise at anything greater than 70 kph. The journey south was largely through the undulating farmland, patches of wooded areas along the rivers and an endless trail of impoverished villages.

This was the first real opportunity that I had had to see village India in the raw, beyond Jammalamadugu and our village clinics. The dusty open road took us through rural South India across a mix of cultivated farmland, mainly rice paddies, but interspersed with other crops such as ragi (a type of millet), sorghum, groundnut and mangos.

There were vast flat expanses of near-desert scrubland, speckled with rigid, almost leafless, bushes struggling against the excesses of sun and heat and the lack of water. From time to time a collection of coconut palms would spring up, which added a pleasing architectural feature to the otherwise two-dimensional landscape. Villages punctuated the route, each of which had grown up alongside the road as a largely unplanned ribbon development. Although the scenes were new to me, I soon began to realise after subsequent return visits to India that this was the norm for rural India and was the way that more than 80 per cent of the population lived at that time. Even today, despite the massive move towards urbanisation, 70 per cent of Indian people are still village dwelling.

A water buffalo cart, 1969. (Author's collection)

Modes of transportation on roads in rural India were relatively limited in the 1960s. Simple two-wheeled carts drawn either by two black water buffalo or two white bullocks remained the dominant form of local commercial travel of the day. The animals were as skinny as their owners; their shiny hides were drawn tightly over a heavy skeleton, making it easy to imagine the bulky bony structure which it concealed. These hand-driven, animal-powered vehicles had rights-of-way over pedestrians and motor vehicles. They often formed major convoys along the road, effectively obstructing all other traffic. Bullocks and cows are sacred beasts of major religious significance and thus must never be harassed or injured. The two beasts were held together by a wooden yoke, which was roped to a long wooden shaft connected to the cart. The sun-drenched, dark-skinned driver sat on a beam at the front of cart, holding in his left hand a rope to steer the beasts of burden which was attached to their rope bridles, and in his right hand he held a smooth wooden stick which he used to encourage the animals in their work. The cart handlers generally sat cross-legged, were dressed in a traditional *khadi* shirt and a *lunghi* usually turned up to knee-level and wore an expressionless face beneath a loosely tied cotton turban. Their simple clothes bore the marks of a working man.

Public service vehicles, mainly single-decker buses, were the mainstay of road transport, often highly decorated in a multitude of colours, usually celebrating the plethora of Hindu religious persona and their rich life stories.

A school bus, 1969. (Author's collection)

These local buses were the dominant mode of travel for village communities moving across the country but were rudimentary in the extreme; hot and dusty, devoid of any form of air conditioning or climate control and archaic suspension which was totally unable to deal with the undulations of the road surface. Most had no glass in the windows, the space being filled by horizontal bars to prevent human entry or exit.

For heavy, longer distance haulage there were colourfully painted trucks, again adorned by motifs of the Hindu deity. They transported vast loads up and down the highway, usually travelling at ridiculously high speeds.

A truck crash, 1969. (Author's collection)

Many came to grief either with a fractured axle due to the excessive load, a flat tyre or worse, a head-on collision with a similar vehicle approaching at high speed from the opposite direction. These narrow roads, without any marked traffic lanes, were dangerous places to be for vehicles, animals and pedestrians.

There were a few private taxis, either the classic Hindustan Ambassador, based on the Morris Oxford of the 1950s with its soft, curvaceous lines or the Premier Padmini, a smaller, more modern but less stylish specimen with sharper lines and perky wings at the rear. I do not recall using taxis at all during this first visit to India, other than the city tour we took during that first day in Bombay, but subsequently I hired them from time to time. On one occasion, when I had taken a car with driver for a three-day tour from Madras via Mahabalipuram to Vellore, the driver asked whether he should switch on the air conditioning;

A truck and goats, 1969. (Author's collection)

the major disadvantage, according to him, was that if we put it on, it would slow us down. Many of the Ambassadors had had air conditioning added as a late post-production modification but this seriously drained the power of propulsion. I opted for it, as I preferred the cooler environment and anything that slowed the driver down on these lethal roads seemed a bonus.

The villages themselves were active commercial and social centres. People were everywhere; walking, talking, eating, drinking, sleeping, working, all happening outside on the street or the sidewalk in front of your eyes. The villages were *alive* day and night. Every village would have its small primitive roadside eating houses providing hot tea and coffee and locally bottled soft drinks. Charcoal fired kitchens provided hot snacks for the long-distance lorry drivers and other travellers. Groups of men would congregate in the social centres, eating, drinking tea or coffee, smoking *beedis* and generally whiling away the day.

Most villages would have a repair shop to deal with roadside breakdowns and simple stores selling the basic day-to-day items of everyday living. The piles of brass or white metal near spherical cooking pots were often arranged on a grand scale, such that they would almost appear to be an artistic installation. Alongside the commercial enterprises immediately at the roadside were simple domestic dwellings, commonly single-roomed buildings constructed of mud walls and a thatched roof formed from layers of dried palm leaves or other suitable vegetation. Animals lived intimately with their owners, forming a highly integrated and inter-dependent social unit. All humans and animals alike seem to be on the edge of survival. This was subsistence living in the extreme. I saw a very thin brown pony foraging in the undergrowth alongside what I presumed to be its owner's house. Each of its twelve ribs could clearly be seen protruding beneath its taught skin; there was no fat to smooth out the external contours. What was remarkable was that the pony remained almost static without any obvious evidence that it was tethered or staked. On closer inspection, it became apparent that its front legs were tied together with rope just above its ankles; it was 'cobbled', ensuring that it was not going anywhere in a hurry.

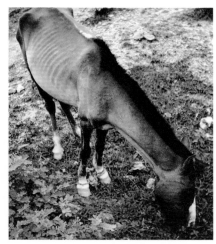

A horse cobbled, 1969.
(Author's collection)

William loved to stop at roadside food vendors to purchase hot sweet milky tea, spicy snacks and orange-pigmented gelebies and other sweet treats. He was an Indian in his heart, having been born in India as the son of a missionary surgeon, and most comfortable keeping close to their simple way of life. We arrived at Tirupati at around midday, after just under five hours on the road.

Our visit was hosted by some of William's Church of South India contacts and academic colleagues at the local university who were working on child health and infant nutrition. I wrote home to my parents on Tuesday 5 August after we had returned to Jammy.

> *Dear Mum and Dad*
> *Thanks for your letters this week. Last weekend I went with the family to Tirupati – the centre of Hinduism. We stayed with a Canadian lady Prof Dorothy Pearson (aged 67 years) who is Professor of Home Science at S V University College, Tirupati. Her special subject is nutrition. She is very kind and a good organiser at the University – quite a thing for a Christian to be offered a seat at a Hindu University especially as they're trying to oust all the missionaries! We went up to the temple – on the Tirumala Hill – an incredible place. They've built housing settlements for the pilgrims – just like Butlin's! Everyone gives their <u>hair</u> to the gods (in 11 A.D. it was their <u>heads</u>!) One sees masses of bald people in Tirupati. It certainly helps to keep down their lice – although as soon as it starts to grow they pick up a fresh lot in the village. The temple is very rich (it built the University) and people give thousands of rupees as offerings. We got back late Monday night – if all is well I should have some good photos.*
> *Love Michael*

Prof. Pearson took us on a tour of the Sri Venkateswara University College and my only memory of the visit was that she showed us some white rats which I can only imagine were used in her research. I never

Sri Venkateswara University, 1969. (Author's collection)

quite worked out the full scope of what 'Home Science' involved but she was certainly engaged in the field of child nutrition which was one of William's main interests at the time. After I left Jammy, William launched The Young Children's Clinic and Nutrition Education Unit at Campbell Hospital on 4 April 1970 and Prof. Pearson was one of the honoured guests who attended the opening ceremony, along with an eminent woman paediatrician from the CMC Hospital Vellore, Prof. Malati Jadhav.

The main university building looked very new and somewhat isolated on a dry, flat piece of land on the outer reaches of the town. Like most similar institutions, it had an impressive pair of iron gates and a dominant clock tower at its heart showing the time as 10.30am. We had started the day with breakfast at 7.30am and then were escorted to the local CSI church in the Chittoor District for the morning service at 9.00am. My notebook tells me that the 'church treasurer preached the sermon on the topic of social responsibility'. I have no memory of this whatsoever. Our spirits suitably uplifted, we then proceeded to visit the local Department of Paediatrics, which was headed by a very large, dominant lady, Prof. Indira Dai. At the time, there was a lively debate underway as to how severe malnutrition in infants and young children should be treated. William was very much part of this and his growing practical experience and expertise was being recognised. Kwashiorkor was still common in South India at the time and carried a high mortality. It was a devastating condition for infants and young children. It was often precipitated by a recurring cycle of infection, which triggered loss of appetite and poor nutrition. The limbs, particularly the legs, became oedematous, the overlying skin was dry and cracked and sometimes called 'flaky paint dermatosis', accompanied by a swollen abdomen, a hallmark of the condition due to ascites (accumulated fluid in the abdominal cavity due to low protein levels in the blood). Most paediatricians were using liquid balanced formulae that allowed progressive nutritional rehabilitation. I was rather surprised to hear that Prof. Dai was recommending quarter-strength buffalo milk, biscuits and fruit!

At 2.15pm we set off again to make the 40 km journey up a rough hill road which wound its way up to the Tirumala temple. This being a weekend, it was not surprising that many others had had the same idea, so we joined a long queue of assorted vehicles that slowly snaked its way up the hillside, un-made road, rising during the journey by 850 metres. It was still early afternoon and the mid-summer sun remained high in the sky. We left the car in a rough parking area and walked towards the main gate of the temple complex. It was a stunning folly; a structure that anticipated the Gateway of India in Bombay but celebrated the country's long religious heritage rather than its more recent participation in the Victorian Empire. The coloured relief across the top of the arch depicted Sri Venkateswara and other lesser deities enforcing their position as temple governors.

Beyond the arched gateway was a rough road which would eventually take visitors towards the inner temple buildings. Either side of the walkway into the temple were a multitude of open shops – a bazaar – selling everything a pilgrim might need on the day, souvenirs that would help transfer the experience back home and sustenance to cover midday repast and the return journey. The walkway between the two rows of shops was teeming with pilgrims from far and wide. One of my earliest discoveries after arriving in India is that the subcontinent is

Entrance to the temple, 1969. (Author's collection)

a collection of many different peoples. Dark-skinned Tamils from the south, pale 'oaten'-skinned peoples from the north and others with more oriental faces from the northeast, close to the Chinese border, such as Assam. I was amazed by the advertisements for husbands and wives in the daily newspapers when the skin shade was clearly a dominant feature in the selection process. Across this vast subcontinent there was clearly discrimination not only by caste but also by skin tone.

I was immediately intrigued by the religious icons, mainly brass or wooden effigies of the full panoply of Indian Gods, incense sticks and their burners that had already begun to appear in ethnic craft emporia in England in the 1960s, gaudily coloured, glazed paper pictures of the Gods and their dependents, and a variety of other brass bowls, plates and utensils, many with religious significance. I lingered at the stalls selling the religious effigies but was hurried along by William who I think felt that any interest in the 'polytheism' and idolatry of Hinduism was anti-Christ and thereby evil. I bought four small brass Gods (Shiva, Ganesh, Vishnu and Sri Venkateswara), two carved wooden representations of Ganesh and a miniature brass cooking pot containing holy water, fortunately sealed by a metal lid which had been firmly soldered in place. My interest in the religions of India had been awakened and would remain extant for many years to come.

Kenneth smiled down at me from his protected observation point in the carry pack on William's back, his pale pink freckled face emerging from beneath his white chaotic, floppy cotton sun hat, quietly pleading with me to get on with the tour. Margot and Catriona were striding ahead and then paused at the barbers' hall. This was one of the high spots of the visit for me. We re-grouped under the main entrance to the hall. Despite being a relatively ancient building of deep significance for Hindu worshippers, the entrance seemed to have some of the features of the European neo-classical period.

Above the doorway to the hall there was another striking bas-relief carved in wood and richly coloured; I presumed to be advertising the activities contained therein. On the left a barber is depicted poised on a length of wooden board, sitting on his haunches in front of a pilgrim, whose head is tilted forward,

Entrance to the barbers' hall, 1969. (Author's collection)

and also seated on a long board close to the ground; his hair is being removed with a cut-throat razor held and steadied by both of the barber's hands, watched by his wife (who is unshaved) holding a young child in her arms; on the right, a woman is depicted having her head shaved, watched by her already shaven husband and their young son standing by his side. Interestingly, the barbers had full heads of hair beneath loosely tied cotton turbans; the barber on the right had enough hair to tie into a ponytail. In the centre, dominating the scene is Lord Venkateswara, portrayed in blue with four arms and the tell-tale vertical black line on a white background in the centre of his forehead. And above the scenic tableau were written the words 'Place of surrendering human hair to Lord Sri Venkateswara Swami'; below these words written in English were respective translations in Telegu and Hindi script.

We entered the hall and were greeted by the unpleasant odour of wet, dirty, oiled hair. I can only liken the smell to that of a warm, wet Labrador. However, the scene set out before us was extraordinary but not surprising, because of the images we had already seen outside, above the entrance to the hall. Rows and rows of squatting, traditionally clad barbers flashing razors across the scalps of a multitude of kneeling supplicants. The hair fell to the floor in front of the pilgrims and when the job was done, it was collected promptly by a team of helpers and taken to a central repository for holding before cleansing and export. Between clients, the barbers would hone the edge of their razors on a leather strop. This hair would become a major commodity, which would be an important contributor to the financial sustainability of the temple; mostly exported to the West to be re-fashioned into wigs for those who could not live without hair. For the shaven, only a stunted tail would be left in the region of the occiput at the back of the head. This, so the legend is told, would enable the pilgrim to be caught and thereby saved by the Gods if there was a chance that the individual might fall from grace.

I was entranced by the scale of the operation. There was nothing I could think of that paralleled any event back home. Culturally, it seemed unique. This was an industry several centuries old which had that magic combination of intense religious significance with the ability to generate vast wealth to support the work of the temple. It did cross my mind that there would be a risk of transferring blood-born viruses, like the Hepatitis B virus between pilgrims, as there was no obvious attempt to sterilise the razors between clients. In their defence, we should remember that HBV was only identified two years earlier in 1967, and the Hepatitis C Virus not until 1989. It would be more than decade before HIV was discovered in 1983 and recognised as a blood-borne infection, but theoretically this was also a risk.

On the return journey to Jammalamadugu we stopped briefly in the village of Chandragiri ('mountain of the moon') to visit the magnificent palace and its fortifications, about 10 km from Tirupati. This splendid stone building in the Indo-Saracen style (the lower floors of the south-facing façade being constructed with numerous Saracen arches whereas the crowning towers are typical of Hindu architecture) was constructed in around 1000 CE and boasts a deep moat and extensive walled fortifications. It is set in an austere landscape; a predominantly rocky terrain with a paucity of vegetation. Originally controlled by the Yadavarayas, in 1367 it fell under the jurisdiction of the Vijayanagara Kings (whose empire occupied the Deccan plateau in South India from 1336). The main building is now a museum, but it is possible to see the original Raj and Rani Mahal's (King and Queen's Palaces) and a scatter of ruined temples.

After a short break, we returned to the car and took the road north back through Cuddapah and Proddatur to Jammalamadugu, where we arrived late in the evening, totally exhausted.

IN THE STEPS OF MOLLY PANTER-DOWNES

One morning at the end of a typical Cutting family breakfast in Jammalamadugu, William announced that he had arranged a special trip for me to visit the 'Queen of the hill stations', Ootacamund. He explained that the Nilgiri hills was a favoured spot for the British to escape in the summer months from the sun-drenched dry plains of Tamil Nadu to this cool, green mountain retreat; Ootacamund (affectionately known as 'Ooty') is set about 2,300 m above sea level. It was a favourite of British Viceroys and Governors of Madras. Even the Maharaja of Jodhpur was pleased to travel from Rajasthan to his summer residence in the Nilgiri hills, aptly named Arranmore Palace, possibly in sympathy with the 'Scottish scenery'. I guess in the 1920s he must have travelled the 2,000 km by train, which would have taken the best part of two days. Although William never referred to the similarities between the Nilgiri hills and the Scottish Highlands, I suspect deep down he felt very much at home there, and indeed soon after I returned to the UK, early in 1970 the family went on a family retreat to Ooty to get some respite from the rising temperatures in Jammalamadugu.

I leapt at the opportunity to visit Ooty, not simply to see some more of the diversity of South India but to fulfil a useful task, that of accompanying William's nine-year-old son Alistair back to boarding school. As the crow flies, the journey is about 600 km travelling due southwest from Jammalamadugu through Bangalore and Mysore and finally a steep mountain climb from Mettupalayam via Coonoor to Ooty. In 1969 most people would not contemplate such a journey by road (which even today would take eleven to twelve hours), making the railway the only sensible option, even knowing that the travel time was in the order of twenty-four to twenty-six hours. Today, one can travel from Yerraguntala (the closest stop to Jammalamadugu on the Mumbai-Kanyakumari Express) to Coimbatore in about thirteen hours, changing to the Nilgiri Mountain Railway, which takes a further, eye-watering, five hours up to Ooty (just 45 km). I am not obsessed by time, but I do mention travel times because it underscores the challenges of moving around the extensive and varied terrain that is India. During the last forty years the highways in India have improved progressively such that car or bus is now a perfectly acceptable option for some journeys. However, from the mid-nineteenth century onwards it was the railways that opened the country for everyone, even for those with relatively limited resources. The train was probably affordable for a large proportion of the population even though travel conditions were not perfect. The British soon realised the importance of a reliable rail network, and although they may be criticised for many things during the British Raj, a rail infrastructure was developed, much of which remains today. The steam train that pulled the 'Madras Mail', which brought me from Bombay to Muddanuru, was certainly a remnant of earlier times. Today the rail networks have matured, steam engines have all but disappeared and travel times diminished markedly.

Alistair and I travelled by train to Madras, where we changed on to the Nilgiri Express at about 8.00pm. We had reserved a sleeping compartment; it was comfortable and permitted a good night's sleep. Alistair was a self-sufficient, rather mature nine-year-old who seemed happy with his own company. We did not talk very much until the following morning when at around 9.30am we changed trains in Mettupalayam (about 300 m above sea level) on to the mountain railway. Refreshed and reinvigorated, we enjoyed the slow, crawling narrow gauge, rack and pinion railway and plotted our progress along the 2,000 m winding climb. The steepest part of the climb is between Kallar and Coonoor when the rack and pinion is operational, thereafter the final ascent is back on the metre gauge rails. This remarkable 'toy railway' is still running today and was the subject of a BBC documentary. Coal-fired steam engines are much loved and maintained by an attentive team of engineers, many of whom come from a long line of mountain railway families.

The Nilgiri Mountain Railway was constructed by a Swiss engineer Arthur Riggenbach who was invited to pitch for the project in 1882 by the Government of India. Construction started in 1891 and was progressed in stages in an upward direction, but not completed until 1908.

In my notebook on Tuesday 26 August, I wrote, 'nice ride up to Ooty – too much cloud – masses of English!' That railway journey was extraordinary; partly because of the adorable ancient steam engine and its historic rolling stock which cranked their way uphill for five and a half hours, relying on a central cogwheel and matching notched track to stop it sliding back. The nineteenth-century engine pushes the

Nilgiri Mountain Railway. (Dethan Punalur / Getty Images)

carriages up from behind, the driver being guided by signal guards on the edge of each of the carriages who inform the driver that it is safe to proceed. The journey was also special because of the extraordinary views, particularly when the train emerged from the forested sections of the route and entered the beautifully constructed, arched elevated viaduct sections of track (about thirty in all) and the 250 bridges to reveal spectacular views of both the hills and plains. Sadly, as my note suggested, the views were substantially curtailed by low-lying clouds and mist. The rickety old carriages were absolutely packed, largely with English, other European and some American children, many of whom were the sons and daughters of missionaries returning to schools in Ooty after the summer break. They did not stop talking from the moment they got on the train to the moment they left.

We disembarked at Ooty, the end of the line, at around 2.15pm and took a taxi to Alistair's school, Lushington Boys' School. I waited while he unpacked and took a bath. The school, based in Lushington Hall (named after a Governor of Madras, the Right Honourable Stephen Lushington), was established as a non-denominational Christian foundation; it was particularly focused on attracting the children of European missionaries. In 1974, Lushington became part of Hebron school, which was co-educational and already had a well-established educational base in Coonoor; it continues to this day with its ethos maintained.

We took a walk around the Government Botanical Gardens (known locally as 'Govvy Gardens'), which are located just behind the school; I had an overwhelming sense that we had actually left India and returned to England. Edward Lear in his *Indian Journal* arrived in Ooty on 5 October 1874. The diary entry of that day includes the following; 'Ootacamund is prettier than I had expected, but it is just like an English place, such as Leatherhead.' He continues, 'got a very good breakfast, beefsteak and claret; afterwards, slept a wink, and then wrote letters. A curious place is "Ooty"; houses stuck all about the hills, and trees everywhere, which is not what I was led to expect.' On 9 October, at 3:20pm he completed a stunning pen and ink sketch with indicative colour wash depicting Ooty's Lake in the foreground with the Nilgiri hills, partly forested, rising behind.

At about the same time, the then Viceroy of India (1876–80) Lord Lytton wrote to his wife from the Ooty 'paradise', inviting her to 'imagine Hertfordshire lanes, Devonshire Downs, Westmorland Lakes, Scotch Trout streams….'

Mollie Panter-Downes published *Ooty Preserved* in 1967, just two years before this visit. She relates her observations during a visit of unknown purpose and uncertain duration; she was enchanted by what she found and with an incisive charm, places twentieth-century Ooty into its historical context. She too was overwhelmed by the Englishness – or indeed Scottishness – of both the natural landscape and the built environment. Panter-Downes penetrates the deepest corners of Ooty and has thereby produced a valuable social document. She tells of the Toda, the indigenous tribal people of the Nilgiri hills and describes their pastoral life, vegetarian diet and deification of the water buffalo and its milk. Their thatched, armadillo-shaped huts seem quite unique. The Toda lived in a polyandrous setting with typically several brothers sharing one wife but taking full responsibilities as fathers for her children. Thus, it is said, no child in a Toda village was ever raised without a father. This 'unnatural' coexistence was challenging for the influx of Christian missionaries to the region in the early nineteenth century. Panter-Downes discovered the Ootacamund Club, which focused on the needs of Europeans, and like most other clubs founded in the British period, did not admit Indians as members. Even in the mid-1960s Panter-Downes did 'not see any Indian sitting in companionable groups on the blue and white linen covered sofas, or having a peg in the bar, or lunching in the panelled dining room.' E.M. Forster put forward the view that 'Indians don't long for intercourse with Englishmen any more, they have a life of their own' (letter November 1921, *The Hill of Devi*). She discovered the Ootacamund Hunt which pursued jackals or 'jacks' rather than foxes on horseback with a pack of hounds, and the Hindustan Photo Films Manufacturing Company which was founded in 1960 as a public-sector company making film for still and moving cameras; latterly it has struggled to be competitive financially and needed a government bailout.

Alistair and I walked into the centre of town and enjoyed the redbrick buildings with typical white trim, many looking like an English bungalow. We looked at a few shops, visited Charing Cross and were delighted to find a bright red British Victorian post box; and then what seemed quite by chance, we met the person who would accompany me back to Coimbatore, the Rev. Roy Martin. He knew we would be in the vicinity and he must have been looking for us. The Church of South India missionary network was strong in those days. Visitors like myself could easily pass from one missionary home to another on the basis that it was always more economic to stay with friends in the faith, rather than risking the financial and possible health hazards of staying in small private hotels, the quality of which in those days could not be assured. We shook hands warmly and he greeted Alistair as one of the family. He had already delivered his son back to Lushington Boys' School and was keen to get back to Coimbatore. William had arranged that I would travel back with him and stay the night at their home, but before that he had one important task still to do which was to deliver his two daughters back to school in Coonoor, at the Hebron school (the girls' campus) which would eventually combine with Lushington in 1974. The 45-km drive down to Coimbatore passed rapidly, largely I believe as I spent much of the time dozing on the back seat. It had been a long day and I was beginning to feel the effects of an imperfect sleep the previous night on the train from Madras.

I stayed that night with the Rev. Martin and his wife Joy in their traditional bungalow that came with his appointment as chaplain of All Souls' Church. He was the last English chaplain of that church serving from 1969 to 1980. The church grew substantially during this period and brought together a mixed community of Tamils, Malayalis, Europeans, Africans and others, many of whom came to study in the academic institutions of Coimbatore city. Roy Martin took on a special responsibility to educate children in Christian virtues and started the All Souls' Junior Church. The following morning, he took me on a lightning tour of Coimbatore, which included attending a meeting of the local pastors at which I was invited to say a few words. I cannot imagine what I might have said to them. That evening the Rev. Martin delivered me to Coimbatore station and saw me safely into a sleeping compartment on the overnight train to Katpadi Junction which arrived on time at about 9.00am. The night journey was uneventful for me although as we were arriving into Katpadi, I learnt that one of the passengers in my compartment had lost Rs. 600 down the toilet. The sanitary arrangements on trains in those days were rudimentary

Ladies' toilet, Katpadi, 1969. (Author's collection)

and lost meant lost forever, as the money would have descended through an open pipe directly onto the track beneath. The victim was deeply distressed.

As I walked along the platform I saw male and female WCs with rather beautiful coloured paintings of a male and female head on respective doors, which were side-by-side each other. There was an accompanying notice, which clearly stated that the key to the door was with the stationmaster. It occurred to me that this was an unhelpful arrangement if one was suffering from an acute intestinal affliction such as 'Delhi belly'. It was just a short 5-km bus ride to the Christian Medical College Hospital in Vellore where I was greeted by my next missionary host, Dr Jim Milledge.

IDA SCUDDER'S LEGACY AND THE MEDICAL MISSIONARIES

Dr Milledge and his wife Betty were kind and generous hosts. After a brief introductory tour of the hospital, which included sight of the dispensary with its manufacturing and analytical functions, I was taken back to their home on the college campus for lunch. I rested that afternoon, wrote some letters, joined them for dinner in the evening and stayed in their guest room overnight. During those first twenty-four hours, particularly over coffee after dinner, I came to understand that Jim Sibree Milledge was quite a remarkable person. Sibree is a Huguenot name acquired from his great-grandfather James Sibree who was a master builder in Hull but who eventually ended up building churches in Madagascar, a sort of missionary builder. Jim was a great raconteur.

'My father was also a medical missionary working in China where I was born. He had to do everything, medicine, surgery, gynaecology, obstetrics, anaesthetics – everything.'

'So how did you get into medicine?' I asked coyly.

'Having gone through the phase of "anything but", and narrowly avoiding working in a jam factory, I eventually studied medicine in Birmingham. It was great, and I feel I owe a lot to Birmingham.'

He spoke in an open forthright way and was utterly credible as he recalled the past.

After house-jobs he sought travel and adventure; he combined the two by joining the Royal Air Force. He was posted to Hong Kong and was inspired to enter the world of mountain climbing and altitude medicine by a senior colleague. He learnt about Sir Edmund Hillary's Silver Hut expedition, which was to study the long-term physiological effects of high altitude. He managed to find his way on to the team and spent about nine months at 6,000 m.

He then made a conscious decision that he wanted to work in the developing world and after 'a meeting under the clock at Victoria station' with an American-trained Indian neurosurgeon from Vellore, both he and his wife moved to CMC Hospital Vellore for the next ten years. There he worked as a chest physician, set up a TB clinic and supported the establishment of open-heart surgery. Milledge was an inspirational individual whose career continued to develop when he eventually returned to academic medicine in the UK.

The next morning, suitably inspired, I took the College bus to the hospital and spent the morning with two giants of paediatrics, Professors Malati Jadhav and Sheila Pereira. Prof. Jadhav was head of the Department of Paediatrics at CMC and Prof. Pereira started as a medical student in Stanley Medical College in Madras (established formally in 1938), joined CMC in 1954 and did ground-breaking work on protein calorie malnutrition and vitamin A deficiency. These powerful women had emerged at a time when women were still in a very small minority in most medical schools and were providing leadership in research and clinical practice; it is remarkable what can be achieved in a relatively resource poor setting by intelligent, driven, hard-working individuals.

The following day I took the staff bus to the leprosy hospital, which was under the aegis of CMC Vellore, located in a small village called Karigiri about 20 km from Vellore. In the local language Tamil, *kari* means elephant and *giri* means hill. At some point, elephants would have roamed this region. The foundation stone of the sanatorium was laid in 1952 by the founder of CMC hospital, Dr Ida Scudder. The initial funding was provided by the American Leprosy Mission and named after its chairman at the time Dr William J. Schieffelin. It was initially started as a research institute with the expectation that the disease, if caught early, could be cured by the new sulfone drugs. I visited busy wards full of patients, some of whom paid for their treatment as private patients and others who received care at low cost to themselves. I was shown the skin smear technique for diagnosis and the electromyography lab for assessing the extent of nerve damage, largely due to the unhelpful immune response to the bacterium *Mycobacterium leprae*, the primary cause of the disease.

Karigiri has from the start attracted some great names; perhaps one of the most important contributors to the surgery of leprosy worldwide was Dr Paul Brand, an orthopaedic surgeon who was working at CMC Vellore but became one of the medical pillars of the leprosy hospital at Karigiri. Like Cutting and Milledge, Brand was also the son of missionary parents having been brought up in the Kolli Hills of Tamil Nadu, which is part of the Eastern Ghats. He was educated back in England and studied medicine at University College London. He was one of the first to recognise that the soft tissue damage that destroyed the body, notably the limbs, in leprosy was not due directly to the bacterial infection but to the immunologically driven nerve damage and loss of sensation in fingers and toes. Lack of sensation in the extremities leads to injury which, when repeated over an extended period, results in their destruction. He also developed some revolutionary reconstructive surgical procedures, such as tendon transplants which restored function to the disabled limbs. Paul Brand had left the hospital by the time I visited, having taken up a position in the US in 1966, but I did meet him once at a CMC reunion event sometime later. He was another remarkable individual who gave his life to treating what was regarded by many as an 'orphan disease' of the southern hemisphere which had little relevance to the industrialised world.

Perhaps the most remarkable person associated with CMC Vellore was its founder, Dr Ida Scudder, who was a third-generation missionary, born in South India in 1870 but who returned to Cornell University in the US to train as a doctor following the realisation that many women in the region did not wish to be treated by a male doctor; and that was all that was on offer at the time. She returned to Vellore in 1900, established a small dispensary and eventually the Mary Taber Schell Memorial hospital, using the $10,000 she had raised from a wealthy banker in New York, Mr Schell. She soon realised the importance of bringing care close to home and started roadside dispensaries. She established a school for training nurses, and by 1918 had established a course for training women doctors, which awarded a Licentiate Diploma in Medical Practice (LMP). By 1928 she had built a hospital on the same site as the current CMC. University level medical degrees were awarded from 1942 and men were admitted to the Medical College for the first time in 1947. She also took on a major responsibility for raising the funding to support the capital development and the core funding to maintain the service which required regular trips back to the US, the major source of philanthropic donations which supported her work. The institution has developed into one of India's premier academic clinical centres with more than 2,000 beds, leading the way in open-heart surgery, kidney transplantation, rehabilitation, non-invasive vascular procedures, and bone marrow and liver transplantation. Ida Scudder died at the age of eighty-nine years in her bungalow in Kadaikanal. This is an extraordinary legacy for a woman who initially planned a life of relative comfort in the US. Ida's grandfather, Dr John Scudder Sr, was the first medical missionary in India, arriving in 1819. His son, Ida's father, was also a medical missionary. Ida was the third generation and there have been another two generations to follow, making a total of five in all.

William Cutting was also born in India during the time that his father, Dr Cecil G. Cutting, was serving as a medical missionary in Chikballapur; a small market town just north of Bangalore in the south-east corner of Mysore State. The mission hospital opened in 1913 but Cecil Cutting did not join the staff until 1932. His missionary colleague, the Rev. Richard A. Hickling, had been in Chikballapur for forty years. Dr Cecil Cutting's parents also gave a lifetime of missionary service to India. In 1962, he published an account of his medical experiences in a book entitled *Hot Surgery*, in which he describes the challenge of treating a massive diversity of diseases, including cholera, malaria, bubonic plague and other fevers and a variety of surgical conditions. Most importantly, he talks about his patients with the love that would normally only be directed at a member of one's family.

Christian missionaries from the UK, some Commonwealth countries and the USA and the missions and missionary hospitals and schools that they founded, played an important role in improving health and literacy during the nineteenth and twentieth centuries before and after Independence. For many people living in the rural regions of S. India, the local mission hospital was all that was available. English medium schools founded by missionaries contributed to the establishment of English as the second language in India (spoken by 125 million Indians), Hindi being the first (550 million, although over 100 million of these list Hindi as their second or third language). This almost certainly explains why Indian students have been attracted to the English-speaking world for higher and post-graduate education. Indian industrialists and entrepreneurs, many of whom received secondary and tertiary education in the UK, have been highly successful in creating business opportunities outside of the subcontinent, including the UK, notably in steel and motor vehicle manufacture.

Missionaries, in addition to giving themselves and their skills to the people of India, attracted major philanthropic gifts to establish and maintain many charitable foundations. Although these individuals were totally committed to improving the health and quality of life in general to the people they served, there is little doubt that it was a way of bringing local people (Hindus, Muslims and others) into the penumbra of a Christian community, thereby increasing the chances of conversion to Christianity. Christian missionaries started arriving in the subcontinent centuries before the establishment of the East India Company in 1600; the first, according to Dennis Kincaid's account, was Father Stevens of The Society of Jesus in 1579.

Most of these Foundations established in the nineteenth and twentieth centuries are now run entirely by Indians, a process of handover which began soon after Independence, but most remain independent of government funding although they continue to be reliant in varying extents to external international financial support.

KUMAR, ASOK AND ROBI

In the following days I was placed in the care of three medical students at CMC; Kumar (eldest son of Dr Ratnaraj), Robi (son of a doctor in Kerala, who I would visit later in the summer) and Ashok. We passed these days in true medical student style, although unlike student life in the UK it was devoid of alcohol. Over the weekend we visited some of their friends, talked about the many topics that are on the minds of young students, but we remained in exclusively male company. Women just did not feature, at least visibly, in the day-to-day social life of these young men. Couples could not be seen in public together, could never be observed engaging any form of physical contact and a kiss or embrace was totally forbidden. Young women when presented as a marital candidate, usually by their parents, would need to have an impeccable conduct record. My friends were reluctant to discuss the details of any relationships with their female contemporaries, but I suspect that furtive meetings did take place, perhaps like that evening when Arthur Samuel met Suseela on the steps of the Womens' Hostel; it was not a subject for open discussion, certainly not in my presence. On one evening, we did discuss early sexual experiences and I came away with the impression that it was expected that most young men, particularly those living outside a major metropolis (where the approach to male-female interactions was becoming more relaxed), would obtain their first sexual experiences with prostitutes.

On Sunday evening, we travelled together by train to Madras, arriving at about 7.00pm. During the next two days, we ate most of our meals in a small traditional 'hotel' in town called Buhan's which provided a varied menu ranging from typical vegetarian South Indian, to biryani and even Chinese. The movie culture was a dominant feature of a young person's life. Each evening, usually around 9.30pm we went to the local cinema and took in a film; on Sunday, it was *Two Violent Men* (a violent 'Western' which centred on revenge, 1964), on Monday, *Thunderball* (with Sean Connery as James Bond, 1965) and on Tuesday it was *The Pirates of Blood River* (starring Christopher Lee and his infamous drinking buddy Oliver Reed, a Hammer film production 1962). We drank coffee, listened to Beatles' tapes and on one occasion smoked cigars. On Monday evening, I spoke to Robi about his home in Mundakayam in Kerala; it sounded beautiful and quite different from the arid plains of Andhra Pradesh and Tamil Nadu. His father was a doctor and through Robi had extended a warm invitation to make a visit to Kerala when I came to the end of my time in Jammalamadugu; we started to make a plan, and I was hopeful that Robi would be free to join us during the visit.

Shore temple, Mahabalipuram, 1969. (Author's collection)

The final stage of our tour in Tamil Nadu was to visit the magnificent shore temples of Mahabalipuram. Early next morning we took a public bus from Madras which routed us in a southerly direction along the coast road. The seven monolithic temples constructed in about CE 700 had extended out into the Bay of Bengal but over the centuries they have been subjected to considerable erosion, such that only one of the temples remains intact. We explored the land-based features of this ancient building complex with incredible life-size granite elephants, bulls and other animals and the precariously perched Krishna's 'butterball' stone (made of granite and estimated to weigh 250 tons) which sits on a stony slope from which it has not moved for many years.

We ate green coconuts (a first for me); the coconut seller would slice off the top of the nut with two or three rapid, elegant strokes of a razor-sharp machete, insert a straw through the hole in the top of the green globe and pass it back to the client. Once the coconut milk had been drained, the coconut man would split open the nut with another single strike of his machete, to reveal the soft pearly white coconut flesh in the centre which we scooped out with a slither of coconut shell; quite delicious. We completed the day with a walk on the beach and at one point were surrounded by children selling seashells. They lived

Riding a bull, 1969. (Author's collection)

Krishna's 'butterball', 1969. (Author's collection)

A boat on the sand, 1969. (Author's collection)

A boat on the sea, 1969. (Author's collection)

in a hamlet of traditional thatched houses at the top of the beach being the children of fisher-folk. At the shore-line we could see fishermen beaching their primitive wooden boats constructed from the trunks of four or five large trees that had been honed into a boat-like shape and bound together with heavy rope.

Some had a mast with a small sail, but the main propulsion energy was by a fisherman with a paddle. They emptied their nets of small- and medium-sized silver fish into large baskets which were carried up the beach and sold directly from their village to traders from Madras and to local inhabitants including hotel owners. The fishermen were shiny skinned, muscular, almost totally devoid of body fat and wore nothing but a scanty loincloth; their bodies were as dark in colour as the night. Once the nets were emptied of their contents they were laid out on the soft fine sand to dry and where necessary, repaired. The scene was one that has been repeated over many centuries; it was history in the present.

AUNTY DOLL, DR DEY AND BILLY CAMERON

I stayed that first night in Bangalore with the Xavier family who had befriended Elizabeth throughout her stay in Bangalore. Elizabeth had already sent a thumbnail sketch of the Xaviers a week or so before I arrived in a letter.

> *He is the general manager and accountant and more-or-less holds the place together! She is in-charge of laundry, weighs about 20 stone (!) And has a heart of gold! They are very nice and have almost adopted me this summer, and when I said you were coming to Bangalore Mrs X immediately offered to put you up without my having to ask her – I think you will enjoy yourself here.*

They lived in a small bungalow on the hospital campus which was an entitlement for key workers. They were Anglo-Indians and very proud of their heritage. I use the term Anglo-Indian to describe people of mixed race which I believe was the original definition of the term. It is also used to describe British people who are living in India for significant periods and Indians who have emigrated to or were born in the UK. The Xaviers came from a long line of railway workers which was a popular occupation for those of an Anglo-Indian background and jobs passed from one to another across generations; just like the porters working in the London meat and fish markets of Smithfield and Billingsgate. They were a warm, generous and a hugely comic family who enjoyed everything they did. They were less reserved and more emotionally demonstrative than a comparable Indian family and dressed as Europeans, which was less common then in Bangalore than it is today. Doll, or 'Aunty Doll' as she became known to us, was a strong matriarch, although her husband Joe, while less effusive was obviously a loyal and caring husband and father. They gave us a wonderful 'English' dinner and during the evening we played with their two children outside on their small veranda. Both Joe and Doll enjoyed a drink and I recall that we all worked extremely hard that evening to drain a bottle of domestic dark rum, which was clearly a favourite with them. It was a warm night and I chose to sleep on the veranda under the stars. It would be an early start in the morning.

During that brief stay with the Xaviers, we talked about some of the challenges that were facing Anglo-Indians and whether indeed there would be a long-term future for their dwindling population as India developed. The community began to grow in the mid-nineteenth century following marriages between British Army officers, railway workers and tea planters and the local Indian women. By 1947, at the time of Indian independence, there were about 500,000 Anglo-Indians living in India; the number has fallen steadily during the past seventy years and is now between 100,000 and 150,000. It has got to the point that the community has now set up a marriage bureau to try and save the dying community. Many within the community feel that they are a distinctive group that should stay together and be preserved. This sense of loss probably emanates from a feeling of 'un-belonging', that is neither Indian or British. Homi Bhabha, the distinguished scholar of postcolonial studies coined the term 'un-homed' to describe the social and psychological dislocation that can be felt by a post-colonial subject, particularly one of mixed race. The individual is not physically homeless but Bhabha's paradigm suggests a life in a 'border zone'. Anglo-Indians are particularly concerned about their portrayal in literature and film. Denis Kincaid caricatures Anglo-Indians in an unhelpful way in his book *British Social Life in India*, and E.M. Forster sharpens the focus when he refers to a chauffeur in *Passage to India* as being 'vexed by opposite currents in his blood'. The Anglo-Indian community has been angered by stereotyping in films such as *36 Chowringhee Lane* directed by Arpana Sen (1981) and *Cotton Mary* directed by Merchant and Ivory (1999). Merchant was attacked in *The Guardian* by the Anglo-Indian community for, 'portraying them as lazy, promiscuous and obsessed with all things British'. Inter-marriage between Indians, Europeans and other Western nations continues apace today but somehow these new relationships do not see themselves as part of that close-knit community living in India but more as part of the growing wider global community of mixed-race people.

The following morning, we took a brief tour around Bangalore in an 'auto rick' and did some shopping. That evening we took the Island Express (Bangalore to Cape Cormorin at the Southern tip of India, via Trivandrum) which left Bangalore City Junction at 6.10.00pm and arrived in Ernakulam Junction (our point of departure) at 11.00am the following morning, a journey of about seventeen hours. Today that same journey takes about eleven and a half hours. We purchased a return ticket to Bangalore at the station and then took an auto-rickshaw to Ernakulam North station on a reconnaissance exercise, as later in the day we would take the bus from there to Mundakayam, where we would stay for a couple of nights with Robi's father, Dr Dey and his wife. We had lunch in a restaurant in the Sealord Hotel situated elegantly on Marine Drive overlooking the sea, which was the first high-rise concrete building in Cochin, completed just three years previously in 1966. We wandered through the endless canals and waterways that are important thoroughfares for people and commerce. The canals were teeming with long low-lying wooden boats with a prow that rose out of the water bearing an uncanny resemblance to the gondolas of Venice; many were overflowing with fruits and vegetables, others carried baskets of recently caught fish.

Some of the boats were open while others were protected by a beautifully structured arch of thatched roofing, not unlike the traditional homes of the Toda people in the Nilgiri Hills. There was a buzz of commerce in the air; we even found a snake charmer who would entertain tourists for a few paisa.

Boats on a canal, 1969. (Author's collection)

Fish in a basket, 1969. (Author's collection)

TOP: A snake charmer, 1969.
(Author's collection)
BOTTOM: Elephantiasis, 1969.
(Author's collection)

Traders would shout at each other across the waterways, passing the time of day with casual chit-chat, doing deals and probably just enjoying the bustle of daily life on the water. There was a sense of purpose and fulfilment which was not always apparent in those working on the land.

I stood for a moment and watched a man unloading his boat at the quayside; he was wearing a blue and white checked *lunghi*, a white sleeveless vest (the 'wife-beater' variety) and a white turban, turned loosely around his head leaving a 'tail' to fall over his left ear. I was immediately drawn to his lower legs, one of which was thin and scrawny the other was three times the size of its mate and had lost the normal muscular and bony contours; and yes, it looked as if it should have belonged to an elephant. This was the first time I had seen elephantiasis. This condition was still quite common in certain parts of India; it is due to a filarial worm infection which takes up residence in the lymphatic system, resulting in chronic blockage of the lymph ducts and this causes accumulation of fluid in the lower limb. This infection, filariasis, is now easily treated with the appropriate anti-parasitic drug but difficult to ameliorate once severe damage to the lymph ducts has occurred.

One of the striking features of people in Kerala at that time, irrespective of their occupation or social standing, was that they and their clothes always seemed clean. Men wore dazzling white shirts and *dhotis* and the women frequently wore white sarees. They seem to have a compelling pride in their appearance which was not always the case in other parts of the rural South. I was also struck by the frequency with which people, usually women, carried an open umbrella, which in this season was to provide protection from the sun rather than the rain. Residents of South India, particularly Tamils, and to some extent Malayalis have darker skin tones compared to those in the north. Walking in the sun every day in the peak of summer would darken the tone which for many would be perceived as undesirable.

Despite having a relatively low per capita Gross National Product, Kerala has for many decades provided its citizens with high-quality healthcare and education compared to many other states with similar economic pressures. Back in the 1990s Kerala had achieved almost 100 per cent literacy rates which compared starkly to other states, particularly in the northeast, where they struggle to achieve 60 per cent. How did this state make such rapid progress?

Kerala, like most of the rest of India in the early 1900s, was gripped by an extraordinarily rigid caste system. By introducing an innovative and progressive education system which insisted that all castes should study together, Kerala made rapid progress in providing equal opportunities for all citizens, thereby widening participation in education and thus maximising the effectiveness of its people. Soon after Independence, Kerala elected a Communist Party of India majority to the State legislature, which immediately led to land reforms and activation and organisation of land workers. Although some of these changes were subsequently watered down, change had occurred. Kerala Land Reforms (Amendment) Act 1969 ultimately turned 1.5 million tenant farmers into small landowners.

By distributing state resources into healthcare, life expectancy is six to seven years longer than the average life expectancy in India overall. Kerala has made these improvements without the requirement of massive economic growth. It has achieved it through education and the creation of an informed society with an overwhelming commitment to fairness in the way in which wealth is distributed. This social culture has continued despite changes in the ruling party; it is what its people now expect.

We took coffee in the Seashells Cafe (Shanmugham Road, Ernakulam) and successfully found the express bus which was to take us to Mundakayam about 100 km from Ernakulam. We were advised by Robi to ask the driver to let us off the bus at 'Dr Dey's house', which he duly did. Dr Dey and his wife were extremely hospitable; after a traditional South Indian dinner, they took us through a two-day travel inventory which would encompass visits to rubber and tea estates, and a trip to their own land much of which was heavily forested. The following day we would take an early morning bus to Thekkady (about 50 km) to explore the Periyar Nature Reserve. It was a delight to sleep in a bedroom with something that approximated to a European bathroom, after several nights in trains and buses and on the sofa on Aunty Doll's veranda.

The rubber estate was located just less than an hour from the Dey's residence. I had never seen such a plantation, as these trees will only thrive in warm and moist sub-tropical environments. Kerala is blessed with both; the right temperatures and adequate rain. Compared to most of Andhra and Tamil Nadu, Kerala is a green, lush state. One of the supervisors took us through the entire process from the harvesting of the glistening white latex which is released from the trunk of the rubber tree, a process called 'tapping', by deeply scoring through the bark with a sharp blade to make a curved downward sloping cut, a sort of spiral, along which the sap can drain under the influence of gravity into a strategically placed collection vessel at its lower end. In Kerala, where coconuts grow in profusion, the receptacle would be traditionally half of a dried coconut shell. These vessels would be periodically collected and taken to a processing point where the processed sap would then be poured into metal trays to cure and then dry. The raw dry latex is rolled to express water from the solidifying material and then often smoke dried to stabilise the rubber for transportation.

Latex drying and curing in Kerala, 1969. (Author's collection)

The British introduced commercial rubber growing in India in the early twentieth century, an industry which has grown substantially such that India is now the third leading producer of rubber globally; when I visited the plantation in 1969 Kerala was contributing more than 90 per cent of the national output, but this has now fallen to around 70 per cent because of diminished yields and increasing competition from other parts of India. Rubber sales still contribute around 50 per cent of the state's annual income.

Our next stop was the tea estate less than half an hour away; we arrived just before midday. We were greeted by the ebullient, magenta-faced, sandy-haired estate manager, Billy Cameron. Yes, a friendly Scot.

'Thank you very much for hosting this visit to your estate.'

'Not *my* estate, laddie!' He blurted in a heavy Aberdonian brogue. 'But you're very welcome all the same! Can I get you a drink before we take a walk?'

Elizabeth and I looked at each other and exchanged a signal that said, 'Yes.' I guessed what was coming next because I had detected a faint small of alcohol on his breath, but before I had a chance to respond, he continued:

'Will it be whisky or … whisky?' he said with a bland expression on his face.

Then he released a wicked smile and before we had had time to reply he was back on his way into the bungalow, returning rapidly with a bottle of home-grown domestic whisky and glass tumblers on a tray. He poured three very generous glasses and placed then symmetrically on a round low table on the open veranda.

'There, not Scotch, but as close as you can get to it here. Not bad though and it seems to work!'

He was clearly enjoying the excuse to entertain guests from the UK and the opportunity to get in a swift peg of whisky before lunch and his afternoon siesta. We struggled to get the whisky down at his rate but before we knew it we were on our feet again and making our way out on to the terraces where endless rows of tea bushes were being systematically harvested by a team of women, each with a basket on her back suspended by a cloth sling which ran over the crown of their heads. Their fingers moved swiftly over the plants, picking the most desired 'tips' that would be selected for the finest teas. The leaves from these Indian tea bushes are dried so that they lose about 40 per cent of the moisture content, rolled and then fermented on trays in a special drying shed before packing for export.

I have never really enjoyed tea in India, unlike green unfermented tea in China which I have come to adore. I think the main reason is that for economic reasons India was exporting its best teas, whereas green tea in China was initially, largely grown for home consumption; the export trade was more limited as the taste for green tea was not highly developed at that time in the West; a situation that has now changed markedly.

Tea is big business in India. The East India Company introduced commercial tea-growing in India in the 1820s, initially in the north in Assam. For over a century India was the leading tea producer in the world, though just recently has been overtaken by China. Production continues to increase year-on-year although Kerala only contributes about 5 per cent of the total from across India.

We eventually left the terraces and walked back to the bungalow.

'Another wee drink before you go?'

A tea picker, Kerala, 1969. (Author's collection)

'No thanks, we need to get back for lunch.' I said without a moment's thought.

'Och well, more's the pity!'

'How does your wife find it out here?' I asked tentatively.

'Oh, she left years ago. Hated it! She could never find anything to do. She got fed up with me; I just worked all the time. She went back to Scotland. I hear from her from time to time. But that's all in the past.'

'How long will you stay?' I was somewhat taken aback.

'As long as it takes. I have an OK life here. Don't know what I would do if I went back. Probably start drinking!'

We said our farewells and were glad to return to the Dey's residence which was a cool stone house and well protected from the midday sun by its tree-filled gardens.

Cameron seemed an isolated person with little to engage him in life other than the day-to-day toil of the tea estate. Like so many people in a similar position, he just had no-where else to go.

We slept well that night and rose early the following morning at 4.30am, drank an exquisite South Indian coffee in the kitchen and waited for the 5.30am bus which would get us to Thekkady by about 8.30am. We saw the sun rise through the gaps between the hilly undulations of the Western Ghats. It was good to feel its warmth after waking into the cool morning air following a night of cloudless sky. Thekkady and the Periyar Game Reserve are located at about 2,800 m above sea-level which brought an exhilarating freshness that we had not experienced in Ernakulam and Mundakayam. On arrival our next task was to locate the person who was to see us safely on to the boat that would show us the wildlife of the nature reserve from the lake.

We found the Hotel Aryana Nivas by the lake, our agreed place to rendezvous, took a light breakfast and waited for our contact, a Mr Wood, who had been instructed to arrange our tickets for a 'Lake Safari'. He duly arrived and took us down onto the jetty to board the rather elderly double-decker lake cruiser. From the shore it looked a little like a 'giant sandwich' and reminded me of a smaller version of one of the Nile cruise ships. We decided that views would be better from the upper deck and positioned ourselves accordingly. There were very few other tourists that day, so we could move around the boat freely from side to side depending on the points of interest.

As the crew navigated us through the lake, it became apparent that this area had not always been underwater, as there were many leafless and barkless trees emerging above the waterline, indicating

Periyar Lake, 1969. (Author's collection)

former forestation. I had an immediate flashback to Paul Nash's World War I paintings of deforested Ypres, such as *The Menon Road* (1919). I subsequently learnt that the Mullaperiyar Dam had been constructed in 1895, which prevented the westerly free-flow of the Periyar River, thereby creating an artificial lake to the east. It now seems extraordinary that these bereft leafless trees had survived so long. This intervention created the Periyar Lake Reserve.

There was a guide on the boat who took a rather relaxed approach to his job but would point out interesting wildlife as they appeared. We saw turtles in the water and on land a variety of small deer such as sambar, wild dogs and an exquisite herd of Asian elephants.

It was not until 1972 that Bengal tigers were introduced into the reserve as part of a conservation project, the 'Tiger Project'; today there are at least forty Bengal tigers roaming free in the jungles of

A herd of elephants at Periyar, 1969. (Author's collection)

Periyar. This is part of a global campaign, the Global Tiger Recovery Plan to double wild tiger numbers by 2022. A century ago there were 100,000 tigers in Asia which has been dramatically reduced to 3,000 to 4,000 through poaching and habitat destruction. In the 1990s the Elephant Project was initiated as part of a drive to increase the number of wild Asian elephants in South India.

After about three or four hours the boat returned to the jetty and we were soon on a bus back to Mundakayam. After a long and tiring day, we enjoyed dinner with Dr Dey and his wife at home and retired early to bed, as at 6.30am we would need to be ready to take the bus back to Ernakulam. From there we were to take the train from Cochin to Coimbatore and finally Bangalore.

The Xaviers welcomed us back as if we were family and gave us breakfast, lunch and dinner before we left the following day to take the three o'clock train overnight to Bombay. The 1,000 km by rail took us about twenty-four hours but today there is a choice of at least six different airlines and a direct non-stop flight takes less than two hours. It was the end of a great adventure; at this point I remember feeling strongly that it was time to get home.

The '60s in the West were a decade of revolution, miniskirts and the Beatles. In India it was a decade when you were constantly told what you could not do and, when for a while, it seemed the very idea of India might not work. The country was pictured as an aeroplane poised for economic take-off.... But soon Plane India stalled so badly on the runway that for a time there were real fears it would collapse – certainly foreign critics wrote it off – while Armageddon was avoided, the decade ended with much of the high hopes of freedom turned to dust.

Mihir Bose, *India Today*, 1999

In his article Bose continues to reflect on the devastating damage to national confidence after the Indian army was massively defeated on the northeast frontier by China; for a moment there was a chance that the northeastern state of Assam might be lost to another nation. Students were required to undertake basic military training to prepare for any future attack. Bose reflects on the economic stagnation and 'a four years wait for an Ambassador, twelve years for a Fiat'. He indulges himself further in the misery of prohibition; 'my father could drink at home in Bombay only after getting a permit from the Collector of Customs. It was obtained after his doctor certified that for health reasons my father required two pegs of whisky every night. My father also used his friends in the Indian Armed Forces to get around prohibition. On Indian naval ships the Gandhian injunctions against alcohol did not apply, and the old British custom of drinking still prevailed; as soon as his naval friends came ashore, my father was off to the Bombay docks.'

This difficult, turbulent and rather sad period of India's progression into the free world is captured in V.S. Naipaul's book, *An Area of Darkness* published in the middle of these bleak '60s, in 1964. This book sparked profound dislike of the author from real Indians who were living through this period of prohibition and deprivation, a man who was regarded by many as a mere 'visitor' since his birthplace was not India but Trinidad. What right did he have to comment on a place that was not his own? However, many of his observations were correct. There were sporadic famines; the rice and milk shortages, for example, had a profound effect on the daily way of life of ordinary people.

PART 5 — A PERIOD OF ADJUSTMENT

There is something beyond our mind which abides in silence within our mind. It is the supreme mystery beyond thought. Let one's mind and one's subtle body rest upon that and not rest on anything else.

6.19 Maitri Upanishad

Relocation back to the UK was not easy. When the moment came, I was content to leave India and return to the life I knew. I was missing friends and family and needed to restart what I can only call 'real life'. However, at the same time, I was appalled by the affluence of my homeland, by the dismissive culture of those that inhabited the tail end of the 1960s and the disinterest of my colleagues who had summered in less challenged places.

It was exactly as Tennessee Williams poignantly posed in his play *Period of Adjustment*, first performed in New York City in 1960, just ten years earlier. His 'serious comedy' examines the dilemmas of two couples, one which had just moved apart and the other which had just come together. I had difficulty separating from a 'new life' that I had come to love and was struggling to re-establish a relationship with the 'old life' with which I was most familiar.

On returning to the UK, I felt distinctly out of place. Not only did I have to shed a superficial oriental mantle (wearing traditional *khadi* shirt and *dhoti* in the evening, burning incense while writing at my desk and practising the tabla sitting cross-legged on the Cuddapah stone floor of my room) that now protected me to some extent from what I judged to be the superficiality and brashness of Western materialism; but at the same time I had to grow with some urgency into a responsible 'student doctor', keen to acquire the knowledge and skills that would guarantee a successful career in the protected and privileged environment of an elite London teaching hospital. I had to find a shirt and a tie, don the short white jacket that distinguished a medical student from a qualified doctor and carry that medallion of medical supremacy, the stethoscope. However, I was the subject of an inexplicable human paradox. I had just experienced several months of deep immersion into the devastating health and social problems of a deprived low-income, resource-poor society in South India, having performed endless surgeries and other invasive procedures on defenceless villagers, learnt more in three months than I would learn in the next three years but had no choice but to buckle down, restart my studies and remember that in three years I had to pass a series of exams to allow me to move forward in my career. Prof. 'Sherry' (Sherwood) Gorbach, a distinguished but raucous infectious diseases physician in Boston is renowned for saying 'travel broadens the mind but loosens the bowels!' Within a few hours of arriving in Bombay I had fulfilled his prophecy. During the rest of my stay in India I had remained extremely well, but within days of arriving back in the UK I had a return of symptoms, although this time it had the characteristics of malabsorption; I self-diagnosed tropical sprue or giardiasis. I was too embarrassed to seek medical advice but just put up with the symptoms and with the passing of time, some weeks I recall, my internal workings gradually returned to normal.

I found it difficult to talk about my experiences of the last three to four months. To be honest, I do not think my colleagues were particularly interested. I saw Elizabeth from time to time, less than perhaps than we would have wanted, as she moved on to complete her clinical training at another London Teaching Hospital. Our experiences had been different; mine focused in a small, isolated village mission hospital which inevitably meant that the community was closed and amenities were limited; her experience was in the relatively sophisticated town of Bangalore (the 'Garden City' much favoured by the British because of its elevation of about 900 m and thus a more temperate climate conducive to English style gardening), in a larger hospital with a more open, mixed community. The engagement she had with the Anglo-Indian family at the hospital added a sense of irreverence and fun which seemed to have diminished the religiosity of a mission hospital experience.

Soon after I returned to the UK, I received a letter from Aunty Doll; I think it was the first letter I received from India after my departure.

Bangalore, 30.9.69

Hi Mike,
Hope you landed home safe – your dear parents and brother must have been waiting for you my dear. We are OK. Joe, kids and myself went to Madras the weekend. How was your dear mother, please let me know by return post as to what does she want from here and if she likes to have a saree and if so what is her height. Also ask dad and your brother. Please do go and see my brother and also if possible introduce your dear parents to him. Poor fellow he is real far from us and we do feel it now and then. The little time I knew you I really took to you. The kids also love you and the Black Beauty [her daughter] is growing fatter day by day. Please send the photos as soon as possible. I have also written to dear Liz. Please do write to me my dear.

Love

Aunty Doll

A letter from William, written at the end of September followed me to Bangalore and finally to home in London.

22nd September, 1969

Dear Michael,
Hope that you have had a splendid final fling in India with an exciting trip down to Kerala and back. Different from Jammalamadugu?!?
The house is strangely empty without you, and the kids often speak of you. We miss the gentle sound of the tabala and the whiff of Joss sticks. . . . .

I wrote to Sam, who eventually replied but without any clear explanation other than,

I was just postponing. Here as you know life is just passing on without any change. This is very boring to me. When you were here I felt for a while 'young' (one must have an equal company to exchange his opinions and ideas) but now again feeling 'old'. Let me not further bore you with my boring life?

I could not see Sam surviving at the Campbell Hospital in the long term but hoped that he would go on to further training in paediatrics and give a few years more to the child health service, as I knew that William was counting on him, knowing that he, himself would not be there forever. William wrote again in November:

8th November, 1969

Dear Michael,
Please excuse the red, but the black on this ribbon is worn to a very pale grey. . . . [The entire letter was typed in red ink! See page 126]

He wrote optimistically about developing future research collaborations with the UK and reported that Margot's fourth child, a boy named Colin, had arrived safely in the maternity unit at Campbell Hospital delivered by Mollie with William close at hand. He went on,

This last week I have had an additional worry in the form of Dr Ratnaraj having a turn of aphasia that started on Monday morning. He had had a pretty busy four days preceding, and it would be easy to label it as largely hysterical. However, it is really the wrong age group, and he did have a little hypertension. He is now much better, but still very slow. I have clutched the one organic sign, raised BP, and I'm trying to give him some simple encouragement around that. It would be nice to be certain that there is nothing organic at all. Looks as if we're going to have to carry him even more than before!

I heard nothing more until I received a long letter from Sam, written in early January 1970.

The C.S.I. Hospital,
Jammalamadugu,
8th, November, 1969.

Dear Michael,

Please excuse the red, but the black on this ribbon is
worn to a very pale grey. First I must thank you for the second
film, and the replacement tape. Also I must add that my folks
were very pleased with the pictures of the kids that you kindly
took for them. Neither I nor you gave them your address, so they
have not been able to get into touch. Do go and visit them if
you can possibly tear yourself away from the wards and the other
destractions of being back in the big city !

Possibly the last time I wrote I did mention that we
had had Dr. David Morley here (Institute of Child Health, 30
GuilfordStreet, W.C.L.). He seemed to be quite pleased with our
efforts, which I suppose is not really surprizing as so many of
the plans are based on his ideas. The most troublesome or
exciting consequence of his visit - whichever way you view it is
that he is pushing me very hard to try and organise a Longitudinal
Survey on the Growth, Morbidity and Mortality of village children,
and apply for a fat grant from M.R.C. for the work, and take on a
team of about half a dozen, including an Indian M.D. in Pediatrics.
I can see many difficulties of getting staff, and further spreading
my limited resources and consequently doing more and more, less and
less well. Nor do I think that my colleagues are likely to be very
excited at the idea. We shall see, anyway at present I am still
thinking about it, but take off for Vellore for advice soon.
We also had the OXFAM overseas aid appraiser here for part of a day,
Bernard LLewellyn, and fortunately he seemed suitably impressed.

Of course the most important piece of news has been already
told you in Catrionas part of the letter. Fortunately all went
very smoothly, and I was able to be present to aid and abet Margot
and Mollie. Catriona is really delighted with Colin despite the fact
she had ordered a sister. "We will have two girls next time to make
up" .. says she ! Progress seems to be satisfactory at present.

This last week I have had an additional worry in the form
of Dr. Ratnaraj having a turn of Aphasia that started on Monday
morning. He had had a pretty busy four days preceeding, and it would
be easy to label it as largely hysterical. However it is really
the wrong age group, and he did have a little hypertension. He is
now much better, but still very slow. I have clutched the one organic
sign, riased B.P., and am trying to give him some simple encouragement
around that. It would be nice to be certain that there is nothing
organic at all. Looks as if we are going to have to carry him even
more than before!

Another disappointment was that I had a letter from a class-
mate who is in a lucrative G.P. on the West Coast of Scotland. One
old dear in his practice had died off and wanted to leave some cash
for a good cause. Fortunately Harry McDonnell had swallowed our
work, and was going to send it here. However he sent it to OXFAM,
who promptly put it in the Nutrition Unit fund, and I had already
planned a new Lab and a new Jeep ! Anyway we are going to apply for
the latter but we need the former too !

Red letter, 1969. (Author's collection)

Michael,

My dearest friend,

I'm so sorry I kept you so long waiting for my letters. Really I feel very bad for this. Please pardon me. I find no cause for my silence all these days. I hope you don't misunderstand me for this.

Many thanks for your greetings and kind letter. Before it is too late, let me wish you a Happy Christmas and a Happy New Year.

This place has not experienced any change except there was a 'rainless' rainy season followed by torrential rains due to some disturbances in the Arabian Sea (weather experts say) both of them are detrimental to the crops here, resulting in increase of 'prices'. People whom you know here will never change excepting getting older. One is Dr Ratnaraj. You must have heard of him already.

One and a half months ago one early morning he just kept 'quiet' without talking. The whole day he didn't talk (aphasia). After two or three days he started talking slowly. Some thought he is 'behaving' (and I too!). Doctors thought some cerebral accident. Anyway, he has been to CMCH, Vellore and was diagnosed as having glioma (malignant 95%) and is being treated with 'cobalt exposure therapy'. He will be back in Jammy next week I suppose. They are (he and his family) very much depressed....

We, the left off doctors (7– 2 = 5) here have to struggle like 'bulls' all the time and I couldn't find proper and leisure time to write you. And this week is my 'night duty'.

So, you are now a clinical student. Remember <u>Eyes first</u>, <u>Hands next</u> and <u>Tongue last</u> (when you examine a patient). For your interest sake I am sending some photos of some of the Indian dances.

Mary is fine and sends you her greetings. Please give my regards to your parents.

Closing with best wishes,

Yours sincerely

Arthur Samuel

Sadly, William's optimism that this was all due to a small stroke related to high blood pressure was not confirmed. However, perhaps Dr Ratnaraj's somewhat unpredictable and irascible behaviour in the operating theatre over the summer months was now explained?

William wrote again in February confirming that Dr Ratnaraj was doing well and had just returned from Madurai where he had collected a new hospital vehicle and was then stopping off in Vellore for a check-up. In 1972, more than two years later, I received a circular letter from Dr Ratnaraj sending 'Easter greetings.' He wrote:

Dear friends

We are very sorry that we couldn't write to you at Christmas time, but you were all in our thoughts. At this time, we wish to convey to you our sincere and affectionate greetings for this Easter tide. May the risen Lord grant to you his bounteous blessings.

On 17th July last year we celebrated the 75th anniversary of our hospital. On that occasion, in my report I said that 'it is impossible for living things to remain unchanged – either they grow and develop or else they shrink and die'. It is the same with hospitals and looking back now over the past twelve years the development seems astonishing. The hospital has grown to be a 300 bedded one and by God's Grace it has become a popular hospital and it draws patients from far and wide and it is known for its Surgery, Obstetrics and Gynae and Ophthalmic treatments. Modern emphasis is on Family Planning and preventive medicine. Last year we opened a Nutrition Education Unit and Under-Fives' Clinic where mothers be shown just how to feed and care for their babies and young children and be taught the importance of immunisation against diseases and we are proud to have one of the first such units in India and it is attracting many visitors. This work is at present supported entirely by OXFAM. All the credit goes to Dr William Cutting's efforts.

Our Nursing School and hostel building is progressing and nearing completion. The ground floor was opened by Miss Mollie Smith, our Nursing Superintendent, on 8th December 1971. We are proud of the fact that last year our first batch of students have qualified as Nurses and Midwives and are now serving on the staff.

By Grace of God my health has been good and I am able to carry on the normal duties in the hospital. My wife too has kept up her health in good state. Our elder boy, Vinaya Kumar, is in Christian Medical College, Vellore and he is working hard at his anatomy and physiology which he will be taking in December this year. He is fairly good in his studies as well as in sports and games. Our younger boy Michael is in first year B.Sc. and hoping to get into one of the Medical Colleges, preferably Vellore but the chances are very remote due to heavy competition. He Is also a keen sportsman.

Wishing you all well and with kindest regards,

Yours sincerely,

Ratnaraj

This is a remarkable story – Dr Ratnaraj's survival of more than two years with a malignant glioma, the stunning growth and development of Campbell Hospital to become a 300-bedded, full-service district general hospital and the delivery of the first cohort of nurses from its nursing school – and all this in one of the most deprived, rural settings in South India. For thousands of impoverished, largely agricultural workers and their families within a 80 km radius, Campbell Hospital was their only reliable healthcare option. The success story can only be attributed to the unswerving commitment of the medical, nursing and ancillary staff, and the international support that provided the lion's share of its funding. Dedicated, locally trained Indians, some of whom had undertaken postgraduate study in the UK and British missionaries who were devoting their professional and personal lives to the service of others. However, this was just twenty-five years after India had gained its independence, and even when I was there in 1969 there were discussions as to how long foreign missionaries would be allowed to stay in the country. Whilst Campbell Hospital was fulfilling a vital function in this part of India, it sat alongside a failing government hospital that many of the locals regarded as a death trap. This was not an isolated situation in India at the time and one could see that it would become an increasing embarrassment for a government that now needed to stand on its own and cut the ties with its former master.

GOODDY, ROSENHEIM AND WOLFF

Transition into the persona of a 'clinical student' was bumpy. Despite the extraordinary experience that I had gained in India, somehow I was not ready to talk to London patients. We were divided into groups of five or six students and sent to different 'clinical firms' in the hospital; we were allocated some in-patients and expected to take their history, examine them and keep up to date with their progress. On Ward rounds we might be asked for recent test results or to comment on their diagnosis and treatment. These were the days when we accepted the process of 'education through humiliation'. Most importantly, we were assigned to take our allotted patients' blood every morning at around 7:30am, having collected the requisite blood test request forms from Sister's desk, written up by the Houseman the night before. I struggled with history taking and physical examination and seemed unable to generate any enthusiasm whatsoever for the process. In retrospect, I wonder whether I was depressed. During those first few months there were, however, two memorable experiences, both of which were generated by charismatic but rather extraordinary hospital consultants. I trained in the days when a consultant, particularly those working in the London Teaching Hospitals, were expected to be 'characters'; extrovert behaviour, idiosyncrasies and other elements of 'performance' were the norm from this elite group of clinicians.

Dr William Gooddy was the senior consultant on my first firm, a neurology assignment based at the decrepit St Pancras Hospital in St Pancras Way, which had all the trappings of a 'workhouse', which indeed was its origin from the second half of the eighteenth century. He never mentioned the poor surroundings and seemed quite oblivious to the decay around him. He also had an appointment at the National Hospital for Neurology and Neurosurgery, Queen Square which probably satisfied the desire in his personality for elegance. He was a skilled clinician, with enormous experience and an astounding breadth of knowledge of clinical neurology. He was gentle with patients and seemed to enjoy building a relationship with them; importantly, he gave them time. His obituary stated that 'unlike most neurologists of his generation, Gooddy was amusing and charming, lacking the austere asceticism and obsession regarded as prerequisites for success. He was also humane and hated to give bad news, leaving much of that to his juniors.'

He was erudite and articulate. However, despite his experience, knowledge and skills, I do not think I was ready for his level of intellect, learning little from the many pearls of wisdom that were offered to us on a weekly basis. He advised against reading heavy neurological tomes but encouraged engagement with Proust for solace. He talked endlessly to us about 'time' and its importance for understanding higher cerebral function; he eventually published a book entitled *Time and the Nervous System* in 1988. Like many of his extraordinarily able contemporaries in teaching hospital medicine, he had many other interests. I refer again to his obituary; he was a potter, organist, he decorated tiles, embroidered, made jewellery, was fascinated by clocks and was a good photographer. With the advent of the CT scan, he proposed that all world leaders should undergo routine neurological (and psychological) assessment before taking up the role!

My next firm was the Medical Unit at University College Hospital, led by Prof. Sir Max, soon to become Lord Rosenheim. Like William Gooddy, he was a private, modest man but a physician of great distinction. He lived much of his life with his mother in North London, and as far as I know never married. He had built up academic medicine at UCH, which had attracted an illustrious group of clinician scientists to work alongside him. He had been a dynamic President of the Royal College of Physicians and was known internationally for his expertise in kidney disease. Despite these accolades, he never missed the weekly teaching session with his new fresh-faced, undergraduate clinical students. I had not had an easy start in the clinical course and rather lacked confidence, particularly in the presence of this great man. During a teaching session he asked me to present one of my patients, the case of a young man in his late twenties who had end-stage chronic renal failure. In 1970 this was virtually a death sentence. Haemodialysis as maintenance treatment became available in the 1960s with units opening at the Royal Free Hospital and Charing Cross Hospital in London; but the service was limited, and patients had to be assessed as to whether they were 'suitable' psychologically to cope with the challenges of this form of treatment and whether there was a sufficiently supportive network at home. In short, there was rationing. In those days, haemodialysis dominated your life, and usually precluded full-time work. It was clear to us all that this young man's days were numbered and Sir Max was agonising as to whether he should or should not be put forward for long-term haemodialysis. He asked me to plot out graphically all the key biochemical and haematological markers of his disease over the last five years, ostensibly to allow us to predict, by extrapolating forward, when the critical markers would move into a zone incompatible with life. On reflection, I think he was deeply troubled by this case and was initiating a delaying tactic to avoid making what could be a hard and a harsh decision. About two weeks later I presented my graphical account, which spanned more than a metre (having stuck several pages of A4 together), at the ward round. Sir Max placed the chart on his desk, said he was impressed and we all gathered around. It was blatantly obvious that the critical parameters such as serum creatinine, potassium, calcium, phosphate and haemoglobin were all moving relentlessly into the disaster zone, despite the usual supportive treatments of the day. The decision could no longer be avoided as the young man's fate was clear.

'I think it is unlikely that this patient will be accepted on to a dialysis programme, but all we can do is to try. Sadly, places are still limited and suitability for this type of treatment must be a factor.' He spoke softly and slowly, such that all of us were moved by the enormity of his responsibility as a physician.

He had looked after this patient for many years and I could see that he was going to be reluctant to accept this difficult outcome. This was a turning point for me; Sir Max gave me an 'A' for the firm which did wonders for my confidence and having idealised UK medicine from afar in resource poor India, I realised that healthcare at home was not always entirely straightforward.

Towards the end of what used to be called the 'pre-clinical' course, we were gifted with a short series of lectures, perhaps just four or five on developmental psychology. The lecturer was a Dr Heinz Wolff, a physician, psychiatrist and psychoanalyst from the hospital. This was the closest we came to the clinical environment but its relevance was profound, as it was something to which we could all relate; yes, it was about us, growing up through childhood and adolescence and hopefully continuing to develop into mature adults. Heinz was a charismatic individual, bold and not frightened to shock but at the same time contemplative. He spoke with a soft but nevertheless pronounced German accent, having come from the west part of Germany with his brother Otto a year or two before the start of the World War II. He was one of the many German Jewish émigrés that escaped to England from Hitler's Germany. During these lectures, he spoke animatedly about the theories of Freud and Jung, particularly as they related to the unconscious mind, dreams, sexuality and human motivations more generally. His soft 'middle European' accent seemed to add gravity to everything he said; almost like having Freud or Jung in the room with us.

When I finally crossed the road to the hospital some months later, I found that Heinz Wolff and other colleagues in the Department of Psychological Medicine were offering some clinical students the opportunity to engage in supervised psychotherapy. A selected group of students each year were allocated a patient considered suitable for student psychotherapy, who they saw for an hour each week, after which they were required to participate in a group supervision session with Heinz or one of the other psychotherapists. There was fierce competition in those days but I was fortunate enough to be selected. I was asked to take on a woman in her thirties with dysmorphophobia; she had a distinct dislike of the size and shape of her nose. At that time, patients who wanted cosmetic surgery under the National Health Service had to engage in a prolonged psychotherapeutic assessment, ostensibly to help them understand any underlying problems that might not be solved by changing the shape of the nose. My patient was not overwhelmed by the results of surgery, largely I believe because many of the other aspects of her life, perhaps not surprisingly, did not change after the procedure, an outcome which made her both sad and angry. The anger was expressed and dealt with during our weekly conversations. I sometimes feel that I learned more through this process than I did from many other parts of the clinical course. Heinz was an inspiration during supervision sessions and subsequently became a good friend. I think he was deeply disappointed when I finally decided not to pursue a career in psychiatry.

NAIPAUL, CHAUDARI AND MRS GANDHI

Once I had settled back into the routine of normal student life, I had more time think about what I had learnt and seen in India. Letters from friends and colleagues at the hospital prompted me to read more about this changing nation. I went back to Segal's treatise, *The Crisis of India*: 'the religion and poverty of India are the two primary materials, out of which the whole structure of the society has been – and is still being – built'. He goes on, 'India has too many people for too few developed resources. It has a mere 2.2% of the world's land area yet supports more than 14% of the world's population.' President Lyndon B. Johnson was keen that India should address the pressing issue of population growth. Mrs Gandhi and her sons, Sanjay and Rajiv, took a firm hold of the problem by establishing a mass sterilisation programme for men and women, often driven by promotions and incentives that many felt were at best morally questionable and at worst, abhorrent. The scale of these sterilisation initiatives outstripped Hitler's programmes in Nazi Germany and other countries in occupied Europe. It was already evident in many countries in the developing world that fertility and population growth declines as employment, per capita income and the social environment improves, but this did not stop the Gandhis and their population control policy.

V.S. Naipaul's account of the nation during the first half of this difficult decade was found to be pretty daunting and, indeed, angered many Indians. He says in the final paragraph of the book, 'the world is illusion, the Hindus say. We talk of despair, but true despair lies too deep for formulation. It was only now, as my experience of India defined itself more properly against my own homelessness, that I saw how close in the past year I have been to the total Indian negation, how much it had become the basis of thought and feeling.'

The following year, 1965, Nirad Chaudhuri published *The Continent of Circe*, which was awarded the Duff Cooper Prize in 1966. His treatise seriously challenges the principles of non-violence and pacifism espoused by Mahatma Gandhi, instead unravelling centuries of violence perpetrated by every Hindu dynasty. This was not well received either by a nation struggling to find its way in the modern world; it was dealt with partly by dismissing Chaudhuri as a 'European' gone over to the other side.

❧

The dominance and dishonesty of the Gandhis' dynastic regime had unravelled disastrously for India during the decade of the 1970s. During the first half of the decade there was a surge in political unrest, resulting in many public demonstrations against Indira Gandhi and the Government. There were allegations of electoral fraud and the Allahabad High Court found her guilty of 'discrepancies in the electoral campaign' of 1971. On 24 June 1975, the Supreme Court ruled that the privileges of members of Parliament would no longer apply to Gandhi, and while she was permitted to continue as Prime Minister she was no longer able to vote. On 26 June there was a Declaration of Emergency by the President, Farhruddin Ali Ahmed, 'on the advice of Indira Gandhi' which remained in place for twenty-one months. Mrs Gandhi made an announcement:

'The President has proclaimed the Emergency. This is nothing to panic about. I am sure you are all aware of the deep and widespread conspiracy, which has been growing ever since I began to introduce certain progressive measures of benefit for the common man and woman in India.'

This declaration triggered multiple arrests of political opponents, censorship of the press and massive diminution of the civil liberties of millions of Indians.

The national setting for an emergency was conducive in the light of the difficult political and economic situation the country found itself, particularly following the recent war with Pakistan, the 1973 oil crisis and the national drought; a perfect storm! However, many regard this event as one of the 'darkest days' of Indian democracy and was not considered to be due to the prevailing situation but was due entirely to Indira Gandhi's 'autocratic and dynastic mindset'.

Indira Gandhi had a difficult relationship with democracy; she is alleged to have said that 'democracy not only throws up the mediocre person but gives strength to the most vocal, howsoever they may lack knowledge and understanding.'

In September 1976, Sanjay Gandhi – who was not a member of Parliament and had never held a position in government – introduced a mass male sterilisation programme; apparently 6.2 million Indian men were sterilised during the first year of the campaign. He became his mother's principal adviser and directed the activities of ministers and other senior politicians.

On 18 January 1977 Indira Gandhi called for fresh elections and released all the political prisoners. However, The Sixth Lok Sabha (1977–9) left Indira Gandhi and the Congress Party behind, electing the relatively newly formed Janata Party with Morarji Desai as the Prime Minister. The emergency officially ended on 23 March 1977. The country waited anxiously for the new government to declare its national and international objectives. The new government simultaneously courted both the Soviet Union and the USA and started to walk a diplomatic tightrope.

However, life at home was not straightforward. The Janata Government dismissed some of the northern state governments and there was increasing civil unrest, some of it driven by inter-caste strife. Once again, Mrs Gandhi demonstrated serious political intuition when she visited Belchi, a village in Bihar where there had been despicable mob violence. It was a challenging journey, the last stages of which could only be accomplished on an elephant. This signalled the beginning of her return to mainstream politics.

Despite the political shenanigans of the 1970s, culminating in the state of emergency, the creative industries enjoyed an apparently paradoxical sense of freedom. Perhaps the politicians ignored this liberal force as a way of distracting the people from the gravity of the political situation? A formerly 'collective' nation was becoming more cognisant of the 'individual'. The film critic and author, Anupama Chopra declared that in the 1970s, 'everything just came together, the scripts, the acting, the emergence of the superstar, the music and the direction'. Notably, the film industry blossomed with some memorable landmarks, such as a relaxation of the onscreen dress code, the on-screen kiss and Parveen Babi's bedroom scene in the film, *Deewar*.

As an aside, it is interesting to reflect that half of India's current one billion plus population was born after 1979.

FILMING IN THE FOOTHILLS

*There is a path of joy and a path of pleasure. Both attract the soul.
Who follows the first comes to good; who follows pleasure reaches
not the end?*

Part 1. Katha Upanishad

TREVOR AND CELIA

Trevor poured us both a very generous 'four fingers' tumbler of whisky, took a hearty swig himself and leaned closer towards me, like a parrot arching forward on its perch.

'So, will you accompany me to the highest cricket ground in the world?'

'Mm...?' He added hastily, clearly anxious for a prompt response.

'Well, of course. But, where is it? Will we have to play cricket?'

I was genuinely bemused.

'Oh, don't be daft! No of course not. We'll go and look, then we'll have a drink and a bite of lunch. Yes, tiffin! They've given me a day off tomorrow. If I don't do something constructive I'll just sit around and drink all day.'

He took another generous gulp from his glass, which was going out like the tide, as if to make his point about the danger of over-indulgence if left to his own devices.

'It's a couple of hours away by car. A place called Chail. A hill station like Simla, but on another hill, across a valley.'

He creased a wicked smile.

'If you know what I mean.' He took another mouthful of the amber fluid.

'Sounds wonderful!' I was genuinely touched to be asked to accompany the great man on this personal pilgrimage.

'And bring that young lady of yours. She always cheers me up'. He turned away, slightly embarrassed at having made this overture.

'She'd love to come, I'm sure. Knows nothing about cricket! Hates it!'

'Well there won't be any. So that's alright then.' He said with a gruffness in his voice.

He looked off into the middle distance, seemed to be focusing on a bed of towering rhododendrons, and added wistfully,

'I adore it! In a funny sort of way, it's my life. I know that sounds ridiculous. But I get my agent to put it in every contract. If there's a test match on, then I always have the excuse to bugger off from whatever I'm doing … filming, TV, anything. I can just drop it and go and there's nothing they can do about it. Good eh!?'

'Sounds brilliant. You must be a bit of a cricket nut?'

'Yes, you could say that. But there we are! I thought I might ask Celia. I think her husband liked cricket. Who knows!'

'What fun! What, just the four of us?' I had an apprehensive moment as to how we would all survive the day together.

'Yes, and the driver of course. I've got Irene to arrange a car for the day. We'll leave first thing in the morning after an early breakfast. There, that's done. Shall we go in to dinner? No doubt it's bloody curry and custard as usual!'

He drained the remainder of his glass, poured in what was left in the bottle, replaced the screw cap and dropped it blithely into the wastepaper basket; he grabbed my arm for support and then led us down the stairs and into dinner.

The morning routine remained unchanged, although I relieved Beli Ram (one of the service staff who rapidly became indispensable to us all) of the responsibility of lighting our bedroom fire during the 'bed tea' ritual as we would be out for the day. The sky was blue as blue, unblemished by even the wispiest of alpine clouds. However, the heavy spring early morning mist still hung about the trees like a dense cobweb. Mountain candyfloss. The mornings were beginning to get warmer but at this relatively early hour you still needed a sweater and a light jacket.

We went down for a modest breakfast of fried egg on buttered toast and tea in the breakfast room and then waited in the entrance of the Guest House for the party to assemble. In the middle distance, I could see Celia taking a constitutional in the gardens before embarking on our travels.

At just five minutes to 8.00am our car pulled into the pick-up area in front of the main door of Woodville. It was a gleaming white 'Ambassador' with white lace half-curtains pulled across the rear passenger windows. The driver stepped out of the car and waited beside the driver's door in a rather stiff military pose awaiting his guests to assemble.

'Good morning.' I said.

'Good morning, Sir. Please may I assist you?' He offered to relieve me of my camera and a small travel bag which contained spare film, emergency rations and a few other incidentals that might be required on the journey.

'No, I'm fine. Any sign of Mr Howard?' I turned half-round to look over my shoulder to check whether he was following me out of the breakfast room.

'No, Sir. Shall I go to Sahib's room and call him?'

'No, he'll be here in due course.'

Indeed, he was, arriving almost simultaneously with Celia's re-entry from her walk around the gardens. He'd taken a turn somewhere else on the estate.

'Good morning, Trevor'. Celia greeted him in a rather haughty begrudging tone; I felt she was saying,

'I'm only here because there's nothing better to do'. Barely a second elapsed before he responded brightly, springing slightly on his toes as he 'landed' with the group.

'Good morning, all.' He gave a playful, rather theatrical swing of his right arm as if he was about to give a respectful bow to his leading lady but then aborted the full movement at the last minute – almost as if he had anticipated Celia's counterblast.

'I trust, Trevor, that everything is under control?' Celia adopted a stern tone and was making a point. She barely took a breath before setting forth again.

'I hope we'll all be able to cope with the altitude. I'm breathless in Simla. Irene put me on the ground floor at Woodville, so I wouldn't have to climb the stairs. Goodness knows how I'll manage at another whatever it is thousand feet.'

'Celia, that is utter nonsense. Chail is no higher than Simla. If you can manage Simla at 2,000 m, you can cope with Chail. In fact, the atmospheric pressure in Chail will be identical to that in the airplane that brought you to India from England!'

By the time he had finished his protest Celia was already walking around the back of the car to get into the near side rear door. As the day progressed this would be a repeating occurrence. Both had a rather short attention span for each other's conversation and neither intrinsically particularly chatty.

Simla, 1980. (Author's collection)

We were ushered into the car by our attentive driver. He had quickly realised that he was the custodian for that day of film royalty. Celia sat in the back with the two of us, and Trevor in the front. Celia had selected a floral day dress and a woollen jacket, and Trevor a short-sleeved shirt, lightweight slacks and his shapeless floppy sun hat, topped off by a knitted woollen scarf wound in multiple turns around his neck. Trevor arrived in Simla with only summer clothes, despite a warning that it would still be the tail end of winter, despite the clear blue skies. Often during the filming day, Trevor could be seen wandering about in an aged, moth-eaten, classic Jaeger dressing gown to protect him from the cold. We had been warned that the temperature might fall even further, as Chail was on a plateau and less protected than the well-populated Simla escarpments.

Chail was only about 50 km from Simla but the journey along the winding mountain roads was scheduled to take at least two hours, depending on the chosen route and the competing traffic. We took the road through Kufri. The territory between the two historic hill stations was heavily forested and an active site for logging hardwoods. The risk of meeting head on an overladen truck carrying freshly cut timber on a tight mountain bend was high or perhaps worse to get stuck behind the same, crawling along the spiral road at a pace that could only create frustration. The area is renowned for the massive deodars, sometimes called the tree of the gods, which cover the rocky landscape leading up to the majestic Himalayas.

The views were spectacular as we crossed from one hill station to another, but the conversation was sparse. Despite their romantic screen debut in Noel Coward's *Brief Encounter* directed by David Lean in 1945, Trevor Howard and Celia Johnson had little in common. There was no love lost between them but at the same time no animosity. I suppose in truth there was little mutual interest. They had been blessed with different starts in life and subsequently different careers. Celia's connections throughout life were gold-plated. She was the widow of Peter Fleming, the brother of the novelist and creator of James Bond, Ian Fleming. Peter had died in 1971 just nine years earlier. He was a great adventurer and traveller, particularly in Asia and South America, and subsequently a travel writer. She had had a good start in life, which had led her towards the glitterati in both the performing arts and the literary world. She was well connected with elite society and apparently had become a good friend and confidante of Her Majesty Queen Elizabeth The Queen Mother. Trevor, on the other hand, came from a more modest background and seems to have had a bumpier experience all round, which was exemplified by his swashbuckling approach to life in his early days as a post-war screen actor. Trevor's social penumbra appears to have been less well-developed, possibly because of his occasional abrasiveness and utter disdain of pomposity and social elitism. I once tried to get him to speak more freely about his family life; he completely ignored a question about his actor wife, Helen Cherry, who must have been long-suffering during his raucous rowdy youth. Somewhat surprisingly she stuck by and defended her man until the end.

In an interview for the *Ottawa Citizen*, Helen paints an interesting picture of the man with whom she stayed for more than forty years. She was very open about his shortcomings; 'Any ordinary woman with the usual standards of an ideal husband would find him impossible to live with. By accepted standards he was a bad husband. He doesn't come home for meals, he stays out all night, and stops in bed all morning (although he never has a hangover). He forgets birthdays and things he's borrowed. Oh, yes, he's wild. But he doesn't break up the home or anything. If he wants to be wild he goes out.' When Howard was criticised for allegedly being misleading about his World War II military career, she defended him to the hilt and is reputed to have blamed his mother for creating the rumour.

On reflection, it was curious why Trevor and Celia agreed to join up on this adventure with a couple of young doctors. When I told my wife Alison that I had got to this point in the story, she remarked that her only memory of our time in Simla was that she felt totally phased and out of place. Completely lost as to how to deal with celebrities like Trevor Howard and Celia Johnson and the glitz of Granada TV and film-making. I must say that conversation did not flow easily on the journey to Chail but the scenic views along the way were more than sufficient to sustain one's interest.

It was with a huge sense of relief when the driver announced our imminent arrival at Chail Palace and the hallowed cricket ground. I had certainly run out of ideas for topics of conversation and was feeling vaguely queasy with the constant twisting and turning along the mountainous pass. We disembarked in the parking area in front of the palace. The driver led us into the grounds of the house and with a flourish presented 'the highest cricket ground in the world'.

Chail Palace, 1980. (Author's collection)

'Enjoy your visit. I will send out a servant to look after you. When you wish to leave, just ask someone to send for me.'

Our driver withdrew, simultaneously reversing and bowing his head politely. We walked from the parking area past two men deep in conversation whilst painting the elegant stone swans and chubby cherubs that adorned a decorative circular fountain outside the main building.

'Splendid! Splendid! What a marvellous sight. Let's grab those seats and have a drink.'

Trevor was clearly invigorated by the mountain air and the opportunity to indulge his lifetime passion. He led us over to four comfy well-cushioned rattan chairs neatly set around a low table positioned conveniently between the palace and the outfield.

He was in fine form and had already removed his jacket, having felt the rising morning sun on his back. A waiter soon arrived and took our order. Trevor and I took Kingfisher beer and Celia and Alison, 'a gimlet'. We had become accustomed to this midday aperitif (gin and lime juice) on the lawns at Woodville. What a superb relic of the British Raj! Trevor drained his glass, rose awkwardly from the low garden chair

Drinks on Chail Palace lawn, 1980. (Author's collection)

and strode off imperiously, with a swagger, towards the cricket green. We could see him in the distance walking slowly up and down the pitch examining every bump and blemish in the hard, dry surface that just about resembled grass. I closed my eyes for a few minutes and let my mind ponder on this extraordinary moment. I thought I might have heard that unique sound generated by a cricket ball being struck by the willow blade of a cricket bat; and possibly the roar of the crowd as the ball flies in a perfect arc towards the boundary. The umpire raises both hands above his head and six more runs are added to the scoreboard.

Today, there were no runs on the board and no crowds hugging the white rope which defined the boundary. Celia showed little interest in the cricket ground and buried herself in a pamphlet that she had found which described the history of Chail, its palace and the cricket ground.

'Quite remarkable!' she exploded. 'Why would anyone choose to set up home on such a bleak plateau?'

'Well, I suppose the views are pretty impressive.' I offered a somewhat pathetic apologia.

'Quite remarkable,' she continued, quoting from the pamphlet with a Shakespearian swagger in her voice. Perhaps the gimlet had started to work.

'This place was built by Maharaja Bhupinder Singh, the Maharaja of Patiala. He succeeded his father at the age of nine years, had at least ten wives, multiple children by them and more by an estimated 365 mistresses and concubines, and drove around the place in a fleet of twenty Rolls-Royces. He reigned from 1900 to 1938 and captained the Indian cricket team that visited England in 1911. He played in twenty-seven first class cricket matches and had his own team, the *Patiala XI*.

'Well I'll be damned! I bet Trevor didn't know that.' She seemed to rejoice in getting one over him.

Trevor, at that moment, sauntered up and re-took his place in the cane chair.

'Bloody awful pitch! Needs water and a damn good raking and rolling.'

He poured himself another beer and lay back in his chair.

'Trevor read this! I bet it'll come as news to you.' Celia shoved a pamphlet in his direction.

Trevor grunted disapprovingly but reluctantly took the tract from Celia and rapidly scanned the contents.

A Rolls-Royce, 1920's. (Rolls Royce Heritage)

'Lucky chap! Nice if you can get it. A man after my own heart.' Celia turned away and lifted her chin in mild disapproval but refrained from verbal comment. It was like they were playing out a scene from *Brief Encounter*. More unsaid than said!

He sank further into the chair and buried himself in the pamphlet, occasionally letting out a muffled chuckle as he came across some new saucy titbit about the Maharaja's eventful life.

'Actually, I know more about the bloody fellow than you give me credit for. He only built the damn thing because he'd irritated Kitchener who then banned him from Simla, which was the British summer seat of Government. So, he said bugger it, I'll build my own bloody summer palace and there it is!' He manufactured his own, expansive Shakespearian gesture, waving his right arm across the landscape.

'In fact, he had to knock the top off the bloody mountain to make it flat enough to take the turf. Bloody marvellous that's what I think, so there!'

After another couple of Kingfishers and some spicy local snacks, Trevor decided that we had seen enough and sent word through our waiter that the driver should re-present himself for duty. I never got used to the idea that a driver in India is only for driving and that they mysteriously disappear when you arrive at your destination and then somehow re-materialise when you are ready to leave. The same happens if you stay somewhere overnight. I never worked out where they go in the in-between times. They seem to get fed out of the kitchen or a small local 'hotel' and then either bed down with the other servants or spend the night on the back seat of the car.

The party slowly began to reassemble and move towards the white Ambassador whose chrome finishes sparkled in the afternoon sun. The effects of the drinks and tiffin seem to have had a retarding effect on the re-loading process. I watched Celia and Trevor wander across the lawn, arm-in-arm, swaying and zigzagging gently in short steps to the safety of our car. A couple of drinks had generated increased warmth between them and for once they really seemed to be enjoying each other's company. I took a final look at the spectacular panorama that spanned almost 360 degrees around the plateau which hosted the cricket ground. The Himalayas stretched away to the north, many of the peaks still bearing their permanent frosting of the heavy winter snow. A trained eye would have been able to identify the rough location of the Everest base camp. It was a dream world. Whoever played cricket at 2,200 m! Only a slightly mad Maharaja would have been able to fulfil that ambition.

This all happened in the late spring of 1980, more than ten years after my first visit to India and thirty-three years since Independence. I spent about six weeks with the cast and crew of the Granada Production, 'Staying On', in Simla as their resident doctor. Granada had decided to film the short Paul Scott Booker Prize winning novel as a pilot before embarking on their magnum opus, 'The Jewel in the Crown', which serialised Scott's 'Raj Quartet'. This was probably the start of what is sometimes described critically as a romantic revival of the British in India. Some might describe it as an indulgent wallowing in our great imperial past. There were also many other offerings that followed, including Richard Attenborough's award-winning film *Gandhi*, *Far Pavilions* and, more recently, the television drama, *Indian Summers*. I had met the producer Irene Shubik at what turns out to have been a timely moment. She had been lauded for producing and directing many acclaimed television dramas in the 1960s and '70s, perhaps best known for producing 'Rumpole of the Bailey'. She soon picked up on what she thought would be the magic combination of my previous experiences in India and the fact that I was a doctor. She was particularly worried about her two leading actors who were already in their seventies but also concerned about the robustness of the Granada crew, most of whom had never been far from Manchester and if they had it was certainly no further than Blackpool or the Isle of Wight. How would they cope with the unfamiliar culture, change in diet, separation from family and friends and the nasty infections that would besiege them all, at regular intervals?

It was an extraordinary experience, for me personally and a terrific success for Granada and the British TV film industry. The cast was brilliant. Trevor was playing a retired Colonel 'Tusker' Smalley and Celia his wife Lucy, 'left-overs' from the British Raj. They had 'stayed on' after Independence and partition. A sad couple in many ways who were in decline physically but, worse, they were struggling financially. While superficially playing the game of being 'British Imperialists', they loved and respected India and for the life it offered them; and they loved and curiously respected their staff (a gardener and a cook). They opted to stay on in India but, they had nowhere else to go. An old folks' home in Bexhill-on-Sea? Not on your bloody life! They would stick it out to the end.

SAEED, ZIA AND SILVIO

However, the others were equally engaging. Saeed Jaffrey (Mr Bhoolabhoy, manager of Smith's Hotel from which the Smalley's rented their small cottage), Pearl Padamsee (his voluptuous, dominant wife) and Zia Moheyddin (Ibrahim, the Smalley's gardener). We got on particularly well with Saeed (former husband of Madhura Jaffrey, the celebrated chef of Indian cuisine) whose friendship we enjoyed for some years after we returned to London. 'Staying On' was directed by Silvio Narizzano. He is probably best known for his directorship of the film *Georgy Girl* starring Lynn Redgrave, Charlotte Rampling, James Mason and Alan Bates.

'Tusker and Lucy Smalley' on set, Simla 1980. (Author's collection)

Silvio was an enigmatic character who at times seemed more interested in his teenage boy consort, who he had acquired during a brief sojourn in Delhi before coming up to Simla, than directing the movie. Although I was always very much on the periphery, I sensed that Silvio was not a great success. I thought on more than one occasion that he was unwell, but he never consulted me, and time would prove me wrong as he went on to out-live his life partner Win Wells, who died in 1983, and survived until the very

Silvio Narizzano (centre), Simla 1980. (Author's collection)

Wolfgang Suschitzky (mid-centre), Simla, 1980. (Author's collection)

Woodville Guest House, Simla, 1980. (Author's collection)

respectable age of eighty-four. Occasionally Irene let slip her frustrations and as far as I could see, Celia, Trevor and the other actors just got on with the job as serious professionals and did their thing.

The director of cinematography, Wolfgang Suschitzky, a consummate craftsman in his own right, famed for films such as *Get Carter*, *Ring of Brightwater* and *Ulysses*, independently ensured that there would be a surfeit of exquisite footage to weave into the final cut. However, as Irene relates in her account of the film-making, there were gaps that required skilful editing to conceal because of the difficulties in getting the 'rushes' back to Simla during the filming. I was never sure where Silvio fitted into the day-to-day work on the film.

I arrived a few days after the main players and was immediately taken to Woodville House to see Celia Johnson for a consultation following a fall in the shower earlier the previous day. There was a suggestion that the gin levels might have been a shade higher than they ought to have been, but that was just 'hearsay'. Like Trevor, there was never a moment when I thought that alcohol crept into the working day and interfered with performance. The production team's main concern was that Celia had an unsightly bruise high on her left cheek which was interfering with the 'shooting schedule'. Could I get rid of it by tomorrow so that they could get things back on track? Well actually, no! Could I not stick a needle in the bruise and remove the blood? Sorry, no; in fact, as I explained this could make it all a lot worse. We consulted with the make-up team and resolved to use the other side of her face when close-up head shots were required.

SOMEONE LIKE 'MISS EDWINA CRANE'

I was initially 'billeted in lodgings' away from Irene, Trevor and Celia, close to the centre of town. I felt isolated and uncomfortable in a house owned by an austere, unmarried, elderly English woman, I imagined something like Miss Edwina Crane, the large-nosed, single missionary teacher who dominates the opening section of Scott's *Jewel in the Crown*; I felt she was still living in Victorian Empire style and resentful that life in Simla in 1980 was not what it was before Independence.

Lady (Lili) Chatterjee, dowager of MacGregor House, says of Miss Crane, 'I think she had no gift for friendship of any kind. She loved India and all Indians but no particular Indian.… I suppose what I am saying is she made friendships in her head most of the time but seldom in her heart.'

I was served breakfast in a poorly lit, over-furnished dining room set in the style of late Victorian England, including the aspidistras, alone and in ecclesiastical silence. The milk jug and the sugar bowl were covered with lace 'shrouds' weighted down by coloured glass beads sewn into the border to protect them from invading flying insects. Although I was attended throughout the meal by a servant, the 'landlady' – if I can call her that – stood imperiously upright a metre or two away from the table and monitored every mouthful as it left the plate and until it entered my mouth. The cornflakes and fried egg on toast, however, were most welcome. English marmalade was there to complete the breakfast experience. I could survive this regime at breakfast but having to re-run the performance at dinner was more than I could stand. At this point Alison had not arrived, which certainly enhanced my sense of isolation. I lasted there for just three days. I made a strong case to Irene that if I was to do my job properly, I needed to be in the thick of it. I needed to be where my patients were; the case was made without a struggle and I moved swiftly into a small but homely room with an open fire in Woodville. It had two small beds, a tub chair covered in chintz (India of course was the primary originator of this style of painting or block printing on calico in the seventeenth and eighteenth centuries), a delicate mahogany writing table and a companion desk chair. A place to sleep at night and to work during the day.

THE MAHARAJA AND BELI RAM

Woodville Guesthouse was the summer palace of the Maharaja, Kanwar Uday Singh of Jubbal. He used one wing himself as his private apartments and ran the rest as a hotel. Once I was with the others and feeling back in the mainstream, life began to slip into a routine. I was woken at about 7.00am by Beli Ram, one of the servants in the guest house. He was a delightful young man who wore a worn, dusty, navy blue high-collared jacket, chaotic crumpled cotton trousers and the traditional Himachal embroidered pillbox hat.

'Good morning Sir. Did you sleep well? Can I bring your bed tea now?'

I was welcomed with the same cheery greeting every morning. While I slurped my bed tea, Beli Ram built a fire in the traditional cast iron Victorian grate and left me with a full scuttle of coal to feed the fire during the day. Beli Ram only looked about fifteen years old, but he was apparently observed in the bazaar by one of the crew with a young wife and an infant, suggesting that he must have been a little older. The mornings were still very fresh and to have the chill removed by an open fire before bathing and shaving was a treat. As the room temperature increased, the heavy condensation on the north facing windows gradually withdrew.

My primary responsibility of the day was to ensure that the crew were fit and ready for work. I had to deal with a variety of minor ailments, most commonly the dreaded 'Delhi belly'. This was often quite debilitating and although we knew that most episodes were due to a gut infection we were rather parsimonious with the antibiotics. You were expected to man-up, take plenty of fluids, salty soups for sodium, bananas for potassium and a source of carbohydrate (rice, crackers, mashed potato) to drive the absorption of the salt and water. I did have a supply of oral rehydration powders but for mild or even moderate illness in adults it is not usually required unless you get cholera! Some years later, my colleagues and I published a controlled trial which showed that a single antibiotic tablet could halve the severity and the duration of the illness, which is what I would recommend now if I was doing the same job thirty or more years later.

One or two crew members really did not fare well in Simla and were repatriated back to the UK. Most adjusted, got used to the new environment, found a new friend but yearned for standard Manchester fare typified by fish and chips, hot-pot or a burger! Granada management, I recall, did request a modification of the hotel restaurant menu to accommodate the tastes of some of the less flexible members of the crew.

Trevor was never ill and never indisposed; he was always available when required for a day's shooting. His rebel-rousing reputation was evident from his early days as a screen actor. Latterly, in the years after 'Staying On', before he died in 1988, he was heavily criticised for the way in which his affiliation to alcohol might have impaired his ability to deliver professionally from time to time. I must say – and I saw him every day for six weeks, morning and evening – I was never aware that he took alcohol during filming or that his performance was ever compromised during working hours. In those days, he impressed me with his utter professionalism. In the evening, particularly before dinner, there is no doubt that he enjoyed a glass of whisky, in fact we would often sit together in his room in Woodville talking about life with a glass of the amber fluid in our hands. On one evening in the latter half of our stay in Simla, I asked him how many more days filming he had to go.

'Haven't got a clue, my boy! But I can find out.' He smiled broadly with a sense of calm satisfaction.

He got out of his chair and went over to the wardrobe. He almost disappeared into the ancient hard wood monster, but after a few moments emerged, smiling.

'Twenty-three!'

'How on earth do you know?' I thought he must have done an audit of socks or underpants.

'Come here!' He bellowed.

'There! One for each day's filming!'

With a flourish, he pulled back a few jackets and trousers to reveal the shelved part of the wardrobe stashed full of imported, unopened bottles of whisky; space which many of us would have used for shirts and 'smalls'. With that we drained our glasses and went downstairs to join the others for dinner.

During the daylight hours between early morning and early evening consultations I would retire to my room to work. I was in the final year of my first serious period of research and I had set myself a target to write up my doctoral thesis by the time filming was completed. Although many colleagues regarded this adventure in the foothills as a bit of a 'jolly' (which indeed it was), the opportunity to write undisturbed was perfect. I made such excellent progress that by the time Alison arrived I could reduce the intensity of the work schedule and enjoy part of the day watching 'Staying On' become a reality. I did, however, come away with the distinct impression that the making of a film is a rather slow, tedious and often boring process, not just for observers like us, but for everyone involved. I am perfectly willing to accept the criticism by the experts that this is a gross simplification of the creative process.

As our time in Simla was beginning to come towards the end, the evenings became warmer, which enabled pre-dinner drinks to be taken on the beautifully manicured lawns of Woodville's 'English' gardens. Whisky on ice or with a little water was the order of the day. Some days we would take a walk along 'The Mall', a famous haunt of the British during the days of the Raj when the government had retreated from the intolerable heat of the plains in the summer months to the cool hill station of Simla. This elegant straight road stretched between the parade square, the preferred site for military extravaganzas, and 'scandal point'. 'Scandal point' is so-named because, as the story goes, the well-known philanderer, the Maharaja of Patiala, Bhupinder Singh is said to have eloped in 1892 from this location with one of the daughters of the British Viceroy of the day, Lord Lansdowne; but more of that anon.

The Gaiety Theatre, a landmark feature on The Mall, opened in 1887. It was designed by Henry Irwin, an important architect of British India (his other works include Vice Regal Lodge Simla, Madras Railway Station and other prominent buildings in Madras, Madurai and Mysore). The Gaiety was an extraordinary

The Mall and Gaiety Theatre, Simla, 1980. (Author's collection)

neo-Gothic building which housed not only the theatre but also a Masonic Hall, a library, municipal offices and at one time a police station. It has hosted many great names on its elegant stage – Rudyard Kipling to name but one – and many others in the auditorium. The Viceroy had a prominent protected seat in the Grand Circle. It remains to this day an extraordinary venue for dramatic productions, most of which were and still are of an amateur nature. The theatre was restored over a five-year period by the government of Himachal Pradesh and reopened in 2009. A good example of how present-day India preserves and conserves its cultural history, including that generated before Independence.

As the evenings became warmer, we would linger in the gardens with glass in hand before finally entering the house for dinner. Traditional Indian fair was the norm, but Trevor became tired of curry every night and longed for a simple traditional English dish. For many of us, appetites began to decline after a few drinks, which for the men were usually numerous pegs of whisky in line with the Indian tradition, which itself had developed in the elite clubs and private homes during British times.

'Come on! Let's go in. I've had enough.' Trevor was tired, had enough whisky on board and a diminishing interest in food.

He would take my arm and lean on me as we slowly ambled across the lawn back into the house. These quiet, increasingly balmy evenings will always remain with me. We had left the tensions of film-making, professional jealousies and transient love affairs behind us and entered another world. It was a world so far away from the one with which we were familiar. At one moment we were indulging our senses in the grandeur of a building that had grown out of the British period in India and the next minute we could look across at the lights of this classic hill station now mainly populated by low income workers, mostly immigrants from Tibet and Nepal who were vital to maintain the service industries of the small town and to support the logging and timber trades.

The lights of Woodville were still alive, outlining and enhancing the interior and external appearance of the building, making it glisten against the clear, black, star-studded sky. Woodville sits in in an estate surrounded by grand deodar pine trees with the snow-covered peaks of the Himalayas as a backdrop. During the British Raj, Woodville was home to senior British military personnel and was soon adopted as the official summer residence of the Commander in Chief of India. In the early twentieth century, Woodville was acquired by the Alliance Bank and in 1926 was bought by the Jubbal royal family, in the name of his Highness Maharaja Sir Bhagvat Singh. Raj Kumar Uday Singh, one of Sir Bhagvat Singh's grandsons, converted part of the house into a heritage hotel which continues to flourish to this day.

As the last days of April approached, we could now see the end of the adventure and were beginning to make plans to go home. Celia and Trevor were desperate to leave. Irene was petrified as to how she was going to cope with so much unseen material in the cutting room, particularly as the director frequently remarked that any consideration of 'continuity' was old-fashioned and out of date. Even more significant for her was the future of the relationship with Granada Television and her friend and mentor Sir Denis Forman. Although Irene was absolutely committed to the project and was always looking ahead to filming Scott's 'Raj Quartet' as a TV series, *The Jewel in the Crown*, she was often deeply troubled by the personal and professional threats of discontent that ran through most of her days in Simla. Irene constantly struggled with the Granada Trades Unions over working conditions, particularly daily allowance rates (which was negotiated upwards from £25 to £30 a day, a rate which was then adopted for *The Jewel in the Crown*), working at altitude and the complex negotiation that took place to start the working day at 6:30am rather than 9.00am to be able to capture the exquisite early morning light which is all pervasive throughout much of the film.

I would say that for most of the time that I spent in Simla the relationship with Irene the producer and Silvio the director was poor, often non-existent. In her book, Irene recalls that 'Silvio seemed to undergo the most extreme character change of everyone.... He chose to lead an independent life far away at the Oberoi Cecil Hotel with the crew.' This meant that he failed to develop any 'off-set' relationships with Trevor and Celia and other key members of the cast and as far as I could see, had no interest in developing a more productive and creative relationship with Irene. The cast and crew were fully aware of these tensions. Trevor constantly repeated the mantra, 'the chap's mad as a hatter'. It subsequently transpired that the production manager, Lars McFarlane, had been tasked to report back to Sir Denis Forman using predetermined codewords on the conduct of the director and producer. This level of distrust with senior management must have been extraordinarily disconcerting and a real downer on creative and collaborative working in an already predefined challenging working environment.

The final days at Woodville were memorable. For the Maharaja, the Granada cast and crew brought new life to his beloved family home. In addition, the production had contributed substantially to his annual income that year, although I am unaware of the scale of the financial transaction. As a reward and as a gesture of genuine gratitude, he decided to throw a farewell dinner for us all. There was, however, one proviso, that the code of dress would be traditional Indian. That aside, like good troopers we staggered through the evening in our regalia. The whisky flowed, the food was delicious and the farewells endless and sometimes tearful. After all it was just a bunch of luvvies. It had been a long tour but an opportunity to experience another side of life that for me would be impossible to recapture. I think Irene was exhausted and at times despondent. This was not how she expected filming in India to be; nevertheless 'the film was in the can' although she knew its quality and usability would only be evident when she got into the cutting room.

SHAH JAHAN AND MUMTAZ MAHAL

Despite what I said about the somewhat duplicitous role that the production manager Lars had been entrusted with, he had become a friend and someone who at the end of the day was good company to share stories with over a glass of beer. During the production, he had taken up with a rather lovely lady member of the crew and suggested that we should accompany them on a post-production visit to Agra and the Taj Mahal. Irene also decided to join the party; I think it was a good opportunity to help her re-group after the ordeal with the director. The plan was that we should hire a car and driver, spend a couple of nights in Agra so that we could see the Taj Mahal at sunrise and sunset and then travel together back to New Delhi. It was a brilliant idea and an excellent way to wind down after a busy six or seven weeks in Simla. We travelled in an air-conditioned white Ambassador in reasonable comfort, although our major concern was that we might be harassed by the dacoits (armed bandits) on the road. The section of the road from New Delhi to Agra was popular with roadside groups of vagabonds who knew well that the wealthy travellers from New Delhi were rich pickings. Our journey, however, was uneventful, and we covered the 600 km in about nine hours. An early start at about 5.00am ensured that our descent from Simla to Chandigarh was accomplished on relatively empty roads and with some spectacular views of the densely tree-covered foothills which were wrapped in swirling mist; I felt this must have concealed many secrets.

We arrived at the Hotel Clarks Shiraz at around 6.00pm. There was time for a shower before a sunset visit to the Taj Mahal. After a short walk along Taj Road we were soon overwhelmed by the sight of this glistening white mausoleum towering into the landscape, still lit by a sun that was just beginning to leave the sky.

This grandiose site of marble, gardens and reflective water pools was, as we soon learned, a place of love. It was, as many writers have suggested, the epitome of love. The Mogul Emperor Shah Jahan had created the Taj to celebrate the life and mourn the death of his third and most favourite wife, Queen Mumtaz Mahal. She died at the age of thirty-eight around the birth of her fourteenth child. Her beauty,

Taj Mahal sunset, 1980. (Author's collection)

grace and compassion were extolled by the poets of the day, she was loved deeply by her husband and regarded by all as the perfect wife. Surely this is the fairy tale, to beat all fairy tales? As the crescent moon rose effortlessly in that evening sky, one contemplated this extraordinary story set against the immense unparalleled beauty of this unique building, 'a poem in marble' or in the words of Rabindranath Tagore, 'a teardrop on the cheek of time'. In the early evening moonlight, the gem-studded marble is white.

Irene Shubik at sunrise, Taj Mahal 1980. (Author's collection)

However, when we returned early the following morning with the sun just rising above the horizon, the initial appearance of the marble is that it is a pale pink in colour. One of the favoured photo opportunities is to capture your lover's image in front of the reflecting pool with the majestic Taj climbing into the sky behind. That famous image of Diana, Princess of Wales sitting alone on a white bench with the reflecting pool at her back retreating towards the mighty Taj as the backdrop, suggested isolation and loneliness; quite the antipathy of her royal counterpart, the Mumtaz Mahal.

Running behind the Taj is the river Yamuna, now a favoured site for Hindu cremations. The juxtaposition of a Muslim burial site with one for Hindu cremations, known as *antyesti*, meaning literally 'last rites', seemed at first sight strange but on reflection just another paradox of life in this ancient continent.

It would have been impossible to go to the north of India and not see the Taj and, likewise, not to indulge in the traditional Mughlai cuisine in the hotel restaurant. I have wonderful memories of a creamy curry with rice followed by a rice pudding adorned with edible silver foil.

Following a second visit to the Taj at sunrise, our driver took us to Fatehpur Sikri just 35 km to the west of Agra. The city was founded in the mid-sixteenth century by the Emperor Akbar. It was built from local red sandstone ('Sikri sandstone') and contrasts sharply with the glistening white marble of the Taj. Akbar moved his capital from Agra to Fatehabad (*Fateh* meaning 'victorious') following territorial acquisitions, and later renamed this place, Fatehpur Sikri. Akbar had an important part to play in determining the architectural style of the city and it remains one of the best-preserved examples of Mughlai construction to this day. The city is the result of a convergence of architectural styles, partly due to the range of craftsmen engaged in the building process. From the ridge on which the city is perched the views across the plains extend for kilometres in all directions. The architecture aside, my most memorable recollection of that day is of a man who exhibited the most remarkable behaviour in a public place. He was dressed in a long white traditional shirt with a unique red-striped collar, white shapeless, cotton trousers and a soft,

The 'clown', Fatehpur Sikri, 1980. (Author's collection)

white cotton pillbox hat. He was barefoot but stood on what I assumed was a cotton scarf. At his feet was a traditional sweepers' hand brush. He can only be described as an entertainer. His favoured location was around the entrance to the Queen's Palace. He would approach crowds of people, contort his body into the most distracted positions and then disrupt his face to such extremes, attempting to bring tears to people's eyes, presumably with laughter. His parting shot was to push his tongue as far forward as possible and to crown it with a left-handed salute. The only Western parallel that I can think of is a combination of clowning and gurning (pulling a grotesque face).

FAMILY SINGH

Although dacoits were discussed extensively during the drive back from Agra to New Delhi, none were seen and again the journey was quite uneventful. We parted company with our travel companions and went our separate ways. Our flight back to London was not for a couple of days and we had been fortunate enough to be invited to stay with family friends of one of my London colleagues, Dr (now Professor Dame) Parveen Kumar. We were privileged to be welcomed into the home of an extraordinarily distinguished Sikh family, the head of the family being Bhagwant Singh. Our driver delivered us to a large house in the fashionable Golf Links area of New Delhi. The residential enclave was essentially a gated community with its own security. The location was perfect, being surrounded by an upmarket golf course and close to the diplomatic zone of the capital. It was within walking distance of the charming Lodhi Gardens and remarkably close to the city centre. The Bhagwant Singhs welcomed us as 'family'. The formalities were soon dropped as they became 'auntie' and 'uncle'. We were shown a delightful bedroom on the ground floor and advised that we had about half an hour before drinks and dinner. I learnt rapidly that as a Sikh family they observed a highly responsible and moral approach to life but at the same time unreservedly enjoyed themselves.

Although the house was substantial with many rooms, it was modern and distinctly utilitarian, built I would guess in the second wave of city construction in the 1930s. Most of the furniture was constructed of traditional hardwood, was dark in colour and highly polished. The floors were covered in elegant traditional rugs. The table silverware appeared well used and I guessed it had been handed down across the generations. The main building was surrounded by modest gardens that

The Bhagwant Singhs at home in New Delhi, 1980. (Author's collection)

were exceptionally well maintained. The house was serviced by a small group of devoted staff, some of whom lived in. I was much amused and indeed entertained by the cooling system of the main living area. The 'evaporative cooler system', used commonly in Indian homes at that time known as a 'desert cooler', worked on the principle that as water evaporates it removes heat from the surrounding environment. Thus, in this system, water constantly permeates straw retained in an open cage through which air is blown by a large vertical fan. I was astounded by its efficacy.

The following morning auntie accompanied us in her chauffeur driven car to Connaught Place. After some window shopping and coffee in a local café, we were given a wonderful illustrated account of the construction of New Delhi, and slowly we began to realise that not only was the family responsible for much of the early construction but that it continued to own substantial chunks of New Delhi real estate. Auntie's father-in-law, Sir Sobha Singh, who had died at the age of eighty-eight only two years previously, was the person who had created this empire. He was introduced to the construction business by his father Sujan Singh; the attraction of lucrative contracts to build Lutyens' new capital city in the early twentieth century, prompted a move from the Punjab to Delhi. Land was relatively cheap at the time and he took the opportunity to buy substantial areas that he judged were ripe for development. Sir Sobha's company was solely responsible for the massive South Block and the War Memorial Arch (now known as India Gate) and contributed to other buildings, including Vice-Regal house. In addition to the construction of municipal buildings, he was responsible for many commercial and residential buildings, including the Connaught Place market complex, Broadcasting House, the National Museum and some colleges, schools and hospitals. Sobha Singh had four sons and one daughter; one of the sons was Bhagwant our newly acquired uncle. I think by the time we had met him he was already partially retired. Nevertheless, he would go to his office in the morning but, being a passionate golfer, would escape to the golf course at almost any opportunity. On the hottest days in summer, golf was still on the agenda but took place much earlier in the day, soon after sunrise. He was a calm, quiet and dignified man, and clearly the head of a traditional Sikh family. Auntie was a more outspoken and communicative but in his presence always followed the traditional rules of engagement. She never called him by his first name in the presence of others and would walk three paces behind him in public places. There was no sense that this represented any form of subservience, as it was clear that their position within the family was very much that of a partnership, but merely an observance of a long-standing tradition within such a distinguished household. She once said that 'I only walk behind him so that I can keep an eye on what he is doing.'

EDWIN LUTYENS

The foundation stone for New Delhi was laid by King George V in December 1911 as part of the Delhi Durbar. He said, 'It is my desire that the planning and designing of the public buildings to be erected will be considered with the greatest deliberation and care, so that the new creation may be in every way worthy of this ancient and beautiful city.' Lord Crewe, Secretary of State for India at the time was keen that the new capital should also signify 'the permanency of British sovereign rule over the length and breadth of the country.' A town planning committee was established under the leadership of the architect Sir

Edwin Lutyens. The Lutyens philosophy for New Delhi seems to be civic grandeur surrounded by green spaces. To help us understand the structure of the new city, auntie took us from Connaught Place to War Memorial Arch. We then took the majestic broad avenue, Rajpath (previously known as King's Way) down to the elegant administrative buildings beyond which sits the domed Viceroy's house, now Rashtrapati Bhavan, which even to this day is regarded as one of the most splendid buildings of the twentieth century. The architect Herbert Baker also made major contributions to the design of the new city contributing Parliament House and other housing for senior government officials. Lutyens also contributed a large area of residential accommodation still known as the Lutyens' Bungalow Zone (LBZ). The architectural challenge was substantial, aiming to merge, according to Viceroy Hardinge's philosophy, Indian and European styles. The city was inaugurated in February 1931 but within just seventeen years it would become the capital, finally, of an independent nation.

We were taken by auntie to a drinks party hosted by a family friend in a luxurious 'mansion apartment' in the centre of New Delhi. Perhaps the most well-known of Sir Sobha's offspring that we met during our stay was auntie's brother-in-law, Khushwant Singh, the acclaimed writer and journalist. He was also a guest at the party, but sadly my exposure was limited to a rather brief exchange of greetings. Nevertheless, he was an impressive man who radiated an aura of high intellect, supreme confidence and possibly a reckless disregard for public approbation.

Following a morning of immersion in New Delhi, we lunched in a traditional North Indian tandoori restaurant opposite the imposing Red Fort in old Delhi. The red sandstone we had seen in Fatehpur Sikri reappeared in the ancient monuments of this grand old city. Shah Jahan was responsible for a major redevelopment of the old city soon after the establishment of Fatehpur Sikri. We also briefly visited India's largest mosque, Jama Masjid, and finally repaired to one of New Delhi's most elite Clubs, the Delhi Gymkhana Club, formerly the Imperial Delhi Gymkhana Club; 'Imperial' was removed following Independence. Located on 27 acres at Coronation Grounds and designed by Lutyens, the Club opened in 1913 and according to local commentators its ethos and purpose have remained largely untouched; established for 'the use of the ruling elite comprising of officers of the Indian Civil Service, the Armed Forces and civil residents of Delhi'. The entrance to the Club is impressive with its white, neoclassical façade.

Although the membership of the club is now almost exclusively Indian, 'Englishness' appears to be an important criterion for membership. The codes of conduct remain strictly applied and exclusivity is maintained. A sign outside the Lady Willingdon swimming bath clearly excludes all forms of domestic help: 'Ayahs, servants, gun men and security guards with members are not allowed at the swimming pool'. A strict dress code is maintained in all public areas with lounge suits, safari suits or several varieties of formal traditional dress being the preferred options. Informal dress is permitted in the coffee shop. Attire which is not permitted includes 'short and tight skirts, sports clothes including jogging shoes, rubber chappals and T-shirts without collars or with figures or slogans embossed'.

Within minutes it became clear that 'auntie' was a club grandee. Club bearers and other functionaries, dressed in a spectacular traditional livery with towering, brightly coloured turbans came speedily to her assistance. We were shown into a private area at the back of one of the lounges and sank back in grand leather club chairs while we were served tea from silver teapots in early twentieth-century cups and saucers of fine porcelain. Members and their guests, as far as I could see were exclusively Indian. They were distinguished, elegant and apparently content to comply with the club's strict rules. It was a joy to sit in that elegant lounge, watching the pageantry of a rather selected group of senior Indian players from the worlds of politics, commerce, the military and other leadership groups in the nation. I suddenly had a flashback to a box of painted model figures, representing all Indian social strata, that I had bought during my first visit in 1969. Not all were represented in the Delhi Gymkhana Club that evening, as this select, influential and wealthy group was just a small fractional sample of wider Indian society.

The following evening, 'auntie' and her driver took us and our luggage to the airport in good time to take a British Airways flight to the UK. It had been an extraordinary six-week adventure: seeing contemporary India in the raw but at the same time being transported back by Paul Scott's narrative to consider those last days of the British Raj; the fate of a group of British diehards who stayed on because they had nowhere else to go and the new India that was more than thirty years in the making, already beginning to grow into the next phase of its development. We had the good fortune of meeting the current generation of the family that had been central to the building of New Delhi, and who continue to be leaders and indeed beneficiaries of its success. However, one cannot fail to be conscious of the gap between the haves and the have-nots in this increasingly modern urban Indian society. Service staff had left upper-middle-class British homes more than half a century ago, perhaps longer, whereas in New Delhi at this time, it was the norm for all professional families to have maids, sweepers, cooks and drivers. In addition, some of these workers would have linked residential accommodation and mostly were well cared for and indeed loved by their families with whom they had served for many years. Although, as Scott tells us in *The Jewel in the Crown*, Lady Lily Chatterjee's cook spends the night on a camp bed in his kitchen, which presumably gets folded up in the morning.

The real question is whether in another thirty years would there be any measurable, material redistribution of wealth that would significantly improve life quality for those poorer sections of society?

I thought for a moment about the residuum of the crew remaining in Simla and hoped their bowels were holding up and wondered as to how Irene was preparing herself for Granada's management and the cutting room. Her account in 'Play for the Day' describes her first meeting with Sir Denis Forman at the Granada offices in Golden Square after returning from India. She was immediately suspicious that the world had changed despite having already commissioned and received the scripts for 'Jewel in the Crown' and had every expectation still that she would be the producer. Sir Denis had clearly changed the plan. Irene continues: 'I began to feel uneasy, like one of Stalin's Generals, fresh from a victorious battle, who is about to be rewarded for his service to the country not with medals but with the firing squad or exiled to a gulag.' Apparently, Silvio was showing little interest in editing 'Staying On', so Sir Denis organised a lunch at the Ritz to bring director and producer together in an amicable alliance. Fortunately for Irene, Silvio reverted to type in the middle of lunch, getting up suddenly without a prompt and then running through the dining room at great speed, leaving the hotel with no explanation or farewell. Sir Dennis was apparently stunned and must have had some sort of a notion of what daily life must have been like in Simla. For whatever reason, Irene was discharged of her responsibility to produce *The Jewel in the Crown*, which had been passed on to Christopher Morahan, a well-established and respected director of television drama perhaps best known for the popular serial *Emergency Ward 10* (1958), *Armchair Theatre*, *The Wednesday Play*, and a long list of *Play for Today*; indeed, a very safe pair of hands.

Salman Rushdie published a piece in the *Observer* on 1 April 1984 (George Orwell's April Fools' Day!) which he called 'Raj Revival'. He noted that 'the British Raj after 3½ decades in retirement, has been making a sort of comeback'. Together with *The Jewel in the Crown* (which was first broadcast in 1984) he cites Richard Attenborough's *Gandhi* and the TV series *Far Pavilions*. His criticism of *The Jewel in the Crown* was, it appears, based largely on the notion that he regarded it as lowbrow entertainment. He writes, 'the overall effect is rather like a literary version of Mulligatawny soup. It tries to taste Indian, but ends up being ultra-parochially British, only with too much pepper.' Despite Rushdie's crisp commentary, the flow of literary and dramatic works describing the British in India and more recently the response of émigré Indians to life in the United Kingdom has continued unabated; the disarming *My Beautiful Launderette*, *The Buddha of Suburbia*, *East is East* and *Bhaji on the Beach*, and many more.

In 2015 and 2016 we had the Channel 4 TV series, *Indian Summers*, which visits British India in 1932 in the hill station Simla, when the Indian nationalist movement, part of the relentless drive for *swaraj* was gaining serious momentum. Created and written largely by Paul Rutman but with contributions from other British writers, it points a critical finger at the repressive policies and laws of the British Government that operated prior to Independence. In 2017, *Viceroy's House* was a major film starring Hugh Bonneville and Gillian Anderson and directed by Gurinder Chadha (of *Bhaji on the Beach* and *Bend it Like Beckham* fame), perhaps informed by, but not based on, the recently published book, *Daughter of Empire: Life as a Mountbatten* by Lord Mountbatten's daughter Pamela Hicks, which relates her recollections of the last days of the British Raj. Chadha was not popular with some Muslims who felt she unfairly attributed blame to Jinnah for the post-partition slaughter and was accused of creating fake history by historians when the question is raised as to whether Churchill was complicit with Jinnah in supporting the plan for a divided subcontinent on the basis that an independent party's stance might be politically advantageous in the evolving Cold War with the Soviet Union.

The desire and possibly the need to explore in fiction and drama the successive waves of thought and understanding about colonial and post-colonial Britain seems relentless. And why not! Just in the way that historians continue their own iterative process of re-telling the history of British India and the way that thinking has evolved in the seven decades that have followed Independence.

Walter Reid's re-evaluation of the last thirty years of British rule (published in 2016) makes difficult reading for those who still think 'we did our best in difficult circumstances', perhaps still sticking to the political line of the day that we had planned orderly liberation ever since the end of the Great War in 1918.

In 1979, just two years after the sixth General Election, the Janata alliance collapsed; Desai had to step down as Prime Minister, being replaced for a short period by Charan Singh. This precipitated a new election and the Seventh Lok Sabha (1980–84), with Mrs Gandhi again at the helm.

The ISRO programme began to develop momentum in the late 1970s and '80s with several successful satellite deployments for both telecommunications purposes and observation of the earth. In 1984 a joint Indo-Soviet space mission took an Indian astronaut, Rakesh Sharma into space for the first time, orbiting Earth for eight days. It was an interesting way of spending what must have amounted to a very large sum of money, when at the time the country had only one TV channel, one metro system in Kolkata, one method of communication, the fixed dial phone and one airline. Mrs Gandhi is reported to have been keen to get an Indian into space before the 1984 general election. The satellite programme continued successfully during the 1980s and '90s, including at least three remote sensing satellites. Since 1969 India has successfully put more than one hundred satellites in orbit. In 2014 India amazed the world when its unmanned spacecraft *Mangalyaan* reached Mars at a cost of just USD 74 million. A second Mars orbiter is planned for 2021–22.

India had planned to get into manned space flights in the years immediately following the 1984 Sharma flight but as yet this has not happened. In 2004 the idea was re-introduced into the space programme, but deadlines were pushed back and then back again. In July 2018 however, there was a successful testing of a crew escape system, but without live human crew members being present. Narendra Modi, in his Independence Day speech in 2018, once again threw down the gauntlet to get a man or woman into space by 2022.

Acknowledging that although India is a major player in the technology and engineering worlds, is this a good use of resources when it could be argued that there are more pressing needs at home? The Indian space programme probably costs about USD 1 billion each year; spending on health is disproportionately low (just over 1 per cent GDP) for an economy that is now ranked sixth in the world by nominal GDP.

MINGLING WITH MAHARAJAS

Do not covet the wealth of any man.

Isa Upanishad

Direct, personal exposure to maharajas has not been extensive. However, the rulers of India's princely states have had a defining role in India's social, political and economic development over many centuries, their origins dating back to the fifth and sixth centuries CE. I enjoyed meeting those whose paths I crossed directly but have been fascinated by some others who I have discovered through other routes.

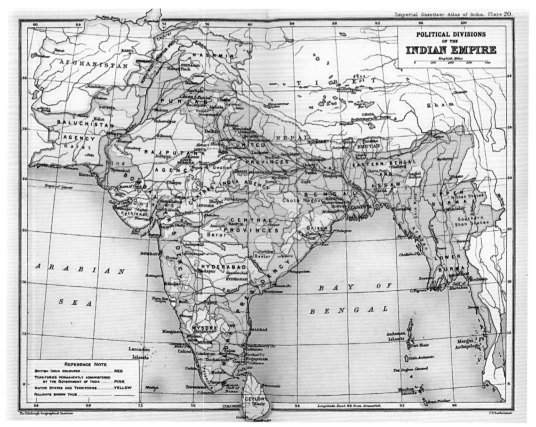

Map of the princely or native states, 1909. (Public domain)

During the period when the British ruled India there were two administrative systems: British Provinces, which were directly under British control, constituted about 60 per cent of the Indian subcontinent and the princely states (otherwise known as the 'native states') accounted for the remaining 40 per cent. The maharajas (some were known as rajas, nawabs, or nizams) and their states were pivotal in the establishment of the East India Company in India. They were celebrated by Queen Victoria, Empress of India and survived largely intact until India gained independence in 1947. The majority were incorporated into the new nations of India and Pakistan immediately, while some such as Sikkim and Hyderabad joined later. The power and wealth of the princely states, whether Hindu, Sikh or Muslim was extraordinary. Indira Gandhi finally saw them off, removing their hereditary rights and titles at a single stroke, but many continued as wealthy landowners, usually retaining their ancient title as a courtesy, and generally remaining caring and benevolent to their former subjects.

European colonists in India – the Dutch, Portuguese, Danish and especially the British – were generally astute in the way in which they engaged the maharajas and nawabs, working on the principle that if you leave an established leader largely undisturbed and provide incentives that encourage loyalty and allegiance, the 'mixed political economy' can work well. The British established such a regime over more than 200 years, with parts of India directly under British control and the 500-600 princely states allowed to continue very much in their own way. This seems to have been a productive compromise.

The British rewarded the princely states by creating a hierarchy which was denoted by the number of 'gun salutes' that each state was awarded by the Crown. When a ruler arrived at the capital, initially Calcutta and then subsequently New Delhi, he would be welcomed by the appropriate number of gun salutes. The ranking according to gun salutes could change with time, depending on whether the state performed well in British eyes or was perceived to have fallen from grace!

At the time of the Coronation Durbar in 1911, there were only three twenty-one-gun states: Hyderabad, Baroda and Mysore. In 1917 Gwalior was upgraded to twenty-one guns and Jammu and Kashmir in 1921, both for their military support during World War I. Jaipur, Jodhpur and Patiala were seventeen to nineteen guns and Dewas Senior and Junior were fifteen guns. I shall return to some of these maharajas and their states in due course.

Queen Victoria's Golden Jubilee was an excellent opportunity to showcase the British Empire and it was decided to invite a selection of be-jewelled maharajas and their maharanis to attend the event. For Hindu maharajas, this presented a problem, as their religion forbade them to travel by sea, thereby crossing the *kala pani* (dark waters). Nevertheless, many seem to have been able to cope with the challenge, including the maharajas of Baroda, Jodhpur, Cooch Behar, Indore and many more. Maharajas paid their own fares but were well-cared for on arrival. The Queen's two new Indian servants Abdul Karim and Muhammad Buksh arrived together with an Indian twelve-man military guard of honour (or escort). These tactical decisions to engage the Indian princes in her Jubilee celebration did much to enhance the Queen's standing as an international monarch.

MAHARAJA RAJ KUMAR UDAY SINGH OF JUBBAL

The 'Maharaja of Jubbal', Kanwar Uday Singh, was my first; these days he refers to himself as Prince Uday; his elder brother is head of the family and resides in the palace in Jubbal. I spent six glorious weeks in Woodville, his summer Palace in Simla which looked more like an English country house than how I had imagined a maharaja's grand residence. The State of Jubbal was established in the twelfth century CE. Maharajas ruled Jubbal state from 1699 until Independence in August 1947. The main city was just 100 km from Simla, in Himachal Pradesh. Jubbal was quite low in the pecking order of princely states, being one of the 'non-salute' states.

By the time we arrived in Simla for 'Staying On', Prince Uday had adjusted fully to his new station in life and seemed to be enjoying running a successful boutique hotel. From time to time during my stay I was consulted medically by others who were not part of the Granada team. Indians are rightly concerned about their health, at times monitoring bodily functions in less than helpful detail, such as the regularity of bowel movements; bowels only opening once a day was regarded by some as constipation. Also, this high interest in the day-to-day workings of the body, in my experience, leads these highly observant individuals to take advantage of the wisdom of any medical practitioner who might happen to be in the vicinity. I got on well with 'the maharaja' who had his own royal suite of rooms in Woodville. Although the Granada invasion must have certainly disturbed his peace, I think he enjoyed being a celebrity amongst celebrities. He would take drinks with us before dinner and would on occasions linger on with us for the meal. The maharani, his wife, would sometimes join us for dinner but she was a shy person and appeared much overshadowed by his position and grandeur. One evening 'the maharaja' came across the room to where we were having drinks, already holding a very significant tumbler of whisky, and asked quietly if he could have a private word. I was pleased to be asked and we moved discretely away from the group into one of the less populated corners of the large reception room.

'I am sorry to disturb you, but I wonder whether I might ask for your ... professional advice?'

'Of course, Your Excellency. It would be an honour and a pleasure.'

'Thank you. Well. What should I say?'

He looked somewhat embarrassed and was struggling as to find his words.

'How can I put this? I always seem to find it difficult to talk about things of a personal nature.'

He paused and took a generous mouthful of his whisky.

'Good stuff, don't you think? Always better to import a decent Scotch than punish yourself with our domestic home brews!'

'To be honest, I quite like your whisky, and the rum, but I am not complaining.' I smiled.

He smiled politely and rather nervously took another mouthful to give him time to frame the next sentence.

I felt somewhat embarrassed for him and made a rather clumsy effort to terminate the silence.

'Nice to be able to have a drink at all. When I was last in the south, in Tamil Nadu, you couldn't get a drink unless you went with your passport to a restricted dim-lit wood panelled tourist bar in the five-star Taj Connemara Hotel in Madras [now Chennai] or got a lawyer to make the case that you were an alcoholic and thereby qualified for a special permit. This enabled one to buy a restricted amount of alcohol from a designated store each week.'

'Yes. Yes! Really!' He seemed unaware of the recent history of prohibition in India and to be honest not the slightest bit interested. I guess maharajas always had a way to get what they needed but I am not sure that prohibition was ever enforced in the state of Himachal Pradesh.

'So, where were we? You see … it is my wife.'

He proceeded in a faltering series of sentences to introduce me to his young wife's abdominal symptoms. His potted account was related with much care and concern but lacked the detail and nuance that I needed to begin to assemble a view; a diagnosis and treatment, if any. He continued to struggle to find the next word.

'Would it be helpful if I had a word with her myself?'

I intervened, as it turned out helpfully, as I sensed he was running out of steam.

'Yes, yes doctor, what a splendid plan. Perhaps at a convenient moment tomorrow, before dinner?'

I saw her discretely in one of the reception rooms in their apartment. Fortunately, I was able to provide some reassuring words, and both were much relieved.

At the end of our stay in Woodville 'the maharaja' arranged a farewell party. The only entry requirement was that we British should wear Indian traditional dress. Although I had a selection of *kurtas* and *dhotis* back in the UK, I had nothing with me and wondered whether I should go to the bazaar to purchase some appropriate items of clothing. I happened to raise the issue one evening with 'the maharaja' and asked for his advice. Without hesitation, he took me to his dressing room and fitted me out with the most splendid gold thread, long below-the-knee Nehru jacket, white trousers and traditional white slippers. I was topped off with a stunning magenta red silk turban. To be honest I looked totally ridiculous, but it certainly brought considerable amusement to the Granada team. Similarly, Alison was provided with an exotic, shimmering red silk saree and a discreet matching blouse, courtesy of the maharani. I suddenly realised why we do not dress similarly in England. It is nothing to do with the climate, but all to do with the colour of our skin. The intense colours drain our already pale complexions and make us look like ghosts, whereas the beautiful brown tones of Indian skin enhance the striking colour palettes and contrasts of their often highly coloured traditional dress.

MAHARAJAS OF PATIALA

I discovered the princely state of Patiala during that memorable expedition to the highest cricket ground in the world at Chail, near Simla, with Trevor Howard during the filming of 'Staying On'. The first Maharaja of Patiala was Baba Ala Singh who was granted the title in 1764; the current Maharaja is Capt. Amarinder Singh who initially served in the army in the 1965 Indo-Pakistani War but subsequently was encouraged to enter politics by Rajiv Gandhi, an old school chum, and is currently the Chief Minister of the Punjab. He lives in the New Moti Bagh Palace in Patiala, Himachal Pradesh. I assume he took over as head of the family and 'honorary maharaja' in 1974, after his father died. Sadly, we did not meet the captain when we visited Chail Palace, most likely because by then he was a serious politician and spent most of his time

Maharaja of Patiala, *c.*1911. (Wikimedia Commons / National Portrait Gallery)

in the residence at Patiala. The last statutory Maharaja of Patiala was Amarinder Singh's father, Yadavindra Singh, who took on the role in 1938 and served until Patiala joined the Indian union in 1947. Like his father, perhaps the best-known Maharaja of Patiala, Bhupinder Singh, he was a first-class cricketer.

Bhupinder Singh was also a renowned polo player and had his own team the 'Patiala Tigers'. His extravagance seems almost limitless. In 1926 he filled a trunk with precious stones and other jewellery and sent them to Cartier in Paris, requesting they be remounted in the Parisian style. The result was the world-famous Patiala necklace, probably still one of the most spectacular pieces of jewellery that Cartier is ever created.

In the centre of Simla at the end of the main street there is a popular location known as 'Scandal point'; so-named because, as the story goes, the well-known philanderer, Bhupinder Singh is said to have eloped in 1892 from this location with one of the daughters of the British Viceroy of the day, Lord Lansdowne. However, many writers including Rudyard Kipling, have pointed out that this was simply fanciful since this maharaja would have been only one or two years old at the time. His father, Rajindra Singh, however, did take a white Irish woman, Florence Bryan for a wife in 1893 and took her to England for an eight-month sojourn. Perhaps it was this event which led to his banishment from Simla by Lord Kitchener and the move to another hill station, Chail, 45 km up the road. However, that does not really explain the building of the palace in Chail which was completed in 1891 and the cricket ground in 1893. Nevertheless, it is a good yarn! It seems much more likely that Kitchener restricted the maharaja's access to Simla at an earlier point in history to enable the ruler to have sufficient time to build the new summer palace.

MAHARAJA OF JODHPUR

I was invited to speak at a nutrition conference in New Delhi in January 1994. I arrived from London in the early morning, waited endlessly for my luggage at New Delhi airport but once at the hotel, I went to my room and caught up on lost sleep. I took tea in the hotel lounge with my host Shiva, an Indian clinical academic working in the Netherlands, and then joined a group of international college colleagues, mostly from the USA, for dinner at the Gaylord restaurant, Connaught Place. The following afternoon we were shown clinical cases at the All India Institute of Medical Sciences. I was most struck by the words at the top of the printed sheet which was completed for each patient as their outpatient department record: NO SMOKING. NO SPITTING, NO LITTER.

We then had a general discussion over tea in the hospital boardroom, followed by a grand buffet supper in the hospital gardens. For the next two days, we 'entertained' local clinicians with presentations

No smoking. No spitting. No litter, All India Institute of Medical Sciences, 1994. (Author's collection)

in a symposium on clinical nutrition. After two days, I had had enough and was pleased when we finally checked out of the hotel and made our way to Jodhpur in Rajasthan. The journey of about 500 km took just over one hour by aeroplane.

Shiva had known His Highness Maharaja Gaj Singhji for some years and pressed all international guests to accompany him to Jodhpur for another 'satellite' symposium and an outdoor clinic for villagers from around the region. However, probably most important of all was that our presence was required to celebrate the maharaja's forty-sixth birthday in the form of a *durbar* at the Umaid Bhawan Palace, his ancestral home.

Umaid Bhawan Palace, 1994. (Author's collection)

Fortunately, the symposium was brief, mainly a re-run of two or three talks from the New Delhi symposium but the 'inaugural function' at the Rajdadiji Hospital, was a rather protracted affair because the Maharaja, who was the principal guest, was delayed. His Royal Highness, Gaj Singh arrived with a delegation which included his wife, son, daughter and his elderly mother, all covered in garlands. He made a beautiful, succinct well-crafted speech of welcome, following which we retired for tea on the lawn.

Kipling notes in his *Letters of Marque*, in 1888, that 'Jodhpur differs from the other States of Rajputana

The maharaja's welcome, 1994. (Author's collection)

in that its royalty is peculiarly accessible to an inquiring public. Men asked in Jodhpur whether the Englishman would like to see His Highness. The Englishman had a great desire to do so, if his Highness would be in no way inconvenienced. Then they scoffed: "Oh, he won't *durbar* you, you needn't flatter yourself. If he's in the humour he'll receive you like an English country-gentleman".'

Once the formalities were over and a buffet lunch had been consumed, we departed in a variety of vehicles to conduct an open-air clinic on the outskirts of town. This event was very much under the auspices of the maharaja and one of, I guessed, many goodwill gestures that he and his staff make on a regular basis for the local community. The foreign physicians were grouped with a local doctor who talked to the patients in their local language and then relayed the clinical problem back to the rest of the group.

Village clinic, Jodhpur, 1994. (Author's collection)

Some patients came with X-rays (mainly of the chest) which we reviewed on a light box, which had been provided for each clinical group. Sometimes we were invited to listen to a patient's heart or lungs and then our local leader interpreted back our findings to the patient.

Man in a blanket, Jodhpur, 1994. (Author's collection)

Village girls, Jodhpur, 1994. (Author's collection)

A small selection of drugs was available at the clinic and distributed when required, while other patients received a prescription which they could take to the local pharmacy.

ABOVE: Dispensary, Jodhpur, 1994. (Author's collection)   BELOW: Arrival by tractor. (Author's collection)

We were all moved by the diversity of wealth and health and often distressed by the degree of suffering and the extent of unmet health needs. Despite the poverty of this Rajasthani community, they had a calm serenity and seemed grateful for the attention, albeit brief, that they received. Some travelled to the clinic on public transport, others had come on foot and one family arrived on their rather splendid red tractor. Many of the older men had spectacular full beards and moustaches, always topped off with the most magnificent brightly coloured turbans. That evening we dined at the palace as guests of the maharaja and Dr R.N. Singh, Director of the Hospital.

LEFT AND CENTRE: Maharaja and maharani. (Author's collection)   RIGHT: Maharaja on throne, Jodhpur, 1994. (Author's collection)

The *durbar* began the following evening in the spectacular surroundings of the Palace. Regal, Rajasthani red was the colour that predominated; sarees and turbans, men and women alike, adorned with brightly coloured jewelled ornaments. Greetings were made in the traditional fashion and then men and women moved apart into separate chambers. The men took a drink in front of a background of classical Indian music and exotic Kathak dancers. After some time, the maharaja, Gaj Singh, accompanied by his son and successor the Yuvraj, were invited to join the ladies, who entertained them with yet more dancing. Eventually the evening ended, only to start again with vigour the following morning.

The maharaja presented himself at a timely hour and took a seat in the back of his immaculate claret-coloured, classic Buick convertible (*c.* 1950) with registration plate RJQ 3206; he was again accompanied by the Yuvraj. They set off, followed by their entourage, on a traditional route towards Mehrangarh Fort, the site of many past historic battles. Once the ceremonials were complete they returned for the Birthday celebrations back at the palace. The maharaja took up a central position on his red velvet throne and formally received his guests and completed a series of ceremonial rituals, which largely seemed to centre around the transfer of money. The crowning glory was the birthday cake which had been crafted in the shape of a star.

The maharaja's Buick, Jodhpur, 1994. (Author's collection)

A Jodhpur experience could not be complete without a game of polo. Suddenly the dress code changed from traditional, royal Rajasthani glitz to jodhpurs for the polo players and Western dress for the rest. The maharaja turned out in a sports jacket, trousers with a crease (I think cavalry twill) and a tie. The contest was fought with vigour, but the outcome was reported to be equitable despite the reported shortage of ponies for the last chukka. This 1994 Durbar was written up as a feature article in *India Today* by Vijay Jung Thapa.

Although we did not spend much time in the company of the maharaja, he seemed calm, gentle and reflective, and fully adjusted to the fact that he no longer receives the privy purse from the Indian government that supported his ancestors. The Umaid Bhawan Palace, built by Gaj Singh's grandfather, is sometimes said to have been the largest private residence in the world with over 350 rooms; like many grand country houses in the UK, it has been transformed into a five-star hotel with much reduced accommodation for the maharaja and his family, a change that was essential to generate sufficient running costs for the beleaguered estate. James Cameron describes his visit to the embryo hotel in the early 1970s in *An Indian Summer*. 'It suggested a very big second-hand seaside boarding-house. Our room, fitfully lit by two 40-watt bulbs, was apparently furnished by the Public Works Department with odds and ends left over from a government hotel. There was great talk in princely circles of cashing in on history and attracting American tourists to these now public palaces, and though much enterprising work was going on elsewhere in Rajasthan, as we were to find out, it had got off to a very dismal start here.'

The following evening James Cameron and his wife were invited to dinner with the young maharaja, his sister and his mother. Cameron describes an interesting phenomenon; he and his wife were served one dinner, whilst the maharaja was enjoying superior fare. After dinner, the Camerons were served 'domestic' Indian whisky, whilst H.H. was served Scotch! As far as I was aware this was not the routine during our visit a decade or so later, and the refurbishment had clearly moved forward at pace. Involvement of the Taj Group of Hotels since 2005 must have rapidly accelerated progress towards five-star status.

The maharaja's father died in an air crash in 1952, just five years after Independence, when Gaj Singh was four-years-old; a very early age to be required to step into his father's shoes. He was educated at Eton and Oxford, where he studied PPE. He was recalled to India by his mother because the family found themselves in financial difficulties; his mother arranged a suitable wife and they worked together very successfully to convert the palace into a flourishing hotel, now also assisted by his daughter Shivaranjani who was just six years old when we visited. His son, Shivraj Singh, who was only five at the time, went on to have a very active life and was well-known for his social antics. Tragically he had a polo accident in 2005 and sustained a severe head injury from which he has made a slow but steady recovery.

MAHARAJA OF DEWAS SENIOR

I was introduced to the Maharaja of Dewas Senior, H.H. Sir Tukoji Rao III, K.C.I.E., by E.M. Forster (known affectionately to Forster as *Bapu Sahib*); not personally of course, but through his autobiographical account, *The Hill of Devi*, published many years after the events they describe, in 1953.

The book is an account through letters and narrative of his time in the princely state of Dewas Senior and his relationship with the maharaja. The details of these visits to India have been embellished with information from Wendy Moffat's biography, *E.M. Forster: A New Life* (2010). I briefly recount this relationship, partly because it underscores much of what fascinated Forster about India and its relationship to the British but also because it is a sad story that ends in catastrophe; wealth and social standing as a maharaja does not guarantee happiness and success.

E.M. Forster made two visits to Dewas Senior, the first in 1912–13 following both critical and monetary success with *Howards End* (he had started already to write *A Passage to India*) and the second in 1921, when he covered for the temporary absence of the maharaja's private secretary. His fare was paid both ways, he received a stipend of Rs. 300 per month and possibly most important for Forster, was given another opportunity to re-engage with Masood and other Indian friends. 'Masood (afterwards Sir Syed Ross Masood) was my greatest Indian friend. I had known him since he was an undergraduate at Oxford, and I stayed with him during my first Indian visit. Later, he became Vice-Chancellor of the University of Aligarh.' Forster dedicated *A Passage to India* to Masood: 'To Syed Ross Masood and to the seventeen years of our friendship.' Although Forster longed for a closer physical relationship with Masood, it was never to happen.

There had been radical change in India since his first visit and Forster has been criticised at his lack of understanding of just how far the mood had swung against the British with the rise of nationalism after World War I. Forster was with the maharaja from the end of March until mid-November 1921. During the visit, Forster fully immersed himself in the Indian way of life; he worked closely with the maharaja, dressed as an Indian and took on the mantle of a senior Indian civil servant. They travelled across India together to Nagpur, Simla, Chhatarpur, Dhar and Bombay. Their relationship deepened throughout the visit. Forster had to cope with the breakdown of the maharaja's marriage which had occurred before his arrival, but which created instability in Bapu Sahib's life, almost certainly contributing to the chaotic administration of the palace and the state more generally. Forster liked Bapu Sahib, a small, impish man whose religiosity replaced any intellectual leanings. After three months Forster wrote in a letter, 'Yes, I love H.H. and he me, and I am glad to have had this extraordinary experience, but it has been disappointing to be given so little that I can do, and so much that I cannot.' Forster took a month's leave during this second visit to Dewas Senior to spend time with Masood in Hyderabad.

Since the first visit to Dewas Senior, Forster had experienced a sexual awakening with Mohammed, a tram conductor from Alexandria. His sexual appetite had increased substantially, such that at times it was almost out of control. He confided in the maharaja that he thought there were rumours spreading through the court about his activities; although Bapu Sahib formally disapproved of homosexuality, he reassured Forster that he had heard none, but that if he was challenged he should just agree with his accuser. He arranged for a young male court barber to come to Forster's room every day to shave him, so that he could have sex with the boy without having to create a conspicuous, special occasion! He reassured Forster that the boy was already 'budgeted for'.

Forster returned to India for the last time in 1945 at the invitation of the All-India PEN conference in Jaipur. Sadly, he was not able to visit either Masood or Bapu Sahib, as both had died within a few months of each other in 1937. Masood had lost his job at the University of Aligarh and suffered a melancholic decline. Bapu Sahib's estate continued in modest disarray but nevertheless he pursued a tactical marriage for his son Vikky, the Yuvraj. It was a good match with the daughter of the Chief of Jath and the marriage was celebrated at the end of 1926. Unfortunately, all did not progress well because the girl's father wanted her to remain with her parents, a demand to which Bapu Sahib eventually agreed. At the same time, the

Yuvraj fled the court, fearful that his father was poisoning him. At this, the maharaja collapsed mentally and despite protestations and support from the Government of India he left Dewas Senior once and for all for the French colony Pondicherry, where he rejected all calls to return and died in penury.

Maharajas and Nawabs can be found in fiction where their extremes of wealth, self-indulgence and bad behaviour can be discussed freely without causing offence to anyone. Mulk Raj Anand creates such a story in his *Private Life of an Indian Prince*, although many commentators consider that there are autobiographical elements to his novel. He writes in the genre of social realism; his young prince is struggling to deal with the consequences of union of the State of Khatm with India and decides to elope with an English woman. Yet again a cross-cultural relationship is utilised to attract additional tension to an already troubled period of history. Anand had been educated in England but returned intermittently during the rise of nationalism and the hopes of self-rule. He writes in English but cleverly incorporates Punjabi and Hindustani idioms into his writing. Maharaja tales have found their way into the cinema in India; one of which was a Hindi supernatural adventure fantasy made in Bollywood 1998, and titled perhaps unsurprisingly, *Maharaja*.

NAWAB OF KHATM

Some of the best literary fiction about the activities of a maharaja, a nawab in this instance, is in Ruth Prawer Jhabvala's Booker Prize-winning novel, *Heat and Dust* which became a successful feature film in 1983, directed and produced by James Ivory and Ismail Merchant, starring Julie Christie and Greta Scacchi. The Nawab of Khatm is a fictional minor player in the world of Indian princely states but he is a romantic, with too much spare time, and manages to woo an Englishwoman Olivia, away from her serious and well-meaning husband, Douglas. As soon as she saw him she was immediately enchanted; 'Olivia's eyes lit up as she was led into the dining room and saw beneath the chandeliers the long table laid with a Sèvres dinner service, silver, crystal, flowers, candelabras, pomegranates, pineapples, and little bowls of crystallised fruits; she felt she had, at last in India, come to the right place.'

He pursued her politely but relentlessly, the relationship is consummated, and Olivia becomes pregnant. She leaves her husband, who subsequently remarries, to live in the nawab's palace alongside his other women, including his mother and his long-suffering wife. Olivia's life story became apocryphal to her family in England and after her death, the granddaughter (Anne) of Douglas Rivers, Olivia's former husband, travels to India to unravel the mystery. As her research progresses and the story unfolds, the young Miss Rivers finds herself in a relationship with her Indian landlord, a government officer, Inder Lal, and is then soon with child. Again, the story line follows the Forsterian metaphor of mixed-race relationships. Thus, two nations and two generations are struggling with love and sex, which for Indians would generally have to be delayed until after marriage. In this case, the ceremonials remained undone in both relationships.

There are many other examples of unbalanced, cross-cultural relationships in both English and Anglo-Indian literature. They can often be misinterpreted but it is nearly a hundred years since the publication of *A Passage to India*; it is easy to be critical and judgemental about fiction writing at that time about such sensitive relationships, but we must view them within the times that they were written and the social mores of the day. Cameron, in *An Indian Summer*, relates a discussion that he had with Nirad C. Chaudhuri, famous for his first book in English, *The Autobiography of an Unknown Indian*. He famously dedicated the book 'to the British Empire...' but sadly, colleagues and politicians in India missed the satire and virtually excommunicated him. Cameron relates how Chaudhuri exhorted Rudyard Kipling but showed 'grave distaste for E.M. Forster'. He continues; 'I began to feel, as I had never done in my first admiration of *A Passage to India*, that it must have been for Forster quite a torment to write, so clearly did he recognise the crude unkindness of the Raj, and so easily could he perceive the Indian evasions and dishonesties that provoked them into their stock responses.... I think Nirad Chaudhuri's error is to judge Forster as though he had been writing in the 1940s.... He was making a novel of India, not *about* India, in the days of Stanley Baldwin and the Wembley exhibition and the death of Lenin and the arrival of Mussolini and the acceptance of the British Empire as a permanent factor in the human order. What Forster had against colonialism (since he was a novelist and not a pamphleteer) was its corruption of individual relations, its destruction of personality.'

It is important not to confuse a nawab, usually a Muslim Indian prince, with a nabob! The latter was a derogatory term applied to a nineteenth century, usually self-satisfied and significantly obese, man who had made a vast amount of money in India running questionable deals through the East India Company. Perhaps the best fictional example of a nabob is Joseph (Joe) Smedley, an oversized, globular swollen gentleman in Thackeray's *Vanity Fair*.

Mrs Gandhi won the 1980 election not on ideological grounds or because of a plan to dispense with poverty, but on her ability to rule. Janata had failed to show that it could run a government, and Gandhi played the card of experience. On 23 June 1980 Sanjay crashed a single-engine plane following a failed aerobatics manoeuvre and died instantaneously with his co-pilot. This was a devastating loss for Indira Gandhi and there was only one way forward but to recruit her other son Rajiv, who was working as a commercial pilot for the domestic carrier Indian Airlines, to join the 'family business'. He had shown no interest whatsoever in politics but within nine months had been elected as a Member of Parliament to represent his brother's former constituency. The 1980s would prove to be difficult years with growing social unrest in the workplace, and across class and ethnicity. In 1981, in the State of Gujarat there were inter-caste clashes and in Uttar Pradesh there were major Hindu-Muslim riots.

The Punjab had continued to be a conflict 'hotspot' which was compounded by the occupation of the Golden Temple in Amritsar by a Sikh militant and his followers. Perhaps the defining moment of Mrs Gandhi's last period in government was 'Operation Blue Star', which aimed once and for all to rid the temple of its pugnacious occupants, who were fighting for land to create a Sikh nation, free of either India or Pakistan. On 6 June 1984 she ordered the troops supported by tanks to enter the temple; at least 500 people are reported to have died, including the leader and many other terrorists, but other estimates are much higher, possibly as high as 3,000 deaths. On 31 October in New Delhi, as she walked from her home to her office she was shot at close range by two of her Sikh security guards; clearly revenge for Operation Blue Star.

Internationally there were concerns that Gandhi's death would create a period of prolonged uncertainty and greater domestic instability. There was a fear that it could lead to a violent meltdown and social disorder which could have wider international implications for world peace. There was a wave of national sympathy following the death of Indira Gandhi, and perhaps not surprisingly her son Rajiv won a landslide victory and became Prime Minister of the Eighth Lok Sabha (1984–9).

Within weeks of being sworn in as Prime Minister, Rajiv Gandhi had to deal with the 1984 catastrophe at Bhopal, the city which was home to Union Carbide, the American firm which inadvertently released the deadly gas methyl isocyanate from storage tanks. This resulted in the deaths of more than 2,000 people, with another 50,000 or more harmed in some way or another for the rest of their lives. Rajiv Gandhi saw the need to improve the economy and appointed V.P. Singh as his finance minister. They reduced taxes, simplified the business bureaucracy and liberalised trade. Industry and manufacturing grew steadily during the late 1980s; while the middle classes prospered, poverty and malnutrition remained endemic. However, social conflicts continued, as did turbulence in the Punjab. In 1988 there was a second occupation of the Golden Temple but on this occasion the situation was resolved without military intervention.

Elections followed in 1989 (the Ninth Lok Sabha, 1989–91) but Rajiv Gandhi's party was not re-elected, and the result was a hung parliament. It was an unsatisfactory two to three years politically and, tragically, in the run-up to the Tenth Lok Sabha (1991–96), Rajiv was assassinated whilst out on the campaign trail. The election was won the by the Bharatiya Janata Party (BJP) and India had its first Prime Minister from the south, P.V. Narasimha Rao. He had the wisdom to make Manmohan Singh his Finance Minister; he would in later years serve as Prime Minister.

India's national finances were in serious disarray. The national debt had reached USD 70 billion by 1991 and foreign exchange reserves were at a catastrophic low. Manmohan Singh was given the freedom to sort it out. Essentially, he was an apolitical technocrat who had written a D.Phil. in Oxford thirty years earlier on the Indian economy; he concluded that the nation's trading arrangements should be liberalised, and this was the opportunity to put theory into practice. Soon after the government was formed, an innovative industrial policy was launched in July 1991 which effectively removed industrial licensing, apart from business deals related to national security and some health areas.

PART 8

INTO MODERN INDIA

A gift is pure when it is given from the heart to the right person at the right time and at the right place, and when we expect nothing in return. 17.20

And a gift given to the wrong person, at the wrong time and the wrong place, or a gift which comes not from the heart, and is given with proud contempt, is a gift of darkness. 17.22

Bhagavad Gita

More than ten years had elapsed since that first momentous and life-changing journey to Bombay and South India. I knew it would be hugely influential at the time and this was reinforced in the months after returning to the UK, but I would never have guessed that it would have had such a profound effect on the choices it influenced in my professional life. Despite having demonstrated some aptitude for surgery as an undergraduate in Jammalamadugu, having won a Gold Medal for surgery in my final year and awarded honours in surgery in finals, and going on to do my second house job in Cambridge with one of the most distinguished professors of surgery in the country, I made the decision to pursue a career in internal medicine, not surgery. Although I really enjoyed the technical challenge of surgical procedures, I somehow did not see myself as a surgeon and never have since. When asked by friends and colleagues why I was not doing surgery, I used to say that there was a history of 'piles' in the family and all that standing up at the operating table would be bad for them. That, of course, was utter tosh, but it was a way of brushing off lightly what could otherwise have become a protracted and for me an unwanted conversation.

The Cambridge professor, my prospective future boss, at an informal interview asked me whether I was going to do surgery or medicine. He was in tennis strip and had found a moment to interview me briefly between sets.

'Have you decided what you are going to do in the future? Medicine or surgery?' He spoke in a low, nasal, monotonous tone, looking down his nose and over his glasses but not quite looking me in the eyes.

The idea that I might want to do General Practice or Public Health or any of the other endless possibilities of medical specialities had not crossed his mind. I thought for a moment as to whether there was a 'right answer' to this question but decided it was best to respond truthfully.

'I'm not absolutely sure, but almost certainly medicine.'

I expected a tirade of criticism, particularly as he knew about my experience in India and might, justifiably, have assumed that I was a convert to surgery. However, his response was rapid and arresting.

'Good! That's fine. We need someone [meaning a physician], to look after the patients!'

With that he left and returned to the tennis court to finish his game. He was indeed right, as I was to discover a month or so later when I started the job. He ran the busiest surgical firm in the hospital, his team was on call for emergencies on alternate nights (there was another houseman who shared the emergency duties with me) but most importantly he and the other surgeons on the academic unit spent most of the day harvesting and transplanting livers and kidneys. Their presence on the wards was limited and we were very much left to get on with the job.

After a brief flirtation with the cardiologists at the renowned Papworth Hospital where the UK's first heart transplant was performed, I returned to my preferred discipline, gastroenterology, and began to develop an interest in gut diseases that were relevant to the developing world, namely intestinal infections; it was this ticket that got me to Simla with 'Staying On' earlier in 1980, as the producer had guessed that many of the crew might succumb to so-called travellers' diarrhoea; she was indeed quite correct. So those months at Campbell Hospital had left their mark.

Since that first visit to Jammalamadugu, I had qualified as a doctor and completed much of my post-graduate training. Exposure to the health problems of South India during those hot summer months had influenced my career choices more than I could have ever imagined. I was developing an interest in intestinal infections, particularly those relevant to the resource poor countries in the southern hemisphere and had decided to consolidate my research training by taking the opportunity to spend time in Boston studying and researching infectious diseases in the Division of Geographic Medicine of Tuft's University School of Medicine headed up by Prof. Jerry Keusch. I was due to start in Boston early in 1981 but was advised by the funder of my 'Tropical Lectureship', The Wellcome Trust, to spend three months at the end of 1980 in a tropical environment to orientate my thinking towards the laboratory research that I was to undertake in Boston. Where else was there to go but back to CMC Vellore and to work in the Wellcome Trust Research Unit, which had been responsible for much of the fundamental work on unravelling the epidemiology and underlying disease mechanisms of the bowel disorder Tropical sprue, a disease predominantly of the small intestine which was common in that region of South India, sometimes occurring in epidemics, and responsible for malabsorption with nutritional complications notably anaemia due to vitamin B_{12} deficiency.

MATHAN TAKES CHARGE

The unit was now headed by a distinguished clinician-scientist and gastroenterologist, Prof. V.I. Mathan, a tall, striking, knowledgeable and ambitious Malayali from Kerala.

Both he and his wife Minnie had trained at CMC and were very much part of the senior establishment. Mathan had taken over as the unit's director in 1976 and was very proud that it continued to be generously funded by the Wellcome Trust in the UK; locally and nationally in India this achievement was a mark of great academic distinction. He had attracted some of CMC's brightest graduates as his trainees and

Prof. V.I. Mathan, Vellore 1997. (Author's collection)

junior researchers, and had achieved national and international recognition for their research. During my three-month visit, the unit was subjected to a quinquennial review by the Wellcome Trust which involved a three-day visit by the Director and other Trust staff; they undertook a forensic analysis of research outputs, particularly their quality. This was a difficult time for Mathan, as loss of research funding would have seriously affected the viability of the unit and his national standing. Fortunately, the panel was convinced and funding was continued for another five years, although I recall that there was some 'horse-trading', which resulted in trimming of the budget.

Mathan's predecessor, an Australian physician, Dr Selwyn Baker came to CMC Vellore in 1956 as the inaugural director of the Wellcome Research Unit, which received its first grant from the Wellcome Trust in 1957. He had worked with Dr David Mollin, a haematologist at the Royal Postgraduate Medical School in London where he was developing an interest in the macrocytic anaemia associated with Tropical sprue. Baker became part of an international consortium for sprue research which included study centres in Southeast Asia and the Caribbean. The vision and scale of this work ensured substantial funding from the Wellcome Trust over many decades. Selwyn Baker caused a minor stir when he took up with a local female doctor and eventually left CMC with her for Canada where they spent the last phase of their lives.

The transfer of power from an expatriate missionary physician to a locally trained graduate was a trend which was rapidly gaining momentum across other similar institutions, such that by the 1980s virtually all leadership roles in the CMC were held by Indians. The directorship of the unit was shared between Mathan and his wife Prof. Minnie Mathan, a gastrointestinal histopathologist.

During this period, I had the opportunity to understand the workings of CMC in much greater depth than I had during my first visit ten years ago, and to appreciate the high-quality care and the important internationally competitive research that was being undertaken in what was still an isolated, predominantly rural environment. At that point Vellore still did not have an European style hotel, a situation which was not rectified for about another ten years, and certainly no airport.

The contrast between CMC hospital and Campbell Hospital in Jammalamadugu was stark. At CMC, it was possible to perform many of the investigations and therapeutic procedures that were available in the hospital that I had just left in London. CMC hospital was undertaking renal transplants, open-heart surgery and was building capacity in other technical disciplines, including gastrointestinal endoscopy. Its approach to the diagnosis and treatment of common disorders was largely identical to the approach that was being used in the West, and so different from the minimalist, 'let's make-do approach' in the resource-limited village missionary hospital setting in Jammalamadugu, just 200 km away. Patients in

Jammalamadugu who needed more sophisticated care would often travel to CMC, but for many the challenge of travel and cost was insurmountable.

September in Vellore was blessed with almost perfect weather. The raging summer temperatures had moderated and the worst of the monsoons were over. From time to time there was the odd short-lived tropical downpour, which, if you were unlucky and unprotected, could soak you to the skin in a few seconds. I stayed on the College Campus a few kilometres from the CMC hospital and the Wellcome Laboratories which were both in the centre of town. The residential buildings on the College Campus, where most of the academics and some of the hospital staff lived, were surrounded by rich sub-tropical vegetation, now flourishing after the monsoon rains. Initially I stayed in the glorious 'Big Bungalow', an iconic structure and very much the centre of campus which was the nexus for short-stay visitors to CMC.

The Big Bungalow, 1980. (Author's collection)

When my wife arrived a few weeks later, we moved to our own house close by. We had help to service the house but took many of our evening meals in the Big Bungalow, so did very little cooking. Lunch was in the hospital canteen. There was a constant trail of visitors from around the world to CMC coming through Big Bungalow, so dinner conversations were never dull. After dinner, we would return to our house where I would spend a couple of hours writing up research papers from the work I had done for my doctoral thesis (written during the quieter times of the day in Simla) which was currently with the University of London awaiting adjudication.

Sometimes we would be invited to a colleague's home for dinner but usually we stayed at home, reading, writing and listening to the BBC World Service. After a week or so, it occurred to me that it would be rather nice to have a beer or a whisky at the end of the day. I had imbibed a rather spectacular glass of whisky at the boss's place the weekend after we arrived, so I knew it was around. At the end of one of our regular morning research discussions in his office within a week or two of my arrival, I casually raised the topic. When I reflected with some pleasure on the splendid whisky that we had drunk together at his home before dinner, he explained that this was duty-free 'booty' from one of his many international trips and that he had never seen the like of it in Vellore.

'Tamil Nadu is a dry state. There's no alcohol here.' He said in a somewhat fatalist tone.

'Oh,' I said genuinely surprised. 'What, no alcohol at all?'

'Well, the locals brew up some terrible stuff known as toddy or arrack. You wouldn't want to touch that. Mainly wood spirit. You know, methanol. Sends you blind!'

'No. Is that really true?'

'Yes, we see it in the emergency department all the time. Absolutely tragic.' He paused and took a long, considered pull on his Benson and Hedges Gold cigarette, no doubt also acquired 'duty free' on a business trip to Europe or the US.

'Look, if you want to buy some drink, you'll need a permit. I'll get our tame lawyer to come over to the unit tomorrow morning and he'll sort you out.'

Sure enough, the following morning a lawyer appeared in his black jacket, black and grey striped trousers, white winged collar and white bands. He left the wig back in his rooms.

'Good morning, Doctor. Professor Mathan says that you have something you would like to discuss with me. We are always pleased to advise.' He spoke in a clipped, clean accent with just a tinge of his South Indian origins. We sat down in Mathan's office which was free as he was doing the morning ward round.

'I did much of my legal training in England, where eventually I was called to the Bar. Not entirely straightforward for an Indian in those days; barristers were part of an almost exclusively white tribe of London lawyers. I adored life in England; the art, the music and the culture in general and was planning to rough it out until I eventually broke into some good chambers. I had a few nice English girlfriends who seemed happy to learn about the delights of oriental men.'

A rather wicked smile crept across his face like an early morning sunrise. He left no space for questions and moved swiftly on.

'I could see England changing and was pretty sure that there would be a need for barristers of my background. Then, largely for family reasons I decided, and was strongly encouraged, to come home. My mother had found me the "perfect" wife!'

'That explains your impeccable English.'

'Well, yes and no. I was educated in English medium schools in India throughout my early life. That gives you a good start, and we spoke a lot of English at home. I think I got through the system in UK because if they couldn't see my face, I sounded pretty much like the rest of them!… So, what can I do for you?'

'Well, I understand that Tamil Nadu is a "dry" state and to put it bluntly I rather like to be able to have a drink in the evening. Prof. Mathan says that I will need a permit.'

'Yes, indeed, you will.' He paused and took a long hard look at me.

'So, does that mean you need alcohol on a regular basis? That you require it for, say medical reasons? As a doctor, you would know what I mean.'

'Oh goodness me, no! No, not at all. I just enjoy a beer or a whisky at the end of the day; not even every day!' I launched into shrill, protest mode.

'Sir, I think, with respect, you should reflect again on my question, and think why I might have asked you the question. I might say as an addendum, that there are a very limited number of reasons whereby the local authorities are legally able to issue a license. Can you follow my line of reasoning?'

I was struggling with his opacity. Then, I finally realised what he was wanting me to say.

'Yes. Yes, I see what you mean. Look. I'm not an alcoholic, no Sir. But we could say I need alcohol to keep on the level, to keep me content, even perhaps to stretch the point, to keep me well! So yes, you could say I need alcohol on a regular basis.'

'Thank you, Doctor. You clearly understand the restrictions applied to the issue of a permit. I have prepared a declaration for you to sign confirming the position.'

He pushed a sheet of low-quality paper towards me across the desk on which there was a pre-prepared statement and a place for a signature and a date at the bottom. I duly signed, dated and pushed it back to him.

'I'll have the permit for you in the morning. You just take it to the government liquor store in town between certain hours; I think 2.00-4.00pm and you can buy up to a defined limit on a weekly basis. You'll see there is a space at the back for your purchases to be logged in and signed for, which will be verified with the official stamp. I'll enclose an account of my fees with the permit. Nice meeting you. Enjoy your stay with us.'

India has had a long and interesting relationship with alcohol and particularly its prohibition. Mahatma Gandhi ran a vigorous campaign against alcohol soon after he returned to India from South Africa in 1915, which has continued after Independence to the present day. He said, 'liquor, as we say, is an invention of the devil'. It has varied from state to state and even within states from time to time, partly depending on the political party in power. As always, there is a love-hate relationship between the State Government and alcohol because, while acknowledging the dreadful consequences of alcohol and methanol abuse, the financial losses through tax revenues and tourism have profoundly affected the economy of some states. Kerala, which had the highest per capita intake of alcohol, reintroduced prohibition in 2015 which closed hundreds of bars except those in five-star hotels; a desperate attempt to protect its tourist industry. The economic consequences, however, have been massive since the tax revenue on alcohol constituted 20 per cent of state income, and an unintended consequence of this decision has been an increase in the use of other drugs. Madras State (from which Tamil Nadu in 1969 and Andhra Pradesh in 1953 were derived) introduced prohibition in 1937. Tamil Nadu continued the tradition but after about two decades decided to repeal the decision. Prohibition has been on and off in the state ever since; quite extraordinarily the state has had periods when it legalised locally produced toddy and arrack.

'Karpagam' The Co-op. Super Market, Vellore.
(A Unit of N. A Dt C. C. W. S. Ltd.,)

Licence No.   15/76-77   Cash bill

Date :   N⁰ 27804

Permit holder's name & address

Dr. Michael
S Gt. Fanthin

Permit No. 083050
Permit date: 13.11.80
Issued by: TWLO
VLO
valid upto: 12.11.81

Brand	Item	ML. per bot.	Equal to Uts.	Total Units	No. of Bottles	Rate per Bottles Rs. P.	Amount Rs. P.
	BRANDY	750	1.00				
		375	0.50				
		180	0.25				
	WHISKY	750	1 00	2	1	86 50	36 50
Me		375	0.50				
		180	0.25				
	RUM	750	1 00				
		375	0 50				
		180	0.25				
	GIN	750	1 00				
		375	0.50	2	2	7 60	15 20
	WINE	750	0.33				
		375	0.17				51 70
	BEER	650	0.08				
	VODKA	750					

No. of bottles Equivalent Units
Total Units   M.J.G. Fan

Salesman.

An alcohol receipt, 1980. (Author's collection)

Once my licence with its bright yellow cover ('The Yellow Book ') arrived, I took a trip down to the liquor store in the town and purchased half-bottles of domestic whisky and a few bottles of Kingfisher beer which I recall was a week's allowance. Although it did not strike me at the time, I did eventually recognise that I had obtained a licence under false pretences as I was certainly not an alcoholic. The only mitigating point I would make is that the law itself is totally daft; the last thing a serious alcoholic requires, for sure, is more alcohol.

After a week or two in Vellore a routine emerged, which would continue in an almost uninterrupted fashion for the next two or three months. The day began with a light breakfast at home accompanied by South Indian coffee, followed by a short trip on the 7.30am staff bus, which took us from the college campus to the CMC hospital in the centre of town. I would divide my time between the laboratory, the clinic and a variety of clinical meetings with colleagues. I took a simple, traditional Indian lunch with friends in the hospital canteen and returned on the bus at the end of the day at about 6.00pm. We had a wonderful housekeeper who kept our house running smoothly, sometimes with the help of her daughter, and who on request would prepare a meal for us from time to time in the evening.

Our southern location meant that nightfall truncated the evening unexpectedly early despite the warm evenings. It felt like summer but was unquestionably late autumn. So, it was easy to take to bed at a relatively early hour. The main challenge, however, was to eradicate all flying insects, particularly mosquitoes, from the bedroom before trying to sleep. We shut the door and the windows, used repellents, red plastic fly swats from the bazaar but usually did not resort to mosquito nets. Setting the ceiling fan on 'Max' created enough turbulence to make small insect flight almost impossible, although the noise

Our housekeeper, 1980. (Author's collection)

it generated hindered the transition to sleep and the asymmetric gyration, that resulting from its imperfect insertion point in the ceiling, was a cause for concern. The vision of being attacked by freely spinning and rapidly descending, cutting blades was deeply alarming; I could see where the helicopter descriptor, 'chopper' came from.

Providing the insects were under control, sleep was ultimately smooth and uninterrupted. However, one night, in the very early hours we were disturbed by a barrage of flashing lights and repetitive cracking sounds; my first assessment was that it was due to an exchange of automatic weapons. I woke abruptly, genuinely believing we were under attack. Alongside the flashing lights and repetitive shot sounds, came blasts of Bollywood movie music, rising and falling as the sound was transported in broken cycles by the gusting wind. Terrorists do not usually herald their arrival with popular music. Yes, of course it was fireworks and music from the bazaar. Only the following morning when we met colleagues waiting in the rain for the staff bus, did we realise that we were blessed by the Diwali celebration, Friday 7 November 1980. Diwali, the festival of lights, is an important time across Asia, especially for Hindus, but also for Sikhs, Jains and Newar Buddhists, signifying the victory of light over dark and good over evil. On the third day of the five-day festival, Hindus offer prayers to Lakshmi, the goddess of wealth. The celebrations continued throughout the night and only began to calm with the advent of sunrise. I have never quite come to terms with the idea that in both Indian villages and cities, life continues almost unabated through day and night. The ability of Indians to snatch a sleep interlude at almost any time of the day, often on a traditional cot outside the house and in a public place, never ceases to amaze me. These behaviours contrast dramatically with the more rigid approach to a dedicated period of formal sleep, more usual in the West.

COMFORT ON THE COROMANDEL COAST

Weekends in Vellore were dull. There was work on Saturday morning, church on Sunday morning and once the Fort in the centre of town had been explored, there was little else to do. We took the opportunity to get away and discover the delights of Madras, the Coromandel Coast, the temple at Kanchipuram and to see again the extraordinary sea temples at Mahabalipuram. Sometimes we would take a train (such as the Trivandrum Express) from Katpadi junction to Madras, which would cover the 130 km in about two and a half hours; on other occasions we would hire a car and driver for the weekend. Our first stop would be the Taj Coromandel Hotel situated on Mahatma Gandhi Road; an elegant quarter of the city, with gardens, a variety of restaurants and a secluded low-lit bar. The walls of this bar were panelled in dark wood and it was furnished in dark brown leather chairs and sofas which had lost the smell of new leather but retained the odour of cigar smoke from across the decades; they were arranged in private clusters. Only tourists could enter, following presentation of an international passport or a liquor permit. Sometimes the weekend would start on Thursday evening, for others it would be Friday. After dinner in the hotel and a night's rest we would take a car and a driver the following morning to Fisherman's Cove about 40 km from Madras, also a Taj Group Hotel but beautifully situated on Covelong (now known as Kovalam) Beach with a variety of options for accommodation; sea-view or garden-view cottages close to the beach or a more conventional room in the main hotel.

Beach cottage, Kovalam, 1980. (Author's collection)

It was an idyllic setting although the days could be almost too warm and humid but being on the edge of the ocean the air never stayed still. I cautiously entered the sea on several occasions, but this section of the Indian Ocean was surprisingly cold and notoriously hazardous with unpredictable tides and undercurrents. I imagined that there might be an assortment of hungry sharks out there venturing in from the deeper waters of the Pacific for a lazy breakfast in the Bay of Bengal.

Fisherman's Cove is an ideal setting-off point for a visit to the monuments of Mahabalipuram. Our driver mysteriously appeared at a timely moment after breakfast the following morning and took us the twenty or so kilometres to the ancient site, dropping us off at the main parking area. We arranged to meet him at an agreed time and then we retraced the footsteps that I had made just over ten years previously. I have never been tired of moving through this diverse collection of carved granite monuments, dating back to around 700 CE. The exquisite architectural detail of the Shore Temple is credited to King Rajasimha who was part of the Pallava Dynasty. This remaining temple is thought to be the last of seven similar constructions (apparently known as the *seven pagodas* by ancient mariners who passed in their ships) which extended eastwards into the Bay of Bengal. The devastating 2003 tsunami hit the Coromandel Coast (the tsunami that took Richard Attenborough's daughter Jane and grand-daughter and many others) and uncovered the remnants of one of these temples, clearly showing its construction from large granite blocks. The complex, in addition to the temple, contains man-made caves, several *rathas* (chariots used in temples) carved from single massive pieces of rock and a series of bas reliefs which tell stories of Krishna and other deities. It was impossible for me not to return to Krishna's 'butterball', the enormous oval globule of rock balanced precariously at about 40 degrees on a sloping rocky escarpment. I can testify that it had not moved during that decade of observation and it has remained stable when I last saw it again some years ago. Visitors cannot resist the challenge to clamber up the rocky slope and enjoy a pause in the shady area beneath the stone. Stone carvers still live in the dedicated village nearby and produce suitably size-reduced replicas for tourists to take away as memoirs. Green coconuts are piled high around every corner, their vendors flashing stone-sharpened machetes to 'uncap' or behead the beautiful ovoid structure and reveal its opalescent milk and soft white flesh for the uninitiated visitors. After the pre-planned two-hour excursion, largely unprotected in the midday sun, we were glad to find our driver and to enjoy a relaxing afternoon back at Fisherman's Cove.

PARLEZ-VOUS FRANÇAIS, MONSIEUR?

During one of our visits to the Coromandel Coast, we decided to return to Vellore by way of Pondicherry (Puducherry since 2006). Pondicherry's recent recorded history can be tracked to the colonial days when it became the headquarters of the French East India company in 1674. The city-state changed hands several times with the British but when India formally became part of the British Empire in 1857, France was permitted to remain in control of its petit colony. France finally handed back the territory to India in 1962, some fifteen years after Independence. Pondicherry is a charming, quite idiosyncratic pocket of the subcontinent and much visited by international tourists. It retains endless relics of its French colonial history and provided us with one of the most amusing lunches we have experienced. Pondicherry retains copious evidence of its colonial past, particularly its churches and cathedral, bilingual (Tamil and French) street signs and its cuisine which continues to have a strong French flavour. In the coastally located French quarter there remains a French community and the French-speaking indigenous population. However, there are also Hindu, Muslim and Christian quarters with their own shops and traditions. We wandered through the narrow streets and admired the quirky architecture and the beachside promenade; then we decided it was time to eat. It was just after 2.00pm but on reflection it was evident that we should have moved earlier. Our driver suggested that we go to one of the smaller hotels, as it would be more likely that they would still be serving lunch. We ended up in front of that I think was called Le Grand Hôtel d'Europe. There were a few tables to the side of the main entrance close to the street, but they did not look particularly inviting. They were not prepared for lunch and were only adorned by heavy glass ashtrays advertising the cigarette Gitanes. We walked through the front door and after some time managed to find a tall imposing Indian who turned out to be the manager. I asked politely whether we might be able to take lunch in the restaurant. He immediately threw his arms in the air and virtually exploded.

'Monsieur, c'est impossible. Le service est terminé. La cuisine est fermée!'

As he progressed through the three short sentences his voice became louder and more affirmative. His accent was utterly indistinguishable from a native of La Belle France.

'But surely Monsieur you could provide something? Maybe some bread and cheese and a glass of wine?' I proceeded cautiously but politely.

'*Impossible! J'ai vous dit, Monsieur, le restaurant est fermé.*'

'Then perhaps a glass of wine? Might that be possible?'

Eventually he descended from his position of great height and agreed to bring two glasses of rosé wine (made in India). They arrived quite promptly, and he waited while we tasted the wine.

'*Bon. Trés bon. Merci Monsieur, vous êtes trés gentil.*' I was hoping for a change of heart.

He seemed mildly impressed with my attempt both to be truly grateful and at the same time polite. There was a pause while he watched us each take another mouthful.

'As a special favour Monsieur, the chef has agreed to produce an omelette with herbs. Would this be acceptable?'

'That would be perfect.' I responded with speed and enthusiasm. 'And maybe some bread?'

'*Bien sur.*'

He departed smartly but was back within about fifteen minutes with an attractive looking omelette, two plates, cutlery and a small basket of French bread. He laid the table, cut the omelette in half and served each of us with the slickness of style commensurate with that expected in a smart bistro on the Champs Élysée.

'*Encore du vin, Monsieur?*'

The omelette was worth waiting for and the second glass of wine made us forget our earlier irritations. As we called for *l'addition* and settled the bill with a generous tip, we noticed our driver pull up discreetly in front of the hotel. He clearly thought it was time to go and I imagined was looking forward to getting back home to his family after three days on the road. Sadly, this magnificent culinary and cultural edifice closed after just over one hundred years of trading in 1996, and to my knowledge has not re-opened.

Le Grand Hôtel d'Europe, after 1996. (Author's collection)

There were plenty of other things to see in Pondicherry, such as the museum, botanical gardens and the *samadhi* (mausoleum) of Sri Aurobindo, the Bengali philosopher who founded the famous ashram in 1926. Just 10 km north of Pondicherry is Auroville, 'The City of Dawn', which aims to create a commune living in harmony. I understand that this is not always the case. Like Pondicherry, Auroville also attracts a very large number of visitors each year.

The day was beginning to cool down and we were glad to get back in the car and start the 150 km journey back to Vellore, which we anticipated would take about three or four hours. Never did I expect to have had such an intense 'European experience' in a former French colony in South India.

On reflection, there is a paucity of fiction which takes its origins and ideas from Pondicherry and it rarely appears as a location in other major novels set in India. Perhaps the most notable exception, however, is its appearance in *Life of Pi*, the intriguing novel by Yann Martel (2001) which describes the magical lifeboat journey of a sixteen-year-old Indian boy accompanied by a large tiger; he was the only survivor of his entire family, the remainder of whom were presumed lost at sea following the unexplained sinking of their ship. The early focus of the novel is a zoo set in Pondicherry, fictitiously based in the Botanical Gardens. The zoo, owned by Pi's (his full name being Piscine Molitor Patel, but you will need to read the novel to find out the origin of this unusual name) father, became a central focus of his early life. His understanding of animal behaviour in captivity became a vital element to his survival at sea with a 200-kg Bengal tiger. In the novel, the zoo does not survive beyond his early years so that Pi, when telling his story, must rely on memories to bring it back to life. However, Pondicherry has never had a zoo as far as anyone knows, and the Botanical Gardens are certainly not of a scale that would permit construction of such an entity. However, the Pondicherry local authority was delighted that the success of the *Life of Pi* appeared to be a major stimulus to new tourism to the area, and briefly contemplated establishing a zoo so as not to disappoint their international pilgrims. There is also Lee Langley's novel, *A House in Pondicherry* (1995) which follows the life of a young French woman Oriane, who plans to change the world. She stays on after her parents have left, but the plot has been described as 'flat and anorexic'. However, here again, Langley explores the then familiar and well worked theme of 'staying on', as did Paul Scott, David Walker in *Harry Black* (1956) and John Masters in *To the Coral Strand* (1962). In *The Life of Pi*, Martel, a French-Canadian extends the metaphor of the French colony in India to the former Franco-British colony of Canada where the story both begins and ends. Martel, like others before him, allows the young teenage *Pi* to explore simultaneously his inherited Hinduism and the newly acquired Christianity and Islam, all at the same time. *Pi* indulges his spirituality without restraint in all three simultaneously and is taunted to have the top of his pecker excised so that he might also become a Jew. Like many other places in India and in Asia more generally, believers in these religions and their respective temples, mosques and churches, have coexisted peacefully for centuries. Pondicherry is no exception with its Hindu temple, the Great Mosque (Jamia Masjid) and the Sacred Heart of Jesus Church being located close by, with just a short walk from each other. Louis de Bernières takes it even a step further in *Birds without Wings*, when villagers in a rural spot in Asia Minor would indulge in religious tourism if they failed to get resolution of a life problem from their preferred spiritual provider by passing on to one or other of the alternatives.

THE PLACE OF KALI, THE HINDHU GODDESS AND CONSORT OF SHIVA

During this working visit to Vellore in 1980, I was invited to join my academic colleagues to participate in the annual Indian Society of Gastroenterology conference, to be held in Calcutta ('the place of kali', subsequently renamed Kolkata in 2001). Mathan had already left a day or two earlier, as he had meetings before the main conference, so I travelled with his junior team on a domestic flight from Madras. I was a relative amateur on the conference circuit at that point in my career and was amazed at the quality of accommodation and lavish hospitality more generally that I was to experience at this gathering of clinicians and medical scientists. I was booked into the Park Hotel in Park Street, central Calcutta. It had a similar but less grandiose feel than other great hotels such as the Taj Palace in Bombay and the Taj Coromandel in Madras. I felt that I had certainly moved up the social strata since that first night in India at the Red Shield Salvation Army Hostel, Bombay more than a decade ago. It was a short walk along Park Street and across Chowringhee Road to get to Garer Maath, a massive expanse of open green space which hosts the Victoria Memorial and Museum and St Paul's Cathedral. It also links up with another green area, the Maidan, by the bank of the Hooghly River, with the massive H-shaped pillars of the second Hooghly Bridge rising proudly in the background. This vast edifice of a memorial, a tribute to the Empress of India following her death in 1901, instigated by the then Viceroy Lord Curzon, took fifteen years to construct and is built of bright white Makrana marble, the same material that was used to create the Taj Mahal. Victoria's dominating statue, depicting her sitting grumpily on a dark throne, is set in front of the building in the gardens. It is now a museum displaying a large collection of paintings, antiquarian books and other imperial memorabilia.

The statue of Queen Victoria, 1980. (Author's collection)

What surprised me most about the conference was that I do not recall having to pay for anything. There were dinners, receptions, lunches and other recreational events, all of which were on someone else's account. Medical conferences in the UK and the US were heavily supported by the pharmaceutical and biomedical industry but the times were a' changing and the concept of ethical funding was beginning to take a grip. The concern that receiving financial and other support from the industry could influence prescribing habits and clinical practice more widely was now discussed openly but it was still about another twenty years before doors began to close on the massive spending on individual physicians that had become the norm up until the late 1990s. In India at the time it was not thought to be a problem and concern about possible coercion and pressure on clinical decision-making had not arisen, at least it had not become part of any professional or public discussion. I remember one special evening that a group of us spent in the company of the conference President, Prof. K.N. Jalan. He was an eminent gastroenterologist in Calcutta who had established his own research institute, The Kothari Institute of Gastroenterology, supported at least in part by the biomedical industry. Mathan was close to the centre of power and I guess it was for this reason that his team, including me, were invited to a luxurious evening at one of the old Calcutta clubs. It was a remnant of the British days in Calcutta, the original capital of British India from 1772 to 1911, because of its importance as a trading centre for the East India Company; hence the dominating presence of Queen Victoria, Empress of India in the memorial gardens. Capital city status was transferred to Delhi in 1911 when it was made a district province of the Punjab, largely to detoxify the freedom-seeking revolutionary activities which were brewing in Bengal, as the empire moved from Victorian to Edwardian. However, it was not until 1927 that it was given the name 'New Delhi', and not officially inaugurated until 1931. Did it really need a twenty-year process to effect the change?

Like all traditional Indian Clubs established during British days, the style (structure, decoration and culture) was deeply conservative, controlled by strict protocols and house rules for dress and behaviour, many of whom only opened their membership to Indians after Independence. Some have only admitted women in the last five to ten years. Highly polished, heavy mahogany furniture filled the capacious lounges and dining rooms, deep pile traditional carpets covered the wooden floors and a multitude of bearers dressed in spectacular traditional livery were deployed at every turn, all desperate to be helpful. Again, I had an important social protocol confirmed that I first experienced in the Woodville Guest House in Simla and later at a traditional wedding in New Delhi when I was taken as a guest by the Bhagwant Singh's. The evening begins with whisky. Scotch whisky, not domestic whisky; and it flows in substantial quantities, tainted only with a little soda water, ice or just water. In fact, the pre-dinner drinking starts at about 7.00pm and may continue until 10.00pm or 10.30pm when dinner is finally served. We moved from a spacious reception area into a massive private dining room in the centre of which was a single rectangular table supported by claw and ball feet with seating for about fifty people. By this time the desire to eat had passed and the need to sleep was rapidly approaching. The drinking then stopped abruptly, and nothing was offered during the meal except water. Our host staggered to his feet once everyone had found a place at the table, said a few words of welcome and then slid back on to his chair, continuing to mumble inaudibly until his head finally rested peacefully on the place mat before him. Within a few minutes his driver arrived and with the help of one of the bearers he was escorted out of the room, presumably to his car and then home.

Many of my fellow diners, almost exclusively male, were by this time also losing capacity and showed only a brief passing interest in the food. Inside an hour they were starting to leave the table on the precept of a visit to the restrooms but then noticeably failing to return. The locals slipped away to find their drivers, while the visitors like ourselves waited to be chauffeured back to our hotels.

What a splendid evening it was last night, I thought to myself, as I picked up the phone in my hotel room to arrest the relentless early morning wake-up call. My own personal contribution to the conference was the delivery of a paper entitled, 'Hypothalamic-pituitary disturbance in coeliac disease', a distillation of some of the research that I had carried out during the last year or so at Bart's. I shall not trouble to explain the whys and wherefores of the research at this point, but it was subsequently published in a learned medical journal a year or so later. I had been allocated the early morning 8.30am slot in one of the smaller meeting rooms. By 8.25am I was the only person in the room other than the technician who was to supervise the slide projector.

In those days PowerPoint remained a dream of the future; we were still making slides by getting our medical artists to create customised artwork, which was then photographed and either transformed into a white on blue diazo slide or a black and white negative which was then tastefully coloured by the artist using a range of coloured adhesive gels. The worse aspect of this process was the delay in production (at least two weeks at our institution) and the total lack of flexibility once the slide was made. If you found a post-production mistake – too bad! If you changed your mind – tough! Today, presenters change their presentations up to a few minutes before they take to the podium.

I had loaded my slides into the carousel and was sitting in the front row waiting for an audience to arrive. I could tell now that this venture into medical science was not to be my finest hour. As the minute hand of the clock moved just past the half hour, I was joined by a very senior Indian colleague who I subsequently learnt was to Chair the session.

'Good morning. You must be the speaker. Welcome. I shall be chairing this session. I don't know where everyone is; must have had too good an evening last night.' He chuckled to himself. 'I saw you at the dinner at the Club last night. Surprised you managed to get here yourself at this early hour. No need to start immediately as others may drift in over the next few minutes.'

It was clear that the topic was of no interest to your average jobbing gastroenterologist and it was far too early in the morning to draw an audience.

He slowly found his way up on to the stage, although there were moments when I thought he was not going to make it. He shuffled some papers, drank a glass of water and tapped the microphone with great gusto to call the audience to attention. By this time, now at least ten to fifteen minutes behind schedule, with only another three or four people in the room, he started us off with the briefest of introductions. I hated every minute of my presentation and was glad when it was over. Why on earth had I accepted this invitation to speak? The Chair invited questions, but there were none. To relieve the embarrassed silence, he asked me a question which I recall required only a one-word answer; this created an opportunity for another elderly attendee to rise to a microphone positioned in the centre aisle and give an extended monologue describing his own, totally unrelated work on coeliac disease that he had conducted in the UK some twenty or thirty years earlier. The Chair eventually cut him off quite abruptly, thanked me for coming and moved on swiftly to introduce the next speaker.

By the end of my presentation another seven or eight individuals had joined us but took up distant positions at the back of the room, largely invisible from the stage. I realised that attending the scientific sessions was not a top priority at this meeting, as other sessions in the early part of the day were also poorly attended, but more importantly that my subject was also totally irrelevant to most researchers and clinicians in India at the time. I tried never to make that mistake again by always asking myself the question before starting a research project, 'How will the results of this work impact on the future health and well-being of people?'

This time in Calcutta was not all bad. To observe the remnants of British India, including the grandeur of this former capital city viewed alongside the impoverished street dwellers struggling continuously in the fight for life, was an alarming but informative experience. This was Mother Theresa's world, to which she devoted so much of her life and importantly brought to the notice of the wider world. Despite the economic and technological growth of this region of India, the streets remain the home of Calcutta's numerous poor and will do so for decades to come.

PANDIT RAVI SHANKAR

An unforgettable highlight of this visit to Calcutta was to attend, as a conference participant, a concert of live music by Ravi Shankar in the Kala Mandir auditorium in Shakespeare Sarani Road, a short walk from the Park Hotel. We were picked up at our hotel at about 5.30pm and taken to the venue for a reception at 6.00pm. After soft drinks and a few traditional Indian snacks (pakoras, Bombay mix, etc, etc) we were ushered into the main auditorium by around 7.00pm. It was a modern, sophisticated space with excellent seating, beautiful lighting and filled with fresh cooled air. The mood of expectation was unparalleled in my experience. Shankar was one of the greats of Indian and especially Bengali culture. He started as a composer in the 1940s, notably by creating the film music for the Satyajit Ray's *Apu Trilogy* and *The Philosopher's Stone*. By 1980 he already had a massive global reputation as a composer and performer both in his traditional genre of classic Hindustani ragas and in East-West fusion dating back to the 1960s when he influenced bands such as the Kinks (*See My Friends*) and the Yardbirds (*Heart Full of Soul*), and following that he worked with the Beatles and directly with George Harrison, to whom he taught the sitar. It is said that Shankar's influence can be found in at least nine of the Beatles well-known songs, notably *Love You Too* and *Norwegian Wood*. The scope of his collaborations extended beyond the world of Western popular music; he worked with jazz musicians such as John Coltrane and classical virtuoso artists such as Yehudi Menuhin. Most Indians accept that Bengalis are over-represented in the long list of talented artists that have contributed to the establishment of Indian arts and culture tradition. Great poets like Rabindranath Tagore, writers such as Nirad C. Chaudhuri, Pulitzer Prize winner Jhumpa Lahiri, and Arundhati Roy, film-makers such as Satyajit Ray, Rituparno Ghosh, Aparna Sen and fine artists from the nineteenth-century Kalighat painting tradition followed by the creation of the Bengal School, which was led by Rabindranath Tagore's nephew, Abanindranath Tagore; all are from Bengal. The choice of Calcutta as the nation's capital at that time was unchallenged. Alongside its cultural power was its economic and trading strengths which had been evident for several centuries. So, sitting in that auditorium, waiting for the master to arrive was like bathing in a pool of culture that had sustained this great nation for much of its history, at the same time acting as a major focus for the creative and performing arts more widely in Asia.

I turned to my neighbour, a local Bengali doctor, and enquired whether the delay was anything to be concerned about; and was there any news of his anticipated arrival time? He explained that there was no cause for concern and reassured me that this was a normal occurrence with great artists in India. He could already be in the building but still preparing himself mentally for the performance. He was expected to be accompanied by Alla Rakha, his closest friend and musical companion with whom he had toured the world with his tabla. My own brief excursion with the instrument some ten years previously had highlighted the importance of the intimate partnership between the sitar and tabla; they seemed to speak to each other like old friends. Both instruments could diversify their outputs of pitch, tone and rhythm. When I returned to England after that first visit, I would listen to albums by Shankar and Rakha for several hours, bathed in the scented smoke of smouldering joss sticks, sometimes sitting on the rug in front of my gas fire. I wore the *dhoti* that I had bought in the bazaar with Sam in Kurnool, gradually beginning to translate for myself the beauty of the language which was intrinsic to the scales and progressions that drove forward the classical Indian raga and then to release the explosive improvisation that followed – the two instruments constantly in intimate conversation, while the musical threads grew in length and complexity; tied together in a magical mist of sounds which will penetrate deeply into any receptive human soul.

I looked at my watch. More than an hour had passed and there was still no sign of the performance. There was a restlessness in the room and an infectious anxiety that bad news may be in the offing. The initial cool tranquillity was gradually being replaced by rising temperature and humidity and the air's initial freshness was now laced with the odours of several hundred closely packed human bodies.

Shankar's influence internationally was beyond reproach. He had written film scores for many classic Indian films notably those directed by Satyajit Ray and *Gandhi* directed by Richard Attenborough. He had produced highly talented daughters with different mothers who would go on to develop fierce musical talent. Anoushka Shankar, his eldest daughter, became accomplished at the sitar (although initially she accompanied he father on the less complex stringed instrument the tanpura) and would go on to play with her father in many distinguished settings; Nora Jones would steal the hearts of lovers of popular music and jazz with her warm deep, sensual voice. He would live to see them both enjoy massive professional and personal success.

During my first visit to South India when I developed an interest in classical Hindustani music and purchased a set of tabla, I took lessons from an expert on the hospital campus and had explored even the possibility of learning the veena, a South Indian stringed instrument, which closely resembles the sitar. I had learnt the violin at school (although never achieved any level of excellence that would allow performance in the orchestra) and had taught myself the guitar; I thought there was a chance therefore that I might be able to manage another stringed instrument. I decided against for several reasons; it was a large instrument and I judged too challenging to ship one back to the UK. They were expensive and probably most important, I was told it was a lifetime's work to gain any sort of competence; it was both a physical and a spiritual commitment.

Suddenly my musing was disturbed by movement on the stage. Stage hands were placing rugs on the wooden floor and distributing cushions somewhat randomly about the place. This all looked very promising. It was by now about 8.30pm. A senior figure appeared in a suit and walked imperiously across the stage and then beckoned to two or three other musicians to take their places towards the back of the stage. The auditorium was silenced by this activity. Eventually the suited gentleman announced the arrival of Mr Shankar and the other musicians who would play with him. The two female tanpura players entered first and took up positions towards the back of the stage, where they tended their instruments in preparation; they were seated behind the centre stage places clearly allocated for Ravi Shankar and the tabla player. The tanpura, like the sitar, is a multi-stringed instrument usually no fewer than four but may have as many as five or even six strings. The instrument used in the north of India is like the sitar being made solely of wood but in the south the body (sound box) is made of carved water pumpkin. The strings can be tuned as required; it is not used to depict a melody but acts as a background 'drone' which blends with and supports the ragas driven by the sitar.

Finally, the moment came, and the maestro slowly walked on to the stage dressed in traditional white *khadi* shirt and plain *dhoti*, carrying his magnificent sitar. He turned around to find that Alla Rakha was not following. He paused and waited for a few seconds for his companion to join him. They said nothing; both held neutral, pensive facial expressions and appeared completely oblivious to the presence of the expectant – and by then somewhat frustrated – audience. The welcome was unbridled but it failed to distract these consummate performers who sat cross-legged on the stage, adjusting their positions until they were totally comfortable and once achieved they then directed their energies to their instruments. The tanpuras were still being tuned in the background, now listening and adjusting to the sitar tuning that was beginning in front of them. Rakha positioned and then re-positioned his two drums, which together constitute the tabla, until he was totally comfortable. The drum at his right hand is usually made of wood, often from a hollowed trunk from the Jak tree and the other has a pot-shaped metal body, and both are covered in cured animal skin. As the sitar was slowly coming to life, he tuned each of the drums sympathetically by tapping down the wooden blocks or metal rings which apply tension to the leather thongs which then pull the diaphragm taut until the desired note is reached – exactly as an orchestral percussionist would tune the tympani. Tanpura and tabla tuning sounds began to diminish as Shankar, cradling his beloved sitar, methodically tuned the instrument for the work at hand, with his accompanists closely following. There is something quite magical when these instruments are tuned together; there are apparently occasions when it is not always clear when the performance proper has started. At the beginning of one concert, when the audience broke into applause after completion of the tuning process, Shankar is reputed to have said, 'If you like the tuning so much I hope you enjoy the playing more.' Well we did, and it was a most exceptional evening. They played and played and played; the audience was stunned in appreciation. His music created a bridge back to India when I returned to London.

On returning to Vellore, I settled back into the daily routine working partly in the clinic, partly in the lab and then enjoying the evenings back at the College Campus. An irritating feature of the working day at the hospital was the plague of monkeys. Like the cow, the monkey is sacred. Hanuman is the monkey god, usually portrayed with a monkey's head on a human body, very well connected to the senior deity and much revered in village India. Thus, it follows that the monkey is deeply respected and must be allowed to coexist peacefully with its human counterparts. On a practical level in the hospital, this meant keeping the windows shut to avoid the wily creatures pillaging food stores, patients' lunches and any other edible delights that could be unearthed. The environment was highly conducive to rapid procreation because of copious food sources in the hospital and lack of any natural predators, combined with a gestation period of about five months; a fertile female could produce at least two progeny a year. In addition to their nuisance value, they could be aggressive; a bite was a serious matter. Although it was not widely discussed, I believe from time to time, when the population had grown to unmanageable levels, the 'monkey man' was invited to come to the rescue. He would catch as many as he could, usually in the early morning before the day had started and move them to a 'place of safety'; wherever that was!

On the evening of 9 November, while drinking a glass of Kingfisher beer and listening to the BBC World Service, we learnt of the death of John Lennon the previous evening at around 10.30pm Eastern Standard Time in New York City outside his apartment block. He was shot several times with a handgun and was pronounced dead on arrival at Roosevelt Hospital. It became another of those incidents which reverberated around the world when many of us remember exactly where we were what we were doing; just like the shooting of JFK and the road traffic accident that killed Diana, Princess of Wales. Somehow it felt wrong not to be home in England where the loss was felt profoundly and there would have been more people who wanted to express their grief.

I returned to Vellore on multiple occasions during the 1980s and '90s, almost exclusively to maintain the productive research collaboration that my group in London had established with the Wellcome Research Unit. Our research fellows would come and go in both directions; some working on new approaches to the diagnosis of intestinal infections, others on the further development of oral rehydration solutions for the treatment of children with acute dehydrating diarrhoea. It was a productive period for me as an early career researcher making his way in the competitive world of academic medicine. Mathan welcomed the collaboration and was a great supporter of our work.

One of his Vellore trainees, David Rolston, came to work with me in London.

He was first author on our initial publication which suggested that a less concentrated oral rehydration solution (ORS) would be more effective in clinical practice. In the mid-1980s the standard WHO ORS had what we would now regard as relatively high glucose and high sodium concentrations. Sometimes this created problems, particularly in seriously dehydrated, undernourished infants and young children; the high sodium concentration could cause hypernatraemia (high sodium concentration in the blood) and the high glucose concentration could make diarrhoea worse, as it was poorly absorbed in the small intestine and effectively acted as a laxative in the large intestine. Our new recipe had reduced the concentration of both sodium and glucose to make the ORS significantly more dilute. After publishing our first paper I wrote to the WHO in Geneva and applied for a small grant to develop the project further. After several weeks without a response, I wrote again. Within a few days I received a telephone call from the Director of the Diarrhoeal Diseases Research Program advising me in no uncertain terms

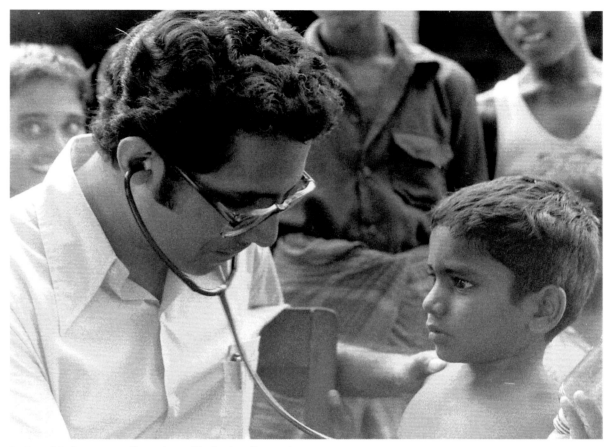

Dr David Rolston in a village clinic. (Author's collection)

that I should cease this line of research forthwith, as it was in grave danger of undermining the highly successful WHO programme which was saving thousands of lives every year worldwide. Frankly, the phone call reached a pitch which I can only describe as harassing and intimidating. There was clearly no future in pursuing this line of funding with the WHO, but the research continued (funded at this point mainly by the pharmaceutical industry).

The case for making the simple but fundamental changes in the glucose and sodium concentrations was reaffirmed time and time again in both animal and human models of diarrhoea. We even created a model of cholera in humans to prove the point. The work with Vellore continued through a productive collaboration with Prof. Ramakrishnan, both in the laboratory and in the clinic. We promoted our work around the world and eventually after some early pilot clinical trials the WHO sponsored several major global studies which confirmed improved efficacy and safety. In 2003, almost twenty years after we had begun our first studies, the WHO formally changed its recommendation and approved the low-glucose, low-sodium and reduced osmolality ORS for use worldwide for the treatment of acute diarrhoea in adults and children, including cholera. Interestingly, the commercially produced ORS preparations re-formulated ahead of the WHO change in policy, wisely in my view because some of them were dangerously over-concentrated. This episode taught me one thing in life; if you think you are right, believe in yourself and do not be put off because you are challenging the accepted wisdom of the day. And I guess, speak truth to power.

Our partnership working in oral rehydration therapy continued under the leadership of Prof. Ramakrishna in Vellore and the collaboration broadened to include Prof. Henry Binder, a distinguished physician and physiologist at Yale; the concept of using low osmolality ORS is still being pursued by replacing glucose with a poorly absorbed carbohydrate source (resistant starch) such as maize which lowers the osmolality still further. The science is compelling and the clinical trials so far look highly promising.

Mathan retired from clinical and academic practice in 1997 and I was delighted to join his retirement celebrations in Vellore at a mid-term meeting of the Indian Society of Gastroenterology, which included a symposium to acknowledge his many contributions to the advancement of clinical science. On this occasion I decided to take my eldest son, Tom, who was nearly fifteen, with me; we planned to spend the weekend in Chennai and then travel on to Vellore by way of Fisherman's Cove and Mahabalipuram. I organised direct flights from London to Chennai International Airport and planned to spend the weekend at the Taj Coromandel Hotel in the city but also made reservations at the beachside hotel at Fisherman's Cove. We arrived at Heathrow and went straight to the check-in desk to discover the most devastating travel error that I have ever made in my life. I had failed to arrange our Indian visas. I had made the plans in somewhat of a rush and on reflection must have been confused by the fact that another country to which I travelled to frequently, Poland, had just removed the requirement for British travellers to hold a visa. We had no option but to go home; it was a Saturday and the Visa section of the Indian High Commission was closed. The following Monday was a Bank Holiday but fortunately not for the Indian Embassy, and we managed to get our visas early in the morning and pick up the flight to Chennai (formerly Madras until 1996, just a year before our visit) later that day. I have never forgiven myself for that error, as we lost two days of our week in South India.

Tom embraced India with enthusiasm. He enjoyed the hotels and developed a deep affection for South Indian cuisine and Indian beer. He had curry for breakfast at Fisherman's Cove, swam in the Bay of Bengal and was deeply moved by the simple way of life of most South Indians. I had arranged a car and driver to take us from Chennai to Fisherman's Cove and Mahabalipuram and then on to our final destination, Vellore. I was pretty sure that he appreciated being part of the trip, but he did verbalise concern and perhaps embarrassment that we could afford to pay for a car and driver for several days. He had rapidly and rightly detected the massive gap in resources between us and the average South Indian.

We shared a simple room in the Big Bungalow, used a communal bathroom and toilet along the corridor with other guests and ate breakfast in the dining room on the ground floor. While I was at the conference, Tom accompanied a team of midwives to their antenatal clinics in neighbouring villages. Overall it was a good experience to share but quite a sharp introduction to some of the challenges of the subcontinent. Subsequently, we travelled together on two occasions to South Africa (Cape Town, Johannesburg and

Durban) and he and a good friend worked with a colleague of mine in a research centre in Lusaka, Zambia. I was glad that he was able to gain some understanding of my work and had engagement with the developing world at this point in his life.

LUCKNOW

In 1998, I spent a week at the Sanjay Gandhi Postgraduate Institute in Lucknow as a Visiting Professor; I was also invited to speak at a neighbouring institution, King George's Medical University. Lucknow, capital of Uttar Pradesh, has a long and turbulent history. The coachman who drove Kim to Kipling's fictional St Xavier's School, said of Lucknow: 'there is no city – except Bombay, the Queen of all – more

Tom in Vellore, 1997. (Author's collection)

beautiful in her garish style than Lucknow, whether you see her from the bridge over the river, or from the top of the Imambara looking down on the gilt umbrellas of the Chutter Munzil, and the trees in which the town is bedded. Kings have adorned her with fantastic buildings, endowed her with charities, crammed her with pensioners, and drenched her with blood. She is the centre of all idleness, intrigue, and luxury, and shares with Delhi the claim to talk the only pure Urdu.'

St Xavier's was almost certainly based on La Martinière College, which is still located in the massive country residence, built in the Indo-European style, by Major General Claude Martin and completed in 1802. It opened as a boys' school in 1845 and quite uniquely was awarded a 'battle honour' for its role in resisting the Indian Rebellion of 1857. Although Major General Martin initially served with French army, he was taken on subsequently as a military leader by the East India Company.

I enjoyed this visit, gave my talks as requested and did my best to answer the penetrating questions of aspiring young post-graduates. Sadly, I had a limited exposure to the city as I was sequestered at the University Campus, away from the city centre. One of my over-riding memories was of feeling devastatingly cold at night; so cold that I could not sleep. The room was spacious, en suite with a traditional bathroom but no heating. The season was on the cusp between autumn and winter; during the day when the skies were clear and with the sun at full power it was wondrous, but at night the temperature plummeted, as might be expected from the city's position on an expansive plain. The other enduring memory is that this was a Mughal place. The grand architecture was created by past emperors over centuries, such as the Hussainabad Imambara, the stunning mausoleum of Muhammad Ali Shah, the Rumi Darwaza a massive ornate gateway built by Nawab Asaf-ud-Daula in 1784 and the Kaiserbagh Palace Complex, built by Nawab Ali Wajid Ali Shah and completed in 1850.

During the first decade of the new Millennium I returned to India almost on an annual basis. I was still fully engaged with the international conference scene in my medical specialty and still apparently a popular speaker with friends and colleagues in India. Medical conferences in Mumbai and New Delhi sustained my interest both in matters medical and my interest in the progressive economic development of India. During this period, I witnessed major advancements in healthcare and a massive development in hospitals in the independent sector. In some ways, it was depressing to see the advancement in hospitals and medical technology taking place in the major cities of India and the constraint applied to our own National Health Service during the latter part of that decade. The economic growth in India was astounding, with GDP increasing at some points by almost 10 per cent annually.

Interspersed between the delights of medical conferencing, I represented my university on a series of missions to many of the major Indian cities, notably to Chennai, Mumbai, New Delhi and Kolkata; I was particularly impressed by a return visit to Kolkata, a city I had not visited since 1980. During the intervening thirty years the place had been transformed. The classic sites such as the Victoria Memorial, the Hooghly River and its iconic bridge, and the Maidan were largely untouched, but a new city had emerged between the airport and old Calcutta. This was a sister operation to the information technology powerhouse in Bangalore which had developed some years earlier. New residential provision and high-tech buildings full of ambitious young 'coders', technologists and managers were creating wealth within this new emerging economy. How narrow-minded was our Home Secretary, Teresa May (until recently our Prime Minister) and her minister, Damian Green, to insist that the bright and highly industrious Indian students who wanted to come to the UK to study at our universities should be regarded as immigrants and invited to complete and submit a fifty-six-page Visa application form. Not surprising, their numbers fell away dramatically as they changed their desired higher education destinations to the US, Canada and Australia. The concern that these brilliant minds and agents of change would want to remain permanently in the UK was a complete misreading of the situation. The majority would want to return to India, the land of opportunity with jobs and economic growth. And when we were finding it difficult to recruit engineers and computer scientists in the UK. During these university missions, we were always well supported by the British Embassy and the British Council who were desperate to rebuild the bridges across our two nations and to limit the damage which flowed out of the foreign policies emanating from the Home Office. On one occasion I went to Mumbai for breakfast. 'Bahjis for breakfast!' I left London Heathrow on Friday, arrived local time in the early hours, slept for a few hours in the Taj Mahal Palace Hotel and was ready for my 9.00am breakfast meeting with one of our distinguished university alumni, Noel Tata. I flew back to the UK later that day.

Despite these incredible developments in health, technology, engineering, manufacturing and growth in urban infrastructure I was aware at every visit that large numbers of Indians, almost certainly the majority, were living under similar circumstances to those which I had witnessed forty years previously. The 'trickle down' effect from capitalism was as yet not widely apparent.

DR AUGUSTINE AND JAMMALAMADUGU: MORE THAN FORTY YEARS ON!

Early in 2012, I knew that I would be visiting New Delhi and Mumbai on university business and wondered whether it might be possible to find a couple of days at the beginning of the trip to return to Campbell Hospital in Jammalamadugu. However, when I looked at the logistics of making a return visit to Jammy I soon realised that little had changed in the intervening forty years. The town, although having expanded territorially and grown in population, was still relatively isolated in the south of Andhra Pradesh and the options for transportation were limited. There were only two possibilities; the first was to take the Mumbai Mail from Chennai Central to Muddanuru (about 300 km taking an estimated six and a half hours) followed by an 18 km taxi ride to the hospital or alternatively to take a car with a driver from Chennai airport, again about 300 km with an estimated journey time of about five hours. I chose the car and driver but either way I would need an overnight stay to make a visit worthwhile. I wrote to the hospital superintendent, Dr Helen Davidson, some weeks before I intended to visit and received a cautious but nevertheless warm invitation to return to the hospital.

I flew directly from Heathrow to Chennai, arriving at about 2.00am, spent the remainder of the night in a basic room in the Trident Hotel about fifteen minutes from the airport and was collected at the hotel at about 7.00am by my kind and courteous driver, Afzal. I did not check out of the hotel and left most of my possessions in the room, as I was already booked on a domestic flight late the following day to New Delhi where I was scheduled to participate in a variety of university events. Afzal loaded my backpack into the boot but before setting off I checked with him whether he was familiar with the route to Jammalamadugu.

'No problem, Sir.' He responded confidently in an almost dismissive fashion.

'But Afzal have you been there before?'

'No Sir, but no problem. We just take Srikakulam highway northwest out of the city and soon we cross from Tamil Nadu into Andhra Pradesh. It's so easy! Really, no problem.'

'But it's not that part that I'm worried about. It's the journey through Andhra Pradesh to Cuddapah and then Jammalamadugu.'

'It's really no problem Sir, I have a map!'

I was not making progress and accepted that I just had to put my faith in Afzal and his map.

It turned out to be one of the most frustrating road journeys of my life. Rather than five hours it took nearly eight. We had made one twenty-minute stop for coffee and some traditional south Indian snacks but had otherwise driven without a pause. Parts of the journey were indeed very slow, due to heavy commercial traffic but there were many occasions when I had serious concerns as to whether we were on the right route. I subsequently checked on the time allocated for the airport bus to travel between Jammy and Chennai International airport and even this relatively slow public service vehicle is expected to cover the journey in about six and a half hours. Something must have gone adrift in the route planning.

Finally, we reached Cuddapah and then Proddatur, both of which I recognised and, at last, with much relief, I saw the familiar gates of the hospital with the same sign above the entrance building, Campbell Hospital.

My impressions of India gained through the journey, particularly those changes that occurred during the past forty years were interesting. Chennai had undergone a transformation during this period, notably the massive development of information technology enterprises on the outskirts of the city which seemed to have replaced much of the rice-growing areas of the past. The multi-lane highways sprouting out of the city had been massively upgraded and were now comparable with city highways around the world. However, once we left the penumbra of Chennai and moved closer to rural Andhra Pradesh, the changes became less and less apparent. Here splendid rural India survived although tractors and other farm machinery had replaced the ox-powered, hand-guided plough. We had driven past an enormous white marble, newly constructed temple which dominated the landscape, the like of which I had never seen before. I asked Afzal if he knew anything about the building; he said he did not but offered to stop so that I could have a look around. I graciously declined his offer, as we were already well behind our expected arrival time but asked him to pause briefly to enable me to photograph the white monster. I subsequently discovered that we had driven by The Oneness Temple which opened in 2008, for 'the spiritual awakening of humanity'. The temple is about 70 km from Chennai in a place called Varadaiahpalem, which is in the neighbouring state, Andhra Pradesh. It was designed by the same architect that created Auroville, the famous ashram in Pondicherry, Prabhat Poddar. It sits on the same campus alongside the Oneness University and has a social outreach programme which supports more than a hundred local villages. The Temple has become a spiritual watering hole for film stars, fashion designers and rock musicians.

We drove into the Campbell Hospital precinct and came to a welcomed halt. My driver spoke to the security guards (most likely in English, as he was a Tamil and would have been unlikely to speak much Telugu) at the hospital gate, presumably describing the nature of the goods on board, and without any further delay we drove through into the hospital compound. After a brief interlude, we were greeted by Dr Augustine Raj who introduced himself as a staff physician. He was an extremely polite, softly spoken

The Oneness Temple, 2012. (Author's collection)

young man, I guessed just five or six years out of medical school and had been awaiting my arrival. From those first moments after meeting I felt he was carrying the woes of the world on his shoulders. I apologised profusely for the late arrival. He seemed unperturbed, presumably because travel times are always unreliable in rural Andhra and immediately took me away for a late lunch. We had simple food; chicken curry, rice, dhal, masala and yoghurt. For desert, it was fresh fruit: grapes, oranges and bananas. He then broke the sad news that unfortunately Dr Helen Davidson, the superintendent, who was to host my visit and who I soon learnt was his mother-in-law, was unfortunately not in the hospital for the next two days as she was having a medical problem dealt with at the Christian Medical College Hospital in Vellore. This was a massive disappointment since I knew she had been superintendent for at least twenty years and wanted the opportunity to explore with her the changes that she had occurred during that period under her leadership.

I am afraid that one disappointment would follow another throughout my stay. The stone buildings that were the fabric of both the hospital buildings and the residential accommodation were largely unchanged on the outside but there was overwhelming evidence that the interiors had been neglected for decades. There was a sense either that no one cared about the buildings any more, or perhaps more likely, that the money was just not there to maintain them. The square in front of the main building, which had formerly been filled with a throng of patients and their relatives, was largely empty. Augustine took me on a tour of the wards; they were mostly devoid of patients, perhaps one or two lonesome individuals lying on a bed with a relative by their side. The Children's Ward seem to have disappeared, but the pharmacy and its adjoining store looked almost identical to the state it was in on the day I arrived at the hospital in 1969, before the clean-up. There was an overwhelming sense of *fin de siècle*!

'Augustine, I really must see the operating theatre where I spent so much time as a student. But maybe everything is changed, and it's no longer were it was?'

'Of course! Come! It's just where it always was!'

We walked along a familiar corridor past some closed and padlocked, double-doors which I recognised, over which was the sign, 'X-ray room', finally reaching another familiar entrance which took us into the ante-room of the operating theatre.

I was appalled. Absolutely nothing had changed. The surgeons' scrub room just inside the operating room looked the same as when I was last there more than forty years ago. There was no evidence of any attempt at an upgrade. The two operating tables which I remembered well (often used at the same time with procedures being conducted in parallel) had decayed over time, although

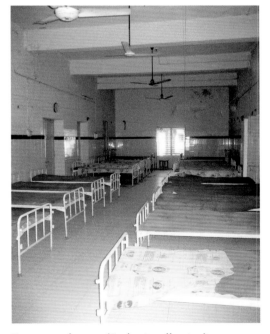

Empty ward, 2012. (Author's collection)

The x-ray room, 2012. (Author's collection)

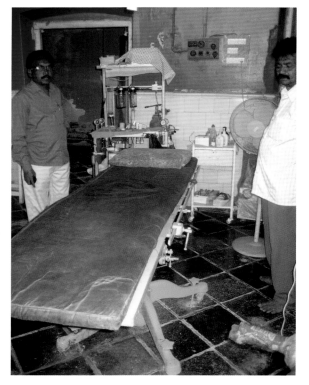

The operating theatre, 2012. (Author's collection)

the old EMO machine, which had been our 'workhorse' for provision of general anaesthesia had been replaced by a more contemporary machine for modern gas anaesthesia. The most depressing of all was that none of the equipment looked as if it had been used in a very long time.

'So how many surgical cases are you doing each month?' I asked gently.

'Much fewer than when you were here. Probably less than twenty cases a month and almost no majors. We do some minor gynaecological procedures, hernia repairs and a few appendicectomies.'

The operating book (which contains the record of the procedures performed each day), a weighty tome, was lying on a shelf inside theatre. I counted the cases in January 2012 and indeed there were less than twenty. Augustine told me that there was no longer a resident surgeon or a paediatrician. There was now only one physician, although a second came from time to time from the Christian Medical College in Vellore. He told me that some years ago they had built an intensive care unit but that this had never become operational. He was enthusiastic about the new Eye Theatre which was working every day under the direction of a full-time ophthalmic surgeon. This was clearly a very sensible move. People are living longer, cataracts are very common as we get older and surgical treatment can be easily performed under local anaesthesia.

'We have invested in a desktop auto-analyser for measuring blood chemistry [such as liver and kidney function] and a cell counter for measuring the blood count including haemoglobin', he interjected enthusiastically.

'But can your patients afford to pay for these blood tests?' I asked.

'We think so, although we haven't had the machines long enough to really know whether it will be a way for us to generate significant additional income. Some patients already have blood and other tests done in the bazaar, and then come back here for their clinic appointment and treatment.'

'I guess you must be struggling with some major financial problems?' I was beginning to sense that he was starting to realise that I had spotted the difference between then and now.

'Yes, it is very challenging. But we still do very good work for poor people and I have no doubt that God will continue to make sure that we have sufficient to continue our service.'

'You still see many outpatients, I guess?'

'Yes, we do; anything from 100 to 200 patients a day'.

I thought to myself that we would see that number of children in a morning back in the good old days. And that didn't include the adults who attended medical and surgical outpatients.

We walked close to the Eye Theatre and I was keen to see how the service ran, but for some reason the ophthalmic surgeon was absent that day and there were no patients in the waiting or the recovery areas.

'We do get some money from the government which pays for anti-tuberculosis chemotherapy and vaccinations such as tetanus. And we still carry out tubal ligations under local anaesthesia.'

'What are the main medical conditions that you are dealing with on a day-to-day basis?' I was struggling to find out what services the hospital was now providing in addition to cataract surgery.

'The main medical problems are patients with fever and respiratory symptoms. Malaria is sadly still rampant from July to December and tragically we still see cerebral malaria. You may have seen neonatal tetanus and tuberculous meningitis in children but thank God these terrible conditions seem to have disappeared.' He was becoming defensive under interrogation.

I thought to myself, yes probably because the tradition of applying a cow dung poultice to the infant's umbilicus has at last ceased.

We continued our tour through the hospital precincts. I was introduced to some of the nurses and technicians but there were no other doctors around on that day. The hospital chapel looked very much as it did in my day and was full of nurses who were having some sort of meeting, possibly a Bible class.

Sister Bhagyamma David with the author, 2012. (Author's collection)

'You must be hungry by now. Come let us take some tea with Sister Bhagyamma David. Maybe you remember her?'

This remarkable woman was working in the hospital when I came in 1969, had 'retired' but continued to work full-time. She seemed to be the rock on which the hospital was built and somehow radiated hope for the future. She talked about her nursing education projects in the community and of the importance of responding to change. It was difficult during this short visit to see much evidence of proactive change. The only change that I could see was that enforced by what seemed to be a decline in external funding and a serious lack of patient demand. It became increasingly apparent that the world outside Campbell Hospital had moved on. Standards of healthcare in the local government hospital had improved substantially, whereas forty years ago Campbell Hospital was the only medical facility that offered a range of services including operative surgery in a 80 km radius. Living standards had also improved and many people even on modest incomes could afford to consult with the growing number of private practitioners in the town. This seemed to be increasingly like a perfect car crash: massive external change in healthcare provision and personal circumstances and a previously wonderful hospital which had failed to adapt to the new environment, compounded by dwindling financial support as an independent missionary hospital.

SAM AND SUSEELA

Dr Augustine appeared to be increasingly uncomfortable by these discussions and suggested we talk more in private over dinner later that evening. As we finished our tea and sponge cake I asked him about Dr Arthur Samuel. He had indeed gone on to train as a paediatrician at CMC Vellore and then returned to Campbell Hospital for several years. Sadly, he had left the hospital and was now working in town in private practice. He had married Suseela and had two boys, now around thirty years of age. I asked if there was any chance that I could meet him again, either this evening or tomorrow morning? Someone made a phone call and within what felt like a few minutes I was being driven to his clinic in the centre of town. He had moved away from the hospital, but not far.

The building was located centrally on a main street, sandwiched between a shop and some other commercial premises and had a deceivingly small entrance to what eventually was revealed as a much larger building that extended way back from the road. There was no formal clinic reception desk, but I walked in and immediately saw a door over which there was a name that I recognised, 'Dr Arthur Samuel'. The door was open, which allowed me to see a simple desk and an examination couch. I penetrated further along the corridor and found another room with a name above the door, this time it was Dr Suseela Samuel. She was sitting at a desk writing a prescription or completing a patient's notes after a consultation; she looked up and transiently acknowledged my presence at the door. She seemed bemused for a moment but soon returned to the task at hand. I walked back along the corridor and there standing alone in the main entrance hall was Sam. He looked lost. Lost and unconnected. Eventually he turned as if to walk back into his office but saw me standing between him and the door. His face remained expressionless and he clearly did not recognise me. I went forward to greet him; to shake his hand. At first, he appeared to have no recollection of the 'Apollo 11 experience' we celebrated on his roof and the ward rounds and clinics that we had done together; but then slowly he made the connections. I do not think he remembered our weekend in Kurnool. Let's say he was non-committal, neither denying nor confirming. Nor did he confirm that Suseela, his wife and colleague in the clinic, was the young woman that I met all those years ago.

'Let me take you for a drink to celebrate.'

He took me by the hand just as he would do in the past and led me across an extremely busy street with two- and four-wheeled vehicles flying at us in both directions. He seemed oblivious to the danger. Once across we moved into a residential precinct and were engulfed by a wall of sound which was emanating from a movie house showing *The Businessman*. A massive poster in glorious technicolour, advertising the incredibly attractive lead actor and superstar, was splashed across a towering billboard. It certainly had all the trappings of a blockbuster. I found out later that this was in fact a Telugu movie made in Tollywood.

The almost unbearable sound drove us quickly on through a narrow passage, eventually arriving at the entrance of a small hut with its door just open. The owner must have seen us coming because within seconds a functionary had brought out two white plastic chairs and placed them on what can only be described as a rather primitive veranda.

'You want brandy or whisky?' Sam seemed agitated and distracted.

'A beer please. A small Kingfisher,' I said. He looked slightly disapproving, perhaps disappointed, but acquiesced. His glass arrived containing a generous dose of amber fluid: it could have been whisky or brandy. I was offered a bottle of Kingfisher or another bottle which I took to be a more expensive premium beer. I took the Kingfisher and asked for a glass. A young boy of about twelve years then arrived with a plastic bag full of chilled water and added some of it to Sam's glass. Sam was clearly a regular and valued customer; they knew just *what* he liked and *how* he liked it. Brandy or whisky disappeared quickly before I had finished a small glass of beer. I could see he was angling for another but before he could summon the waiter, another young man arrived on the scene from the direction of the street. Sam introduced me to his son. He barely acknowledged me but stood with arms folded across his chest, glowering at his father. When it looked as if he might be about to order another brandy he looked at him sternly, shaking his head. I still had some beer left in the bottle and Sam was pleased to tidy it up before we were led back across the street to his clinic. I had an overwhelming feeling that the events that I had just witnessed were everyday occurrences.

As we walked back towards the clinic we overtook a round-faced, chubby man speaking animatedly on a mobile phone. Sam interrupted him so that he could introduce me to the owner of the Picture House. Then again our lives were in peril as we crossed the street, dodging between cars, vans, auto-ricks, bicycles and other mobile weapons. With some pride but with a dose of disinterest, he walked me around the clinic. It did not look very different from Campbell Hospital; facilities were very basic and although clean, it was untidy. An extraordinary contrast to the modern private hospitals in Mumbai, New Delhi, Chennai and Bangalore that I had visited in recent years. I followed him back into his office where he was greeted by a couple of worried parents with an eight-week-old baby who had been waiting for a consultation. He calmly took his place behind the desk and picked up his stethoscope; he sat the parents down on two chairs on the opposite side of the desk and asked them to describe the problem. They spoke in Telegu; any words that I had acquired my first visit had long gone.

Dr Arthur Samuel in his clinic, 2012. (Author's collection)

'The baby cries all the time,' he explained. 'And they are worried that the protuberant umbilicus is the cause.'

He smiled so lovingly at the baby while he prodded and poked the soft, floppy umbilicus. The baby was silent and appeared unperturbed.

'She only has eyes for her mother – see?'

The baby ignored Sam's eyes and his prodding and just looked up at the young mother who was probably still in her mid-teens.

'This is a healthy baby,' he said. 'Mind you, if the umbilicus is not closed by six weeks there could be a problem with herniation in the future.'

He said some more reassuring words and I think he also mentioned the possibility of an operation. However, they just smiled, gave their thanks and departed. No money changed hands and there was no prescription.

'The trouble is the parents get anxious, then the grandparents increase the anxiety and they end up coming to see me.' He smiled at me, then turned away and almost laughed.

'Is the baby's weight okay for her age?' I asked.

He thought for a moment, then called them back from the corridor and got the mother to place the baby without its shawl on the scales. They were extremely rickety, and I did wonder about their accuracy. He pulled a torch from the drawer of his desk and shone light on the oscillating needle beneath the pan on which the baby lay.

'Fine!' he said with a smile. 'Fine for an Indian baby!' This time he really chuckled.

It was wonderful to see him again. He walked me down the corridor to Suseela's office to introduce me. I had another go at reviving memories of the Kurnool weekend, but she did not recall the visit either. She was a charming, intelligent and well-spoken woman who radiated immense respect for her husband and fellow professional. We shook hands and Sam led me out into the small dusty courtyard in front of the hospital.

'It's been good to see you after all these years.' I held his hand for longer than I would normally do at home and looked him straight in the eyes.

'Yes.' he said. 'Yes, it has.'

I put my arms around him and gave him an embrace. He took my hand again, just as he had done all those years ago in the hospital compound and out in the bazaar, and this time was slow to let it go. We were no longer the young men of great expectations; both getting older and thinking about the end. Two very different lives, in very different places – but a sort of bond survived.

I said I would give more notice when I made another visit. I took a page from his prescription pad which had his name, address and telephone number in Telugu. He did not have a business card in English. My driver translated for me and I wrote it out on the prescription sheet where he would normally have written the name of a drug and the dosage regimen. Was this my prescription for the future? He stood for a moment and watched our car make its way out into the advancing traffic. He turned after a last wave and disappeared back into the gloomy corridor that led to his office. Will I see him again? I really do not know. I might. I might just do that.

Within a few minutes we were back at the hospital where Augustine was waiting to show me where I was to sleep. Initially he took me to a room in one of the staff houses which seemed to be currently unoccupied. It had only a very primitive bed without a mosquito net and no ceiling fan. There was a basin in the corner of the room with a single cold tap that did not work, and I was puzzled as to where the toilet facilities might be. I was most uncomfortable about the accommodation on offer and thought quickly of a reason that would not offend. I said that I did not feel safe sleeping without a mosquito net, particularly because I was not taking antimalarial prophylaxis as this was such a short visit. He rapidly realised that this was not going to be adequate and quickly said that I must use the guest room in the superintendent's house. I was delighted and even more overjoyed when I found that the superintendent's house was now what was the Cutting's house, the very same building where I had spent several months during my first visit.

The light was fading rapidly. As we walked across from the hospital to the stone bungalow in which I had stayed during my first visit in 1969, it became clear that the compound itself was also seriously neglected and no longer had the look of a well-kept garden that it had all those years ago. There were many random weeds and overgrown bushes and I could just see in the twilight a group of wild pigs snuffling in some piles of rubbish behind the house. I enquired as to whether there were any snakes in the compound, but I was reassured that this was still a rare occurrence.

'And what about scorpions? I seem to remember they were quite frequent visitors to my bathroom!'

'Yes, of course. But they are normal. Just remember to turn the light on and look carefully, before you walk into your room'. He smiled at me. He had reiterated the advice I'd been given during my first visit.

We entered the house not through the main door as we always used to, but through a side entrance which necessitated us walking through the kitchen before entering the main house. I could think of no obvious reason why they should have changed the main route into the house. He showed me into the guest bedroom which had its own small bathroom, a ceiling fan and a bed with a mosquito net.

'Perfect. Thank you so much.' I said with a huge sense of relief knowing I was sleeping in a house with others.

'Can I see my old room? I seem to remember it came off the main living and dining room.'

'Yes, come over here.' He pushed open the double doors and there was my room, totally unchanged except that it no longer contained a bed and now seemed to be being used as a storeroom. It still had the saloon style doors into the bathroom through which I could see that the bathing area had received some attention over the years. The low wall which defined the bathing area had now been replaced by a tiled relatively high walled tank.

We walked back to my bedroom and I looked longingly at the bed. It had been a long day and a relatively early start.

'Take a bath and then we will have dinner.'

'What about Afzal, my driver? Does he have somewhere to stay; maybe he could join us for dinner?'

'I will make sure he has a bed and of course he must eat with us.'

I was tired and could easily have gone to sleep there and then, knowing that I had a long journey back to Chennai Airport in the morning. However, that would have been the wrong thing to do and a huge missed opportunity for there was still much to talk about over dinner together.

We sat at quite a large table, probably the same one that had been there for decades. A variety of vegetarian foods had already been placed on the table but were covered awaiting our arrival. Before revealing the contents of the dishes, Augustine proceeded to deliver a long *ad libitum* grace which must have lasted about five minutes and demonstrated his deep religious beliefs and commitment to a life of duty and service. It transpired that two of his relatives had been treated at the hospital and his decision to make a commitment to work there at an extremely low salary was his opportunity to give something back.

Once the grace was over he lifted the aluminium covers from the food bowls to reveal curried eggs, cauliflower, potato, masala and a pile of very oily chapattis. During the meal, I learnt much more about the family circumstances. We were joined by his wife who was also a doctor and the daughter of superintendent, Dr Helen. She was a delightful person, calm and capable. They had two daughters, a three-year-old and an eight-week-old infant both of whom were living with them in Jammy. Apparently, the plan was that she would go away for two to three years to train as a gynaecologist and the children would be looked after by Augustine's parents. I thought that sounded quite challenging, but it is not unusual in India for professionals to live apart for quite long periods during training and the establishment of their careers. She radiated the same unbending commitment to the service of the poor in the name of God in a hospital with a religious foundation. It was difficult to establish exactly when Dr Helen took over as Superintendent, but I suspect it was in the early 1990s. She had married a retired tennis coach from Hyderabad, I would guess in the 1970s, from the ageing black and white photograph of the two on their wedding day which hung on the wall in her bedroom.

Apparently, he lived most of the week in Hyderabad but would travel by motorcycle to Jammalamadugu (some 350 km) at the weekends. On one tragic day, he had a road traffic accident and died; it was at this point that she took over as superintendent. Augustine described her as 'getting old' (probably now in her sixties) and he intimated, although not said explicitly, that she had lost the drive to effect change. She was also struggling with her own health problems.

As the evening went on I learned more about the challenges that were facing Campbell Hospital. Mission hospitals were the subject of regular government inspections. They were given an extremely robust examination and were regarded as a special target in need of eradication. Forty or fifty years ago these hospitals fulfilled an extremely important function and in some areas completely superseded anything on offer by the Indian government. However, healthcare had moved on and Campbell Hospital had been left behind. It seemed to me that failing hospitals outside the system were an embarrassment, such that the government might even pay to make them go away. The other main enemy, so I was told, was 'the Bishop'. Ultimately, he had total power over the hospital and apparently exercised this by not releasing significant funds that have been donated specifically for the use of the hospital. Augustine suggested that on occasions it might be necessary to 'encourage' the bishop to release the funds. He acknowledged that the hospital compound was in a poor state but said that they had to seek permission from the bishop to clean it up. This indeed sounded that it was a very difficult, or even an impossible environment in which to operate. Even back in 1969 I recall conversations with William about the increasing vulnerability of the expatriate missionary community.

We talked about his ideas for the future. He saw a role for himself as superintendent at some point; perhaps with his wife beside him as senior colleague and gynaecologist. I asked him how he saw the future and what would be his strategy to get the hospital back on its feet. He still felt that the new technology, such as the auto-analysers could generate valuable income, but he also wanted to offer ultrasound examinations and at some to introduce endoscopy. What I felt he had not done, was to look objectively as to what his patients wanted, needed and, realistically, what they would or could pay for. The hospital had fallen too far behind to be able to offer twenty-first-century surgical services and the cost of setting up core modern medical investigative services would be prohibitive. There was, I thought, a future if the hospital focused primarily on general practice and primary care. There was a problem, however, as I suspect a change of this magnitude would put the nursing school in jeopardy because of the inability to offer a broad clinical training experience to student nurses. I am afraid that I left the dining table in a most despondent mood, partly because of what I judged to be the hospital's relentless decline but also because of a complete lack of strategic thinking about the future. Perhaps worst of all was that both the Indian Government and the bishop, representing the hospital's main sponsor and governor, the Church of South India, were totally disengaged and disinterested in the future of the hospital. An unadulterated catastrophe!

Despite our long and engaged discussion, I was asleep by about 9.30pm and already on the road heading towards Chennai soon after 6.00am. I was taking no chances this time. The journey passed uneventfully and after a rapid turnaround in the hotel, I returned to the airport, and boarded my Jet Airways flight to New Delhi and by about 8.30pm was having dinner with colleagues in the Taj Hotel. The following day I had meetings with the British Council and hosted an event for University of Sussex alumni to celebrate our fiftieth anniversary. The following day I travelled on to Mumbai for more meetings and a delightful dinner at the home of an Indian alumnus and his family.

During those days that followed, I agonised about the predicament of this once successful mission hospital, which in the early days had been all that was on offer in terms of rural healthcare, to what can only now be called an anachronism. An embarrassment to a modern Indian Government and maybe even a barrier to progress. Perhaps also, it might be viewed an unwanted vestigial remnant of British India that was now surplus to requirements, but how do you tell that story to altruistic young doctors who want to serve the poor and their God and in some way pay back the goodwill that they themselves have witnessed and received?

From the 1990s onwards, the Indian economy finally took off on a grand scale due both to the massive increase in growth of the indigenous software industry initially in Bangalore and the opening of the economy to foreign investments. Notable multinationals who came to join the party were Ford, Honda, Samsung, Pepsi and Coca-Cola, Philips, Microsoft and General Electric.

The BJP would remain in power until they were finally defeated by the United Progressive alliance (UPA) in 2004. Sonia Gandhi (Rajiv's Italian widow) was offered the role of Prime Minister but declined; she had always been against Rajiv's involvement in politics but had been persuaded to take over as Congress Party President in 1998. Her place was taken by Manmohan Singh who had been in waiting for nearly ten years. UPA was re-elected again in 2009 and Manmohan Singh continued as Prime Minister. However, in the lead up to the Sixteenth Lok Sabha (2014–19), the UPA was accused of corruption and the BJP was successful in achieving an outright majority, the first time in Indian Parliamentary history since 1984. Narendra Modi was installed as Prime Minister. Modi came in as a 'development visionary' and a leader who would drive out corruption from the top. His de-monetization programme has been judged by many as having been a charade, he has failed to create the jobs badly needed by India's young population, but many business leaders support him. His dislike of 'minorities' driven by his Hindu-Nationalist background has aggravated muslim-Hindu relations. Nevertheless, economically India has moved forward.

Despite this progress, many Indians continue to live below the poverty line (estimated to be between 15 to 35 per cent of the population), and agricultural growth has been slow due to a range of issues, including inadequate irrigation. The failing agro-economy had resulted in an increasing tendency for farmers to despair and commit suicide, usually by ingesting pesticide but hanging or electrocution are other alternatives. Infant mortality is still at an unacceptable level despite having decreased during the last twenty to thirty years; literacy, however, increased during the period of economic growth but not universally across all states.

The death rate has decreased, partly due to improved medical facilities, and the nation's average life expectancy has increased from thirty-two years in 1947 to sixty-eight years in 2014. However, the economic reforms of the 1990s coincided with a tremendous rise in population – in the census from 1991 to 2011 the escalation was from 888.5 million to 1.2 billion. In his book, *Social Development in India*, Prof. Ramesh Chandra states, 'India currently faces 33 births a minute, 2,000 an hour, 48,000 a day, which calculates to nearly 12 million a year.'

Overall it is a good story, but future Indian leaders and their Governments will still have plenty of work to do. The headline figures of success probably fail to paint the more detailed picture of the depth and breadth of the impact of India's economic growth and its penetration into the lives of the many millions of Indians still trapped in the traditional village setting and the growing numbers that have flooded into the peri-urban shanty developments of all its major cities.

GAZING BACK AT THE HORIZON

*Where there is creation there is progress. Where there is no creation
there is no progress: know the nature of creation.*

*Where there is joy there is creation. Where there is no joy there is
no creation: know the nature of joy.*

7. 16-25 Chandogya Upanishad

The past is a foreign country: they do things differently there.

L.P. Hartley, *The Go-Between*, 1953

Although it is impossible to think and speak about India without including a socio-political dimension, it
has not been a central theme of this collection of thoughts so far, although I have added a brief political
time-line which has run along throughout the narrative at the end of each part. However, as the pieces of
this jigsaw have come together, I discovered gaps that needed to be filled. Without attempting to create
some bridges across time, there would be intellectual voids that would trivialise the importance of major
national and global developments that have had such profound relevance to the evolution of this great
nation and its emergence as the world's largest democracy. I learnt about many of these vital elements
late in my journey but have relished their discovery because they have helped me understand, but not
always fully explain, the events that have made India, Pakistan and Bangladesh what they are today.

The relevance of democracy to life in the twenty-first century has never been more actively discussed.
Commentators have noted the speed with which the non- or quasi-democratic emerging economies
can make political and financial decisions. China is now often paired with India in the 'compare and
contrast' debate. Democracy in India, at least superficially, appears to be losing out to the faster moving,
less constrained autocratic administration of China. Economic growth and life expectancy are greater
in China and it is unlikely to be superseded by other emerging nations in the coming decade. India is
considered by some commentators to be behind China in the advancement and accessibility to healthcare
and education. India still struggles with the desired level of internal corporate regulation and the extent
to which external joint ventures can be part of its economic growth strategy. India, for example, has the
legislation on the shelf, ready to allow foreign universities to open campuses to help meet the demands

for the expansion of higher education but is still agonising politically as to whether it is the right thing to do. By converse, the UK has welcomed the Tata Empire, which has contributed in a major way to the reinvigoration of our steel and motor vehicle industry. Similarly, there seems to be little concern about encouraging China to be key investor in the UK's telecommunications and flagging nuclear power industry.

Whether India's reticence to work closely with external parties to hasten its development is really a consequence of being a timid democracy or just a cultural caution to engage with outsiders (a consequence perhaps of its experience of imperialism) remains to be seen. China, on the other hand, seems to be in the driving seat and in full control of its economic and financial destiny, despite the slowing of growth and emerging economic uncertainties in recent years. What must be acknowledged however, is that the imperial century running up to Independence and more than seventy years of democratic independence, have not been without event for India and are worth a comment in these last reflective moments.

There have been many comprehensive political histories of India across the twentieth and twenty-first centuries but there a few critical events in a 400-year timeline that seem to me to be pivotal in understanding the evolution of this great nation. I became interested in fictional accounts of these events to understand the human impact of some of the key nodal points in history which can lose their poignancy in bland factual historical accounts; and there may be more than one version of the record, depending on an individual's or a nation's view of the outcome.

Historical fiction went into decline towards the end of the nineteenth century and only re-found its voice in the 1960s, perhaps as the force of post-modernism was running out of steam. The separation of literature and history was challenged, with suggestions that they have more in common than the elements that separate them. India has captured the British imagination in a unique and incomparable way. This is true for each of the dominant periods during the British presence in India and has continued since Independence. During the first ten years of the Booker prize, four of the winners went to authors who set their stories in India spanning nineteenth and twentieth centuries. Novels and screenplays have continued to flow from the pens of Indian and British writers, with no sign that this creative force is coming to an end. Films and television dramas have attracted large audiences in the UK and beyond during the seventy years following Independence. There is no comparator that has had such a compelling influence on British literary and cultural life. What is evident, however, is that great writers that have entered this space from outside and from within the subcontinent, have gone way beyond the traditional limits of the historical novel, venturing into the deeper sensitivities of politics, justice, human rights, cross-cultural inter-personal relationships and magical realism. I have considered some of the complex interfaces between history and literature looking back at four broad epochs of the Anglo-Indian relationship spanning more than 400 years: (i) Independence and partition and the seventy years that followed, (ii) the journey towards Gandhi's *swaraj* (self or home rule), including defining events such as the Amritsar massacre, (iii) the period which Kipling called the 'Great Game' when Queen Victoria's empire was at its peak, and (iv) the establishment and growth of the East India Company until its nationalisation in 1858, providing the economic driving force which sustained the British presence in India.

L.P. Hartley (*The Go-Between*, 1953) and Sir Walter Scott (*Waverley*, 1814) have argued that the ideal time to produce fictional accounts of historical events is forty to sixty years after it has occurred; not too close for the tale to be acceptable to the human imagination but sufficient to provide objective distancing. However, close enough to the historic occasion to still be within the lifetime and memory of living people as a way of testing validity.

INDEPENDENCE AND PARTITION: THE REINVENTION OF INDIA

> *The summer of 1947 was not like other Indian summers. Even the weather had a different feel in India that year. It was hotter than usual, and drier and dustier.*

> Khushwant Singh, *Train to Pakistan*, 1956.

The Indian Independence Act 1947 received royal assent on 18 July 1947. Indian independence came into being on 15 August that year, accompanied simultaneously with the creation of a new state, Pakistan (subdivided into West and East sectors), the so-called partition of India.

The British were finally forced to retreat to their 'green and pleasant land' and this 'Jewel in the Crown' re-emerged as a free, unfettered nation. However, the British left their mark. Sir Cyril Radcliffe QC (later in 1949 to become a life peer, Baron Radcliffe of Werneth and in 1962 a hereditary Peer as Viscount Radcliffe of Hampton Lucy) was appointed Chair of the so-called 'Boundary Committees', despite never having been to India; after just five weeks of deliberation and some wider consultation, his committee drew lines on a map of the subcontinent that divided the nation into two self-governing countries, India and Pakistan, aiming to solve once and for all the Hindu-Muslim problem. Did it hell!

Partition displaced ten to twelve million people along religious lines and initiated bitter conflicts, resulting in the deaths of at least several hundred thousand, but some estimates suggest that it could have been as high as one to two million.

Over sixty years after the event, Howard Brenton's new play, *Drawing the Line*, was performed at Hampstead Theatre in 2013. The drama takes place during those summer weeks of 1947 and explores Clement Attlee's resolve to right the social wrongs and restore India to an independent nation, Radcliffe's inexperience and ultimate regrets about his final conclusions, and, unnecessarily in my view, exposes and to some extent trivialises the relationship between Nehru and Edwina Mountbatten. In the closing scene Nehru and Jinnah make peaceful prophecies in front of Gandhi while Radcliffe and his wife Antonia have the final words:

Antonia: Darling, it's coming on to rain, what are you doing?

Radcliffe: Burning it all, the papers, all the maps …

Antonia: Cyril, my dear, it's settled, it's done.

Radcliffe: You think so?

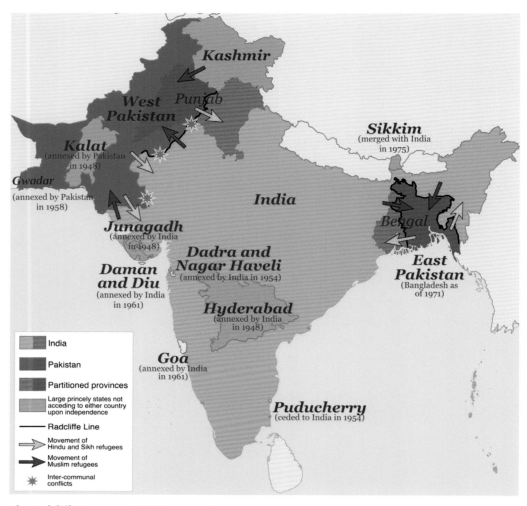

The Radcliffe Line, 1947. (WikiCommons)

What is even worse is that it was not a durable result. India and Pakistan have continued to engage in armed conflict across their joint northwest border, they continue to fight over the ownership of Kashmir (currently mainly in India but a predominately Muslim area) and there was a further bloody conflict in former East Pakistan (formed initially from the division of Bengal) to create an independent Bangladesh in 1971. Both India and Pakistan have a substantial nuclear capability but for the present seem content to maintain it as a deterrent, using only conventional weapons to create and respond to border aggravations.

The story behind whether the subcontinent of India should have been divided along religious lines is a long and tortuous journey. Once the British had finally come to terms with the idea that India would eventually emerge as an independent nation, probably as far back as the end of World War I, the desired and expected outcome was considered by the majority to be a united India. Attlee, the Labour Prime Minister who finally oversaw the creation of an independent India, and who had announced soon after taking over from Churchill as Prime Minister in 1945 that India would be free at the latest by July 1948, certainly believed that this would be the ideal solution.

However, as early as 1944 during the Simla Conference, Muhammad Ali Jinnah, President of the Muslim League, had suggested that for Muslims the most desirable outcome would be a separate independent Muslim state, and effectively torpedoed any further progress at the conference at which Nehru and Gandhi were important contributors. The proposal for an independent Muslim state had been made more than ten years earlier by Choudhry Rahmat Ali, a Muslim activist and a student in Cambridge who published a pamphlet in 1933, 'Now or never; Are we to live or perish for ever?': 'At this solemn hour in the history of India, when British and Indian statesmen are laying the foundations of a federal constitution for that land, we address this appeal to you, in the name of our common heritage, on behalf of our *thirty million Muslim brethren* who live in Pakistan – by which we mean the "five northern units of India", Viz: Punjab, North-West Frontier Province (Afghan province), Kashmir, Sindh and Baluchistan.' The neologism, Pakistan, also means in Urdu and Persian, land of the pure.

As discussions progressed during the next three years, Jinnah did agree to a 'united India' solution, providing it was dependent on a strong regional government. Nehru rejected this proposal as he was a 'centralist' and realised that such a move would put his own power base, as the majority Hindu leader, at risk. The current viceroy, Field Marshal Archibald Wavell, did not hold the confidence of the Indian leadership and following Attlee's announcement of closure on the independence debate by summer 1948, then drafted in Lord Louis Mountbatten, Queen Victoria's grandson, to find an early resolution. Mountbatten, a pragmatist, could see that by then Jinnah was absolutely determined to lead a new Muslim state, Pakistan, and that this would be acceptable to Nehru who would be the senior partner and rule the majority of the subcontinent, including much of the most prosperous regions.

As discussions continued and new information came to light, it had become clearer that this would be not a bad solution for the British. Mountbatten was able to work to an even tighter deadline (summer 1947) than that originally set by Attlee, allowing the British to exit from what was rapidly becoming a nation racked by riots driven by religious unrest. At the same time, during the run-up to independence he built a relationship with Jinnah to ensure that the British continued to have a military foothold in the region to ward off the political aspirations of the Soviet Union. There was concern that it was positioning itself to step in once the British had left and to build on their territorial and political gains at the end of World War II. Churchill, in particular, anticipated the 'Cold War' and immediately before partition began to build a discreet, personal relationship with Jinnah.

This was not the first time that territorial lines had been drawn on a map in a hurry by amateurs. After World War I, the allies supervised the break-up of the Ottoman Empire largely to ensure protection of their own political and economic interests; like the partition of India, this territorial realignment also resulted in mass movements of Turks and Greeks back to their historic regions.

Britain was already in Basra, Baghdad and subsequently Mosul, and with the authority of the League of Nations behind them, Mandatory Iraq was created under the guidance of Winston Churchill, recently appointed as Secretary of State for the Colonies; he failed to fully understand the consequences of drawing straight lines on the map to create a new state of Iraq by confining divergent groups within these new territorial borders. Another failure was to realise the consequences of placing Faisal, a Sunni on the throne of a kingdom that had a very significant Shia majority. Mark Sykes and François Picot carved up the Middle East between Britain and France in 1916 (The Sykes-Picot agreement) which, combined with the Balfour Declaration of 1917, created the Palestine-Israel debacle which is still with us today. The model of placing a 'Britain-friendly' king in place to rule under British sponsorship was repeated with Ibn Saud in the Arabian Peninsula and Abdullah (King Hussein's son) as King of Trans-Jordan.

There is a painful story even closer to home in the UK, which Spike Milligan, writer and humourist who was born in India in 1918, describes in his novel, *Puckoon* (1963) an innovative, collaborative approach to creating a new national border to divide a nation. The action takes place in an upstairs room of the Duke of Wellington Hotel, 'Ireland' where a group of interested individuals were trying to draw the line between north and south. Mr Ferguson says, 'May I make a suggestion? We only have this bit here to partition and the pubs close in an hour. Why not let's all put one hand on the red pencil and draw a line that falls naturally and peacefully into place?' The suggestion was approved unanimously, and everyone placed a hand on the pencil and pulled it slowly across the map. Voices become raised!

'Steady, someone's pulling to the benefit of Ulster.'

'Lies, all lies.'

'Who gave that jerk?'

'Ah! I felt that.'

'Swine!'

'Finally, the pencil reached its destination. Faces broke into relieved smiles, and a series of rapid unplanned handshakes ensued.' The line, however, neatly bisected the town of Puckoon.

At one level, the transition to independence and partition was a disaster. Even during the bloody Calcutta riots the year before when Muslims and Hindus were slaughtering each other in the streets, the British had already appeared to have lost interest and were seriously constrained financially because of the scale of the war debt; Viceroy Wavell's request for additional military support to control the violent conflict did not materialise. This was partly due to lack of money but also because of Attlee's reluctance to run immediately to military solutions rather than negotiation. Criticism continues that the British-led military did too little, too late, resulting in many deaths. The scale on which Muslims, Hindus and Sikhs moved across the newly created borders which delineated the new Muslim state of Pakistan and the Hindu and Sikh areas in the new India was extraordinary and created such desperate instability that it triggered another round of slaughter. These devastating events have been documented by historians but perhaps even more poignantly captured by novelists and filmmakers.

Khushwant Singh's 1956 novel, *Train to Pakistan*, says it all. This book was published less than a decade after partition when memories were still fresh and anger and resentment still dominated the relationships between Muslims, Hindus and Sikhs. The story is set in the fictional Punjabi border village, Mano Majra, where for centuries these diverse religious groups have lived together. Singh's account of the devastation of partition is told in fiction, as social history and through metaphor.

Within the first few hundred words of his story he tells us about an object in the village that unifies all religious groups. 'This is a three-foot slab of sandstone that stands upright under a kikar tree beside the pond. It is the local deity, the *deo* to which all the villagers – Hindu, Sikh, Muslim or pseudo-Christian – repair secretly whenever they are in special need of blessing.' Unification and re-unification are a theme that he drives through the narrative, seeking goodness and love during and after a period of intense hatred.

The rhythm of village life is dominated by the regular arrivals and departures of the daily trains; morning mail from Delhi to Lahore, the mid-morning passenger train from Delhi, the midday express, the evening passenger train from Lahore and the goods train. As the story unfolds, the trains emerge as a metaphor of disharmony as they become the vehicles of terror as Hindus and Sikhs escape to India in the East and Muslims move west to Pakistan. Tragedy of mass movement of estranged parts of a population is sadly not new; it was a major feature during the disassembly of the Ottoman Empire with Greeks (largely Christians) and Turks (Muslims) moving to safety in their countries of origin, and the transportation of Jews both within and outside Europe before, during and after World War II.

Armed robbery by the dacoits (so-called dacoity), resulting in the death of one of the only Hindus in Mano Majra, appears early in the plot, more as an example of background lawlessness in a rural outpost in the 'North-West Frontier', rather than religious fundamentalism.

Singh uses a love story between villagers, a young Muslim woman (Nooran) and a Sikh man (the rough rogue Juggut Singh) as another metaphor of hope for the future; a reminder that religious boundaries are not insurmountable, and that harmonious coexistence is not so difficult. A British-Indian friend of mine once said to me, 'Michael, you know that the future is brown, light brown!' He was anticipating a world in which relationships across national, ethnic, cultural and religious boundaries would increase and become the norm. Dark-skinned people mixing their genes with pale-skinned people would strengthen humanity and progressively move us towards a middle tone. It has been predicted that this will be a sizeable majority of the world's population by the end of this millennium.

This inter-racial metaphor has been widely used in literature and film. such as Forster's *A Passage to India* (Dr Aziz's relationship with the Englishwoman Adela Quested who alleged to have been sexually assaulted in the Malabar Caves), Scott's *The Jewel in the Crown* (the English educated Hari Kumar and Daphne Manners, who was raped in the Bibighar Gardens in fictional Mayapur, a relationship which ended badly for both) and most recently in the film, *Viceroy's House* directed by British Indian, Gurinder Chadha, whose Sikh relatives were among the 14 million Hindus, Sikhs and Muslims displaced during partition. Here the love story focuses on two of the viceroy's household; Jeet, a Hindu and Aalia, a Muslim. This widely used metaphor in fiction can be found in novels from other geographic locations such as in the central Asian story set in Baku in 1914, *Ali and Nino* by Kurban Said. Ali is a Muslim from Azerbaijan and Nino an Orthodox Christian from Georgia. Across the globe, inter-racial liaisons are on the rise but these love stories in fiction during periods of massive community disharmony help us find optimism in those otherwise grim moments of despair; hope has no borders.

Singh uses another device to persuade us that there are more similarities than differences between religious communities and uses it possibly as a motif to bring warring factions together. Early in the story a slim young man arrives in Mano Majra on the 10.30 slow passenger train from Delhi. We soon learn that he is educated, well-spoken and is called Iqbal. 'He did not have to say what Iqbal he was. He could be a Muslim, Iqbal Mohammed. He could be a Hindu, Iqbal Chand, or a Sikh, Iqbal Singh. It was one of the few names common to all three communities.'

Iqbal has its origins in Arabic-speaking countries where it means 'fortunate' or 'blessed'. It is a name that can also be given to girls. In Hindi, it means 'prosperity'. A name that crosses cultures, religions and even gender. Again, Singh leads us to celebrate equalisers, albeit symbolic rather than dividers. Whatever 'Iqbal' he is, he was welcomed by the Bhai to stay as a guest in the *gurdwara* (literally, the residence of the guru), but in practice the place of communal worship for Sikhs.

Trains arriving and leaving Mano Majra throughout the day give a dominant framework for daily life; trains punctuate the simple life of this sleepy border village. The tale moves slowly, inexorably forward until the horror contained in a train travelling to Pakistan becomes apparent. Singh resists the temptation to attribute blame to any party; 'Muslims said the Hindus had planned and started the killing. According to the Hindus, the Muslims were to blame. The fact is both sides killed. Both shot and stabbed and speared and clubbed. Both tortured. Both raped.' Although there is a sense in his writing that partition should never have been allowed to happen, the architects of partition are never mentioned and blame is not attributed.

Manohar Talegaonkar's, *A Bend in the Ganges* (1964) is replete with facts surrounding the process and outcomes of independence and offers graphic descriptions of the violence associated with partition. It expresses some anti-British sentiment and rails against the non-violence espoused by Gandhi. Talegaonkar explores ideas of nationalism and opens a debate around the justification for terrorist acts for the love of 'mother India' but mollifies this by confronting the dangers of fanaticism.

Azadi (Freedom), the story of a young woman caught up in the violence written by Chaman Nahal, (1975), still within thirty years of the event which took place when he was a college student in New Delhi. The central character is heavily based on the author's sister, Kartar Devi, who perished in the riots of 1947, which gives the author profound legitimacy to write this historical fiction.

Salman Rushdie explores the tragedy of partition in *Midnight's Children* (1980). Interestingly, he applies a light touch to the subject of Muslim-Hindu violence in August 1947, whereas earlier in the book, Saleem's grandfather, Aadam Aziz provides a detailed account of Brigadier R.E. Dyer's massacre of innocents in the walled compound, Jallianwala Bagh in Amritsar. He also reflects on the violent outbursts in Calcutta the year before; 'all the way from Calcutta, on foot,' he was saying, 'covered in ashes, as you see, Begum Sahiba, because of my shame of having been there for the Killing – last August you remember, Begum Sahiba, thousands knifed in four days of screaming....'

Richard Attenborough's film *Gandhi*, released in 1982, deals with partition and the consequent human relocations on a grand cinematographic scale. Thousands of people, many in family groups, carrying everything they own; their homes abandoned for the new arrivals. Then as two columns of migrants pass by each other, one Muslim the other Hindu, violence breaks out, blood is shed and lives are ended.

Attenborough leaves us in no doubt that this is a devastating tragedy on an unprecedented scale which can never be explained as a condition of war.

Paul Scott, in the last novel of the Raj Quartet, *A Division of the Spoils*, which covers the final two years of British rule in India, describes two symbolic violent episodes that took place in 1947. Colonel Merrick, a man utterly confident of his racial superiority, is strangled with his own sash, then mutilated with an axe and the symbol of Indian resistance drawn on the ground beside his dead body; the true cause of death was initially concealed, having been attributed to a 'riding accident'. At this late point in the regime, Scott permits the release of hatred and aggression. Many of the British are leaving Mirat, a fictional princely state within a fictional Punjab-like province and making their way by train to Delhi. Ahmed Kasim, the playboy son of a prominent politician Mohammed Ali Kasim and secretary to the Nawab of Mirat, has arranged to travel with them. During the journey, the train is forced to stop because a cow has been tethered to the tracks. Rapidly it becomes evident that an attack on the train and its occupants is imminent; the Hindu assailants demand that Kasim reveals himself. He promptly and honourably steps forward and is immediately killed, as are all other Muslims on that train. These two fictional episodes capture the mood of hatred and anger that for those weeks after partition just bubbled over uncontrollably. These were not just historical facts and figures but 'real people' who were lost in the struggle.

Despite the proximity of Ceylon to the Indian Peninsula (about 80 km), it had for many centuries been an independent nation. In the eighteenth century it was colonised by the Portuguese and then the Dutch, before coming under British administration as a British Crown Colony in 1802. Independence finally came in 1948 and its name was changed to Sri Lanka in 1972 when it became a republic within the Commonwealth. Although there was no process equivalent to the partition of India, the achievement of peaceful and democratic independence was not an easy journey; this might have been better anticipated when the British departed. In the same way that India had Hindus, Sikhs and Muslims living together, particularly in the north, Ceylon also had three national groups: the Sinhalese (largely Buddhist), Ceylon Tamils (Hindus and long-standing immigrants from South India) and more than one million Indian Tamils who were introduced into the island to support the country's agriculture. Under the British, Ceylon had become the world's largest producer of tea. Soon after Independence the new government decided to remove many of the rights of Indian Tamils, including Ceylonese nationality. This resulted in the development of a powerful group of activists, the Tamil Tigers, who until 2009 fought for an independent Tamil state in the north of the island. This tragedy has been recounted in many forms but most recently in the debut novel by Anuk Arudpragasam, *The Story of a Brief Marriage* (2016) which has, as a backdrop, the massive suffering of thousands of homeless, encamped refugees as the Sri Lankan army launches a final major armed offensive from the land and the air to drive the Tamil activists into the sea, but at the same time places centre stage a transient relationship of two young people caught in this violent drama. Yet again tragic history is captured poignantly by the novelist.

MAHATMA GANDHI'S *SWARAJ*

The period between the two world wars framed the endgame for British India. Following the Indian mutiny and the incorporation of the East India Company, Victoria and her successive governments created a level of stability that enabled a period of peaceful coexistence. However, following World War I (in which incidentally more than one million Indian troops served overseas supporting the Allies and about 75,000 died), the mood on both sides began to change. Mahatma Gandhi had returned to India from South Africa in 1915, which for many marked a new beginning for India's final struggle for independence. He started work in Bihar and Gujarat, exploring inequalities and unfairness in employment conditions and setting local agricultural workers against their British landlords. At the same time, he worked tactically with the British to aid recruitment of servicemen for the war. Religious disputes between Hindus and Muslims were creating undesirable instability in British India and Gandhi worked tactically with both sides to try and gain a common understanding of what self-government, *Swaraj*, would mean to all Indians. He was getting old enemies, Hindus and Muslims and political opponents, to work against the common aggressor, the British. Gandhi's plan was for political decentralisation; he regarded 'the state' as a 'soulless machine' and wished to discard what he saw as corrupting administrative bureaucracies. He detested the increasing dependence of Indians on British-made cotton cloth and promoted home-spinning and weaving to produce Indian cloth (*khadi*). He raised the spirit of nationalism and created a movement which became unstoppable.

This was a time when cracks began to appear in the British administration at home, with reformers on one hand like Edwin Montagu, Secretary of State for India, 1917–22 (who went on a six-month, fact-finding mission to India with a ten-man delegation in October 1917) and diehard imperialists like Sir Michael O'Dwyer, a pugnacious fiery Irishman, then serving as Lieutenant Governor of the Punjab from 1912–19. These two clashed immediately they met; their approaches to India's future were totally opposed. O'Dwyer believed that India would never be fit for self-rule whereas Montagu had already entered the endgame and was seeking ways to achieve a responsible and peaceful transfer of power over a reasonable but finite period.

Indian leaders were fully aware of the diversity of views within the British Government and the tension was further enhanced when, in response to escalating civil unrest, the Government of India introduced the Anarchical and Revolutionary Crimes Act 1919 (known as the Rowlatt Act, after the British judge Sir Sidney Rowlatt who chaired the committee that developed the new legislation) in March of that year. This extended the emergency measures in the Defence of India Act 1915 by including preventive indefinite detention and incarceration without trial and judicial review; having been enacted during World War I because of concerns about a growing threat to the Government of India from revolutionary nationalist organisations. O'Dwyer supported this authoritarian approach, seeing it as the only way to teach India a lesson and to demonstrate once and for all who was in charge.

Meanwhile, Gandhi's approach to gaining independence for India was gaining momentum. He deplored the Rowlatt Acts and promoted a new philosophy to change the government's approach, namely 'soul force' or *satyagraha*. Essentially, this was peaceful civil disobedience; within days he had called for a national strike. Gandhi worked tirelessly for the next thirty years to find a peaceful resolution to achieving independence. R.K. Narayan, perhaps India's premier novelist writing in English (discovered and promoted by Graham Greene) captures the tone of Gandhi's remarkable approach in his pre-Independence novel, *Waiting for the Mahatma* (1955) set in his fictional South Indian town of Malgudi. Within a few pages we experience the sincerity and simplicity of Gandhi's way of challenging both the British occupation and rule of India (and his passion to restore home-spun cotton to India and dispense with imported cotton cloth from England) and the inequalities so deeply embedded within the Indian peoples exemplified by poverty and caste. He leads us in the company of Gandhi to a sweeper, Dalit ('untouchable') settlement as a metaphor to banish this centuries-old tradition. Siriam, the young protagonist, is drawn towards the Mahatma, not because of a desire to adopt his humanistic principle but because of a deep physical attraction to one of his young attractive female helpers.

Gandhi was fatally shot on the 30 January 1948, just six months after the re-birth of an independent India.

DYER'S DAY IN AMRITSAR

The Amritsar massacre changed the course of British rule in India for ever and laid the foundations for the path towards *swaraj*. A massacre of Indian civilian protesters took place in Jallianwala Bagh, a walled garden in the Sikh holy city of Amritsar in the Punjab (close to the Golden Temple) on Sunday 13 April 1919. There are many historical accounts of the events of that day and a variety of interpretations of the rights and wrongs of the actions of the British army officer Brigadier-General Reginald E. Dyer who authorised the killing (379) and wounding (1,500) of protesters (Muslims, Sikhs and Hindus), because they had contravened an order that there should be no public demonstrations. There are many accounts which have found their way into important fiction and films which contribute to our understanding of the disaster.

Rushdie, in *Midnight's Children* – which he has described as 'a love letter to India' – uses magical realism to expose the horror of the Amritsar massacre. He describes Dyer's arrival with his fifty men at the entrance to the alleyway which leads into Jallianwala Bagh: 'the waxed tips of his moustache are rigid with importance'. As Dyer gives the order to open fire, Dr Aadam Aziz, Saleem's grandfather, develops a tickle in his nose, 'he sneezes and falls forward, losing his balance, following his nose and thereby saving his life'. The contents of his doctor's bag fly into the air. 'He is scrabbling furiously at people's feet, trying to save his equipment before it is crushed. There is a noise like teeth chattering in winter and someone falls on him. Red stuff stains his shirt. There are screams now and sobs and the strange chattering continues. More and more people seem to have stumbled and fallen on top of my grandfather. He becomes afraid for his back. The clasp of his bag is digging into his chest, inflicting upon it a bruise so severe and mysterious that it will not fade until after his death, years later.... The chattering stops and is replaced by the noises of people and birds.'

'Brigadier Dyer's fifty men put down their machine-guns and go away. They have fired a total of one thousand, six hundred and fifty

Brigadier-General Dyer. (Alamy)

rounds into the unarmed crowd. Of these, one thousand five hundred and sixteen found their mark killing or wounding some person.'

When he got home his wife remarked, 'I see you have been spilling Mercurochrome again, clumsy...'

....'It's blood' he replied, and she fainted.

'Good shooting,' Dyer tells his men, 'we have done a jolly good thing.'

Attenborough's film, *Gandhi*, includes a sequence of the slaughter. He portrays Dyer, acting military commander for Amritsar, and an accompanying officer being driven, sitting bolt upright in the back of a comfortable army staff car at the front of the military column, which was led by an armoured vehicle bearing a machine-gun. The alley to the Bagh was too narrow to accommodate the armoured vehicle, so Dyer and fifty ethnic soldiers (it is uncertain as to whether they were specifically selected for the grisly task), armed with .303 Lee-Enfield bolt action rifles, left their vehicles and marched down the alley into the Bagh; they lined up in formation (some standing, others kneeling) and when the order was given, opened fire on the crowd of about 10,000 without warning. They reloaded and kept firing for about ten minutes until most of the ammunition was spent and the order to ceasefire was given.

What is the explanation for 'machine-guns' in Rushdie's fictional account and for rifles in Attenborough's film 'drama documentary'? A machine gun was present on the day but was outside the Bagh mounted on the armoured car. Was this a mistake or merely the fictional licence of magical realism? When Dyer was cross-examined by the Hunter Commission in October that year, he was asked whether he would have opened fire with a machine gun if he could have entered with the armoured car. He answered, 'I think probably, yes.' Is this what Rushdie is alluding to?

Although initially there was some limited support for his actions, it soon became apparent that Dyer had lied about the circumstances of the demonstration and following a debate in the House of Commons led by the Secretary of State for War, Winston Churchill, MPs voted against Dyer and considered that he had committed a grave error. Sir Michael O'Dwyer, the British Lieutenant Governor of Punjab, was the other villain in the piece. He wanted martial law in the province and wanted to crush the rebellion once and for all. He fully supported Dyer's actions and considered that they had succeeded in this aim. Dyer was relieved of his command in March 1920 and died in 1927.

O'Dwyer was assassinated with a handgun in London in March 1940 by Udham Singh, an activist who had witnessed the events in Jallianwala Bagh and been wounded in the massacre more than twenty years previously. He told the court, 'I am dying for my country,' and was considered a martyr by India. He was hanged in London for murder in July later that year. This story has recently been researched and retold by Anita Anand in *The Patient Assassin*, 2019.

There are other powerful fictional accounts, including the young persons' novel by Bali Rai, *City of Ghosts*, and a mention in Julian Fellowes' TV series 'Downton Abbey' (season 5, episode 8). A conversation takes place at Lord and Lady Grantham's daughter's wedding in 1924:

Lady Grantham: Tell us more about British India.

Lord Flitshire: It's a wonderful country. Bombay is a marvellous city. I'm not sure how long British India has to go.

Mrs Crawley: We heard about that terrible Amritsar business.

Shrimpie: Amritsar was a very unfortunate incident, ordered by a foolish man.

Lord Sinderby: I can't agree. General Dyer was just doing his duty.

Shrimpie: You haven't got that quite right.

The Jallianwala Bagh massacre has attracted filmmakers for the past forty years. These include Balraj Tah's 1977 film, *Jallianwala Bagh* and *The Legend of Bhagat Singh*, the story of a young activist who witnessed the event, directed by Rajkumar Santoshi in 2002. Most recently, in 2017 the Hindi fantasy comedy, *Phillauri*, directed by Anshai Lal, captures screen lovers returning to the site of the massacre, ninety-eight years to the day after the event.

Sadly, Amritsar would witness another shocking moment of conflict when in June 1984 Prime Minister Indira Gandhi sent in the military with tanks (Operation Bluestar) to remove a Sikh militant extremist, Jarnail Singh Bhindranwale and his followers who had occupied the Golden Temple for about two years; they were protesting about what they regarded as longstanding discrimination against Sikhs by Hindus. This action resulted in the loss of many lives (estimated to be about 500 Sikh militants and hundreds of other Indian army soldiers and civilians). Five months later, Indira Gandhi was assassinated in Delhi by two Sikh bodyguards.

VICTORIA'S 'GREAT GAME'

> '*Show me the cuts.*' *Kim bent over Mahratta's neck, his heart nearly choking him;*
> *for this was the Great Game with a vengeance.*

> Rudyard Kipling, *Kim*, 1901

Queen Victoria, Empress of India, died in 1901, the year that *Kim* was published, an event which many would believe signified the end of 'the great game' (a term immortalised by Kipling which described the tense relationship between the British and Russian empires over Afghanistan and other Central Asian territories) and the decline of the British Raj, although it limped on for nearly another half century with Indian servicemen serving with the British in two world wars. Although her government oversaw the tragedy of what might be now regarded as the first war of Indian independence (sometimes referred to as the Indian Mutiny), the incorporation of the East India Company into the state in 1858 and her formal appointment as Empress of India in 1874 – an intervention prosecuted by Benjamin Disraeli – the last years of her reign were perhaps the most peaceful and productive for both nations. Victoria and Disraeli grew to like each other during his two spells as her prime minister (February to December 1868 and 1874–80). He called her 'Faery', referring of course to Spenser's poem, *Faerie Queen*. Taking the Royal Titles Bill through the House of Commons was an uncomfortable experience for Disraeli but Victoria had applied heavy pressure on him and he delivered it for her.

Although Victoria travelled regularly to Europe, notably Germany, Italy and France, she never left the continent to visit other parts of her expanding empire, such as India and Canada. It is unclear as to why she never made the journey to what became her most treasured imperial asset, her 'jewel in the crown', as the passage by sea had during the latter part of her reign been reduced to just eighteen days following the opening of the Suez Canal in 1869. The Peninsular and Oriental Steam Navigation Company (P&O line) had sailings every Saturday in the 1890s from London, with a first-class fare of £55 and a second-class fare of £35, and a stated journey time of twelve and a half days. Victoria was, however, represented in India during a visit by the Prince of Wales in 1877 when he attended the Delhi Durbar, the year after she assumed the title, Empress of India. She sent a message to her subjects anticipating the Delhi Durbar: 'we must trust that the present occasion may tend to unite in bonds of yet closer affection ourselves and our subjects, that from the highest to the humblest all may feel that under our rule the great principles of liberty, equity and justice are secured to them'. Then followed a period of intense change, notably the development of an extensive railway network joining all the major cities within the subcontinent.

Despite the lack of physical presence in the subcontinent during twenty-five years as Empress of India, Victoria developed a deep interest and an extraordinary love for both the place and its people. Perhaps the earliest direct contact that she had with India was at the time of the Great Exhibition in 1851, organised by Prince Albert in the Crystal Palace, erected as a dedicated home for the Exhibition in Hyde Park. It was at this event that the Koh-i-Noor (Mountain of Light) diamond was first displayed in Britain following its somewhat seedy acquisition from the Maharaja of Lahore, the ten-year-old Duleep Singh. After signing a document releasing the diamond to Lord Dalhousie and thereby to the British Crown and watching the British flag rise over his inherited territory, the young boy was brought to England in August 1854 by his new guardians, John Spencer Login and his wife Lena (to avoid him developing any aspirations to regain power in his princely state and thereby cause difficulty for the British Raj) and was immediately befriended by her Majesty. She almost adopted him as a son and he became quite a close companion at court. The diamond had had a long and tortuous history, changing hands many times between leaders in India, Persia, the Mughal Empire, the Afghans and finally arriving in the possession of his father and predecessor as the Maharaja of Lahore, Ranjit Singh. This extraordinary story which spans more the three centuries has been skilfully and critically captured in *Koh-i-Noor* by Dalrymple and Anand (2016).

Duleep Singh, 1854 by Franz Xaver Winterhalter (1838–93). (Alamy)

The Great Exhibition was used as an opportunity to display the diamond publicly in England for the first time. Before it was displayed in the Crystal Palace, it was determined that it should be cut to enhance its true brilliance. Prince Albert, under the supervision of Dutch experts, made the first cut. Although the circumstances by which the diamond was acquired by the British were questionable, Duleep Singh subsequently decided to make a formal presentation of the diamond to Queen Victoria at a special ceremony. His life-size portrait was painted by the court painter Franz Xaver Winterhalter and this still adorns the Indian corridor in Osborne House. In later years the relationship soured but Singh eventually apologised and was formally pardoned by the Queen for his previous 'bad behaviour' (running up debts, trying to escape back to India and insisting on being re-united with his mother). Interest in Duleep Singh has remained high and was the subject of a comprehensive BBC 4 TV documentary in 2018, *The Stolen Maharaja – Britain's Indian Royal*, which reviewed his life and revealed interesting new information based on previously unseen personal correspondence.

Victoria's interest in India came to a crescendo during the period running up to her Golden Jubilee in 1887. The celebrations marked her limited return to public life (since the death of Prince Albert in 1861) and she was insistent that her empire should be fully represented, particularly that increasingly loved part of her empire, India. She hosted numerous Maharajas and their Maharanis at events in London and Windsor, all classified according to their wealth, and their strategic importance of their principalities and level of obedience to the Empire and ranked by the number of guns salute. This was a new departure for British royalty to have so many Indians at court. She was particularly drawn to the Maharaja and Maharani

The maharani of Cooch Behar, 1887.
(Author's collection)

Abdul Karim, 1889 by Rudolf Swoboda (1859–1914).
(Alamy)

of Cooch Behar. According to Lytton Strachey, they had a modern approach to life, were both relaxed and respectful when in audience with the Queen and must have been sufficiently attentive to warrant their portraits being commissioned in Jubilee year and finding a place in the corridor of Osborne House. The Maharani appears most glamorous in a rich red saree and, surprisingly, is captured on canvas without any covering on her head.

Early in the celebrations, the Queen acquired two new servants from India. The most influential of these was a twenty-four-year-old handsome young man from Agra, Abdul Karim, who had been personally selected by John Tyler, superintendent of the Agra jail. During the subsequent fourteen years he would become her closest companion and *munshi* (meaning clerk or teacher, in Urdu) and be known as Hafiz Munshi Abdul Karim, CIE, CVO.

Within a very short period he had replaced her close companion, John Brown, who had died four years previously in 1883. Abdul Karim, by all accounts, brought new joy into the monarch's life during her last two decades. His portrait was painted by the Court artists, Rudolf Swoboda, Laurits Tuxen and Heinrich von Angeli. Swoboda's portrait is displayed to this day in the Indian corridor at Osborne House, but the Queen disliked the Von Angeli portrait as she considered Abdul's complexion to be too dark and it was banished to Frogmore Cottage, Windsor where Abdul lived with his family. The painting remained within the Royal Collection and at some point found its way into the Durbar corridor of Osborne house where it can be seen to this day.

The closeness of his friendship with the Queen brought great distress to the Royal Family and her Majesty's Government. This extraordinary relationship has now been made the subject of a new film, *Victoria and Abdul*, directed by Stephen Frears and starring Judi Dench and Ali Fazal, which is based on the book of the same name by Shrabani Basu, first published in 2010. Basu stumbled on the story when she was researching a book about the history of curry; the great dénouement came when she discovered Abdul's personal journals which describe his fourteen-year association with Victoria. Two years after the book was published, Channel 4 produced a documentary written and directed by Rob Coldstream, *Queen Victoria's Last Love: Abdul Karim* which appears to draw heavily on the story described in Basu's book, but I was unable to find any acknowledgement that this was indeed the case. The TV documentary was well reviewed at the time, but it took a feature film on general release to bring this extraordinary story to full public attention – yet another example of how the personal intimacies of the British-Indian relationship continues to unravel after more than a century.

Queen Victoria was taught Hindustani (Urdu) by Abdul which enabled her to communicate more freely with visiting Indian Princes, and under Abdul's instruction she completed a daily Hindustani journal. Interestingly, although all the letters that Victoria wrote to Karim during their fourteen-year relationship – often sent daily – were destroyed immediately on her death, on the orders of Victoria's son the Prince of Wales, by then King Edward VII, Abdul's own entries in her Hindustani journals were not. His personal journals were not confiscated but surfaced many years later in his home town of Agra; these commentaries are beautifully woven into the story depicted in *Victoria and Abdul.*

Osborne House, on the Isle of Wight, was one of Victoria's favoured residences which she and Albert bought together in 1845; even after Albert's death she continued to use the house as a personal retreat. During a trip to Osborne House it became increasingly clear to me that this house was not a royal palace but a home, a retreat where life could be more relaxed and a place for family life. Her children had their own territories in the house and in the gardens, perhaps allowing them to have a more normal childhood than might have been possible at Buckingham Palace or Windsor Castle. Victoria's interest and love of India grew progressively during her reign, with important nodal points being the Great Exhibition and her Golden Jubilee when she met many of the rulers of the princely states. In one of the rooms on the first floor of Osborne House is a photograph of Prince Alfred and Prince Arthur dressed in Sikh costume dated September 1854. It has been suggested that the costumes may have been a gift from the boy Maharaja, Duleep Singh who had arrived in England just one month previously. Subsequently, the creation of Indian *tableaux vivant* became a popular activity for the royal children, encouraged by Abdul Karim and the other Indian courtiers.

Victoria's commitment to India was reaffirmed in 1890 when she built an extension to Osborne House, the Durbar wing. The Durbar room is of Indian design; much of the interior was constructed in Lahore under the supervision of Lockwood Kipling (Rudyard's father). It is a grand room and blatantly Indian in style. Today, many of the gifts that she received from India are displayed there, including a miniature portrait of the last Mogul Emperor of India, Bahadur Shah II, which the British displaced in 1858. The Durbar corridor is adorned by endless portraits of Indians who Victoria regarded as important to the Empire, including a variety of maharajas and maharanis, and her *munshi*, Abdul Karim. Many were painted by Winterhalter in Britain, but she sent Rudolf Swoboda to India to capture the faces of ordinary people which are hung alongside 'the royalty' in the same corridor.

Victoria developed an intense interest in curry and always ensured that the increasing numbers of Indian members of the household had their own kitchen to prepare traditional meals, recognising the special needs of Hindus and Muslims. An Indian menu was always available at lunch wherever she was staying at the time, although more traditional British fare was *de rigeur* at dinner. Apparently, this tradition was adopted by many British expatriates after the 1857 revolution, demonstrating that the British rulers 'had not completely gone native'. Only now do I realise the significance of the daily routine in the Cuttings' house in Jammalamadugu; curry for lunch but English kitchen at dinner.

Many of the difficulties that Victoria created within her own family and her government were driven by her desire to ensure that Abdul Karim would be well provided for after her death. She provided separate cottages for him and his wife on three of her estates, he was gifted a large parcel of land close to his native Agra, and the medals and titles that he acquired during his period of service with her Majesty ensured high levels of respect when he ultimately returned to India after her demise.

King Edward VII lacked many of the attributes that kept Victoria close to the hearts of ordinary Indians. She had been a devoted wife and mother, was respected for her interest in Indian language and culture, and had built bridges across the two great nations which had softened the blow, at least for some, of colonisation. Towards the end of Lytton Strachey's biography, *Queen Victoria*, he summarises her contribution: 'the final years were years of apotheosis. In the dazzled imagination of her subjects

Victoria soared aloft towards the regions of divinity through a nimbus of purest glory. Criticism fell dumb; deficiencies which, twenty years earlier, would have been universally admitted, were now as universally ignored. That the nation's idol was a very incomplete representative of the nation was a circumstance that was hardly noticed, and yet it was conspicuously true.'

King Edward and his successors, George V and George VI, continued to use the title King and Emperor of India, a convention that was finally dropped in 1948, the year following independence; only George V visited India on one occasion in 1911.

ROBERT CLIVE, THE EAST INDIA COMPANY AND THE GREAT REVOLT: 1857

Britain's relationship with India began more than 400 years ago. Queen Elizabeth I awarded the East India Company its Royal Charter in 1600. For the first hundred years of its existence, the focus was on trade, notably tea, salt, indigo, cotton, silk and opium. The scale of this activity was remarkable, such that at its peak the company accounted for about 50 per cent of all global trade. During the first half of the eighteenth century, the Mughals were finally driven out of India by the Persian leader Nadir Shah who returned to Persia with vast riches. This created a political vacuum in which the East India Company thrived. Robert Clive (1725–74), the British military officer and agent for the East India Company, was responsible for establishing political and economic control of Bengal, which led to the elevation of Calcutta as the British capital city of India. With time, the company progressively occupied many key strategic regions in India, such that by the last quarter of the eighteenth century it maintained a standing militia to protect its assets of over 60,000 troops, largely Indians, divided between Bombay, Madras and Bengal. These forces received substantial resistance from local rulers and their princely states, and additionally from other would-be colonisers such as the French and the Portuguese. By the early nineteenth century the company had control of the old Mughal capital Delhi and had a standing private army of 250,000 men.

The need to control the company's massively expanding assets became unmanageable and eventually India hit back in 1857 with 'the Indian Rebellion' (also known as the Great Revolt, the Indian Mutiny, the Sepoy Rebellion and First War of Independence). The armed conflict was focused predominantly in north India but was not restricted to just the sepoys. Nevertheless, it was a devastating period for British India and the company was held responsible for the tragedy. In 1858, the East India Company was nationalised, taken over by the Crown and formerly incorporated into the British Empire. Although resistance continued, the second half of the nineteenth century was a more stable period in Anglo-Indian relations, due in part to Queen Victoria's calming influence.

The Indian Mutiny prompted a flow of fictional works within twenty years of the event, initially from British authors but soon followed by Indian writers; by the time that India had achieved independence there were almost fifty novels on the topic. The style of fiction which emerged during the latter part of the period of the 'great game' tended to follow the heroic model, perhaps without giving due emphasis to the deep underlying rifts in Anglo-Indian relations that prompted the sepoys to rebel. The straw which broke the camel's back was the enforced use of pork and beef fat to grease the rifle cartridges; this caused massive offence to Hindus and Muslims alike but was a symptom of a more profound discontent. The novels which emerged later and became leaders in the field were John Masters' *Night Runners of Bengal* (1951) and M.M. Kaye's *Shadow of the Moon* (1957). Bhupal Singh in his scholarly *Survey of Anglo-Indian Fiction* (1975) forensically analyses the plot structure of *Night Runners* and *Shadow of the Moon*, exposing what could be distilled down as relatively superficial, heroic British military love stories. Both explore the tension of Anglo-Indian 'affaires de coeur' which has remained a point of interest for novelists up to the present day. However, the Booker Prize-winning, *The Siege of Krishnapur* by J.G. Farrell (1973) is widely regarded as the best post-Independence mutiny novel and clearly sets Farrell apart from other authors. The novel was published more than a century after the historic event in which the novel is set, and hereby breaks the L.P. Hartley/Walter Scott forty-sixty-year rule. The strength of Farrell's work lies in the depth of his research. In the 'Afterword' to his novel he acknowledges this: 'those familiar with the history of the time will recognise countless details in this novel of actual events taken from the massive diaries, letters and memoirs written by eyewitnesses, in some cases with the words of the witnesses only slightly modified; certain of my characters also had their beginnings in this material.' He writes with an openness and an honesty and without the triumphalism that has been seen in some of the work that preceded him. Heat, sweat, excrement and the all-pervading noxious odours of mortality possess you from the page. He might be criticised, however, for his relative lack of knowledge of Indians, compared to say, Masters and Kaye, whose roots in Indian culture were more firmly established. His success, however, is to portray not just the violent events of 1857 but to explore and expose their impact on people.

If the UK leaves the European Union in 2019, it will be the first time it has truly been alone as a trading nation for more than 400 years, except for the brief interlude of twenty-five years before it formally joined the European Economic Community. It took less than fifteen years, however, before we as a nation realised that, following Indian Independence, there was a great danger of political and economic isolation; we started to apply for entry in 1961 but were blocked twice by the French in 1963 and 1967. I am surprised at the confidence of those proclaiming such a triumphant future for a nation which will have had no experience of going it alone since the sixteenth century. Asa Briggs, our eminent social historian, said to me a couple of years before he died in 2016, that he lamented the fact that most politicians had such a poor grasp of history.

༄༅

I do not think it presumptuous to say that India and the United Kingdom continue to have what might be euphemistically called a special relationship. British politicians still regard our relationship with India as important both for trade between our nations and for its wider geopolitical implications. Prime Minister David Cameron, when he led a large British trade delegation to India in 2010, talked about creating a 'new special relationship'; he reiterated this again during a follow-up visit in 2013. The majority of British Prime Ministers serving since Indian independence have visited India, including Margaret Thatcher, John Major, Tony Blair, Gordon Brown and most recently Teresa May in 2016. Margaret Thatcher and Indira Gandhi struck a chord – 'we both felt the loneliness of high office', Thatcher recalls in her memoir. Similarly, many Indian leaders have made state visits to the United Kingdom over this period, starting with Jawaharlal Nehru in 1953 for the coronation of Queen Elizabeth II and followed by Indira Gandhi (1969, 1973, 1978 when she was out of power, 1981), Morarji Desai (1977), Rajiv Gandhi (1985, 1986), and more recently Manmohan Singh (2004, 2005, 2006, 2009) and Narendra Modi in 2015.

British royalty has also seen it as important to visit India, although there was a fifty-year gap between the 1911 visit by George V and Queen Mary soon after their coronation, and the first visit by Queen Elizabeth in 1961, following which she made two further visits, the last in 1997 to celebrate India's fiftieth anniversary of Independence. The Prince of Wales has visited India on five occasions; in 1992 with the Princess of Wales and in 2013 with the Duchess of Cornwall. The Duke and Duchess of Cambridge were the last to visit India in 2016. It can be argued that these visits are largely ceremonial and do little to build a modern balanced relationship, fit for the twenty-first century. Nevertheless, the two countries have sustained a durable accord of benefit to both nations.

PART 10

MEMORIES, DREAMS AND REFLECTIONS

From delusion lead me to the truth.
From darkness lead me to light.
From death lead me to immortality.

1.3.28 Brihad-Aranyaka Upanishad

In the 1960s, psychoanalysis was still the rage. Despite the emergence of R.D. Laing, the controversial, existentialist moderniser of psychological thought, many students of my generation were happy to immerse themselves in the works of Jung and Freud. There was still a belief that psychoanalysis, including the analysis of dreams, which at the time was thought to be the preferred method for penetrating the subconscious, was the route to eternal happiness. Academics were using psychoanalytical techniques to understand the novel and other forms of creative writing, and indeed many built substantial scholarly reputations on the back of the application of Jungian and Freudian notions to their critical analysis of literature. After my return to the UK from India in autumn 1969, I became more curious about what others had found in the heart of this great nation. Carl Gustav Jung was interested in the philosophy and religions of the East and took the concept of the mandala, an ancient Indian construct, to supplement his own thinking about the human mind and its deeper functions. The word 'mandala' is derived from the Sanskrit word meaning circle; when used in Hinduism or Buddhism it is a symbolic way of showing graphically the journey to the 'centre'; which could be a deity or 'the self'. Jung considered that 'a mandala is the psychological expression of the totality of the self'. Jung used the mandala concept to explore the psyche of his psychotherapy patients by getting them to create their own mandala, which he believed could reveal some of their own, perhaps unexpressed, life challenges and possibly guide his psychotherapeutic interventions.

He wrote, 'A book of mine is always a matter of fate. There is something unpredictable about the process of writing, and I cannot prescribe for myself any predetermined course. Thus this "autobiography" is now taking a direction quite different from what I had imagined at the beginning. It has become a necessity for me to write down my early memories. If I neglect to do so for a single day, unpleasant physical symptoms immediately followed. As soon as I set to work they vanish and my head feels perfectly clear.'

He was referring to *Memories, Dreams, Reflections*, written jointly with Aniela Jaffé, which was published in English in 1963, two years after his death. Although it was a co-production, it is perhaps his most intimate, personal work in which he comes closest to placing himself and his feelings into the wider world. Some thirty years previously in 1932, Jung had delivered a seminar on kundalini yoga to the Psychological Club in Zurich. The notes and lectures from this seminar have been reconstructed and published, with the consequence that we now have an exquisite understanding of Jung's fascination with Eastern thought and symbolism, and how this could be a model for the developmental phases of higher consciousness. R.D. Laing acknowledged the importance of Jung's leadership in developing this theme in human psychology but was clearly not overwhelmed; 'it was Jung who broke the ground here, but few followed him'.

Hermann Hesse, a German born in Calw, who was expected by his father, a cleric, to enter the church, collided with Jung in early life when he developed significant mental health problems (probably depression) as a young man and was treated in 1916 by one of Jung's disciples, J.B. Lang, and with whom he subsequently underwent formal psychoanalysis. Subsequently, Hesse met Jung in a hotel in Bern the following year. Entering Jung's penumbra influenced Hesse's thinking and almost certainly steered him towards an engagement with eastern philosophy and religion which had a profound influence on his writing, generating the Buddhist/Hindu novel *Siddhartha*, the story of a young man's search for peace and perfection. Eastern religious themes can be found in other novels, including his masterpiece, *Magister Ludi* (*The Glass Bead Game*); Jungian 'archetypes' surface in many of Hesse's novels including *Demian* and *Steppenwolf*. Jung developed the concept of a 'collective unconscious' which spanned nations and generations, and which could be sub-categorised into a variety of personality types, his so-called 'archetypes'. Interestingly, Hesse's grandparents were Christian missionaries in Kerala, and his grandfather was a scholar of the local language, translating many books into Malayalam, including the Bible. Was this an example of Jung's archetypes playing out in real time?

I discovered Hesse in the early 1970s when new translations of his novels flooded out of the doors of Jonathan Cape and filled the shelves of Dillon's Bookshop in Torrington Place, Bloomsbury just around the corner from where I was a student. His stories collectively charted the life of a young man growing up and finding purpose in life; I was glad that we had met.

It is without shame that I take the title of Jung's autobiography for this final part, modified only slightly.

MEMORIES

The accuracy of memory can always be contested. Recollection of the details of an event are seldom fully corroborated by all observers; we just do not always observe and recall phenomena in the same way. Memory gaps can always be filled. Yes, we confabulate; and not just when suffering from thiamine deficiency, the eponymous Wernicke's encephalopathy. This was most commonly due when I was a student both in London and during an elective in a neuro-psychiatric hospital in West Berlin, to the ravages of alcohol abuse. The reawakening of memories is a creative process, irrespective of the time interval that has elapsed from the remembered event or the integrity of the central nervous system.

Reviving memories across these magical years has been a delight. The day I received the letter from the Rev. Todman, telling me that there was an opportunity to visit India, and the relief that ensued, will always be with me. I was becoming embarrassed by the delay in finalising the arrangements for this much talked of, proposed trip to India and was becoming lost for words when constantly asked, 'And, what are your plans for the summer?'

Magic glimpses back in history through India's ancient monuments, like the stone relics at Mahabalipuram set close to a traditional fishing community still dependent on the most rudimentary of sea-going craft; and the collision of nationalities, cultures and religions in places like Pondicherry. The massive diversity of human phenotypes across the subcontinent, due entirely to the serial invasions, occupations, and colonisations with their inherent mass movements of tribes and their tribulations. I can celebrate the grandeur of some of the most wondrous buildings in the world (seven of which have been awarded the status as UNESCO World Heritage Sites), like the Elephant Caves in Maharashtra, the Taj Mahal and Agra Fort in Agra and other great Mughal constructions in Delhi (Humayun's Tomb, Jama Masjid and the Red Fort) and Lucknow (The Rumi Darwaza or 'Turkish Gate' and Imambara); but at the same moment I can recall the intimacy of sitting, after a clinic, on a dry, cow dung smeared floor in a simple village house in Myaloor, drinking warm, untreated fresh buffalo milk. I still live with the image of watery eyes and the tight neck muscles of the elderly villager with severe asthma, struggling for every breath, who I treated in his village with an injection of adrenaline.

We can gaze with interest and perhaps some wonder at the preserved remains of the British Raj – the clubs, government buildings, Lutyens' New Delhi, the numerous stony tributes to Victoria (such as the memorial in Calcutta and the Victoria Terminus in Bombay) and the quaint, cottage-like residential constructions in the hill stations, such as Simla and Ooty, much of which remain and continue to be preserved. What an extraordinary privilege it was to become a small part of the Singh family of Golf Links Area, New Delhi; a family across four or more generations, which played such an important part in the creation of that new modern capital city of India and then continued to contribute to the nation's cultural life in so many ways.

Despite the massive expansion of new low-cost airlines in India, the railways still have a major role in national communication, of connecting people across this vast and distributed land mass. The laying down of that infrastructure, which began in the mid-nineteenth century, was paramount in the economic development of the subcontinent.

Alongside the main rail arteries were the boutique hill railways like Ooty and Darjeeling which enabled permeation of the less accessible but highly desirable mountainous regions for commerce, comfort and pleasure. I remember those journeys on the mainline express trains, travelling north and south and east and west, and the slow tortuous climb to Ooty on the 'rack railway'. These were magic moments. Today, more than twenty million people travel by train each day in India and the national railways employ more than two million workers.

There will always be a special place in my heart for the weeks I spent with Trevor and Celia in Woodville Guest House and the funny times we passed together, especially the day we did not play cricket on the

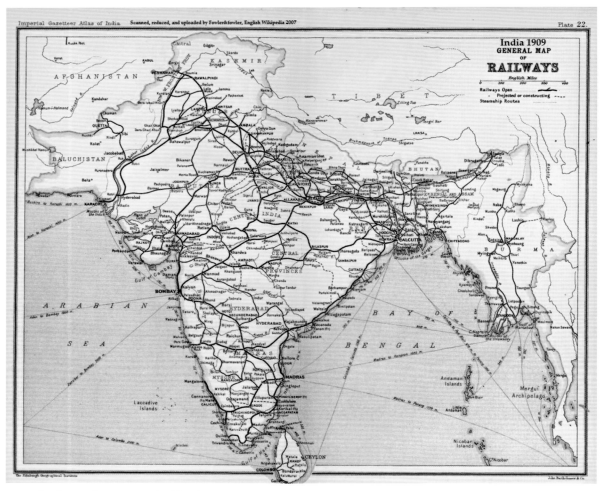

Map of Indian railways, 1909. (Public domain)

highest cricket ground in the world. And the 'wickedness' of the wealthy man that created it, the Maharaja of Patiala. Despite the economic growth that India has enjoyed during the last three or four decades, I shall never be able to forget the unbelievably difficult circumstances under which many Indians still exist. Yes, much of the poverty of India has just moved from the village to the city. The population has continued to grow faster than any other country in the world but, despite this, average standards of living are rising – but of course not for all. I would still say, and it was one of my earliest impressions on arrival in Jammalamadugu nearly fifty years ago, that many aspects of traditional village life do come with a peace and tranquillity that is certainly not evident in the impoverished, peri-urban slums that are a feature of all of India's major cities. As I said at the beginning of this book, I have always felt safe in India.

Characters in the novels of Forster and Scott often expressed the desire to meet 'real Indians' and see the 'real India'. Perhaps they were embarrassed by the danger of living in some sort of 'imperial bubble' which allowed them to enjoy the exotic and exciting aspects of life in the Orient, without having to face up to the realities of being a part of the ruling empire, protected by the privileged colonial life and all that that entails, and the consequences for the indigenous recipients. I am glad that I went when I did; close enough to the achievement of Independence, but not so far forward as to miss some critical points on the journey into the next Millennium. You could say, that I have obeyed the 'Scott/Hartley forty-sixty year rule'!

DREAMS

A dream is a series of thoughts, visions or feelings (sensations) that occur in our minds during sleep, but why do we dream? Is it necessary for us to consolidate memory or for emotional regulation or for the simulation of threats; or is it about wish fulfilment, the 'pipe dream'? Dreams occur during deep sleep when we exhibit rapid eye movements (REMs), anything between twice and five times a night. Most dreams are forgotten. Some believe that dreams are important for human creativity while others consider they have important meaning which help us to address our place in the world. Recently, there has been increased interest in the phenomenon of daydreaming, which is an altered state of consciousness, usually brief, in which there is a period of detachment and an opportunity for visionary fantasy. However, we also use the word 'dream' to encapsulate a cherished aspiration, an ambition or an ideal.

Dreams and dreaming have had a central place both before, during and after India's development as an independent nation. I sometimes think that there are elements of religion that have dreamlike qualities and components, particularly the mythical narratives, that are so important for telling the stories of the gods across time.

The Enduring Presence of Brahma

As soon as I returned from India in September 1969, I bought *Hinduism* by K.M. Sen and an edited translation of the *Upanishads* by Juan Mascaro. Sen's short account of Hinduism was a perfect way for a complete novice to begin to understand the origins, developments over more than four millennia and the complexities of its metaphysics and philosophy. Although the oral tradition in Hinduism began much earlier, the Upanishads are the oldest spiritual treatises, the earliest of which are thought to have been written between 800 and 400 BCE. The Bhagavad Gita – or as it is affectionately known, the Gita – usually considered to be another Upanishad, was composed later between 400 and 200 BCE.

Even earlier are the Vedas, which are thought to originate from around 1500 to 1000 BCE; these are hymns and other religious writings thought to have been brought by the Aryan migration into India from central Asia. These texts teach belief in one supreme God, Brahma, the creator of the universe. Hinduism is often wrongly regarded as a polytheistic religion. The confusion comes when Brahma's three personified powers (namely, creation, preservation and destruction) are attributed to Brahma, Vishnu and Siva which then become a *Trimurti* or Trinity, not dissimilar to the Father, Son and Holy Ghost with which we are familiar in Christianity. There is further confusion because Vishnu and Siva each have numerous avatars, which are merely different incarnations or bodily forms.

Although social reformers in India have worked hard to remove the concept of caste, it is unfortunately deeply embedded in the origins of the Hindu religion and its traditions. At creation, so the myth says, the mouth of Brahma gave rise to the *Brahmins* (priests), his right arm the *Shatriya* (warriors) also known as *Rajputs*, and the left-arm the wife of the warrior. Brahma's thighs created *Vaissyas* (farmers and traders) and his feet the *Sudras* (labourers). Within each of the main castes there were many, perhaps hundreds, of subdivisions – the so-called *jati* – which define an individual's community, their *biradari*. There was a strict hierarchy across the main castes and an expectation that there should be no cross-caste intermarriage with the understanding that you would marry within your *jati*. Only the fourth of the main castes was permitted to eat beef, the first three being expected to be strict vegetarians. If intermarriage did occur, then it automatically created a fifth even lower caste, the pariahs now more commonly known as *Dalits* (formerly as 'untouchables'). These people were expected to be sweepers and cleaners, and the cremators for the higher castes, from whom they were socially and religiously isolated. Although progress has been made in breaking down some of these long-established traditional taboos, the challenge is not dissimilar to the reluctance of some parts of the Christian church to accept women clergy and same-sex relationships and marriage.

In parallel with these writings from the Indus valley, there was the emergence of the early books of the old Testament (Genesis, Exodus, Leviticus, Numbers and Deuteronomy) emanating from the Hebrews, a nomadic community that lived in the ancient Middle East in an area called Canaan, now modern Israel, Jordan, Lebanon and Syria. In Judaism, these ancient writings constitute the Torah. The New Testament was written much later, starting at about 40 CE.

Having read the Upanishads and the Gita, I decided to select some words that could sit at the beginning of each part of the book; I cannot pretend that I believe everything that they impart but I like the way they express something about the world which we would not consider to be part of our normal day. For me they seem to have dream-like qualities.

REFLECTIONS
Partition

Could it have been different? Was it inevitable that Jinnah would stir up Muslim-Hindu hatred the year before Independence and partition, resulting in a massive death toll on both sides? Should the British have found the military resources to quell the violence and not apparently to have turned a blind eye? Would delaying the Independence date to 1948 have made a difference? The Mountbatten Plan, however, had local political support; Gandhi was unhappy as he had always planned for a united India, but it was not imposed and was agreed possibly reluctantly by the other leaders. Lord Mountbatten wrote in the Viceroy's Personal Report No. 9, dated 12 June 1947 (Top secret and personal) – 'I have spent most of the last week in consultation with the Indian leaders…. Gandhi was in a very unhappy and emotional mood … feared that he might denounce the plan.'

Why was there mass slaughter in the year running up to Independence and in the weeks that followed?

I needed to try and understand India's long history of conflict, occupation and imperialism. Does it matter what happened during the Mughal invasions of the eighth, tenth and twelfth centuries? What about the atrocities associated with the later Mughal invasions and occupations of the sixteenth and seventeenth centuries? Paradoxically, it was the British that finally discharged the Mughal rulers in 1858 and ended the Muslim empire. Although India had often been invaded and occupied by military force, some of the leaders, notably Akbar (1556–1605) and his son Jahangir (1605–27) showed remarkable religious tolerance to their Hindu neighbours; some of those that followed, however, such as Aurangzeb (1658–1707) were largely intolerant, which heralded the decline of that empire. At its peak, the Mughal Empire extended from Afghanistan and the farthest reaches of northern India to the southern extensions of the Deccan plateau. Thus, within this long period of invasion and occupation, there were periods of intense conflict, together with times of relatively peaceful religious tolerance.

'Staying On': The Remains of British India

When asked by the P&O agent, during the purchase of her tickets to Bombay, when she would like to return, Adela Quested, the femme fatale of David Lean's film of Forster's *A Passage to India*, pauses and says, 'I don't know; I shall be staying on.' She buys an open ticket. This scene is a key stepping-off point in the screenplay but does not appear in Forster's novel. Adela was going to meet her fiancée, the local city magistrate Ronald (Ronny) Heaslop in fictional Chandrapore, and anticipated that she would marry him while in India. However, quite early in the narrative we learn that 'India had developed sides of his character that she had never admired. His self-complacency, his censoriousness, his lack of subtlety, all grew vivid beneath a tropical sky.' The drama takes place in the early 1920s, probably before Amritsar and well before Independence. This was a different sort of 'staying on' to that described by Paul Scott and Ruth Prawer Jhabvala and one that was not borne out as the story unravels.

Despite the havoc that endured after the British withdrawal, some remained. Those approaching retirement and those who have already crossed that line are over-represented in those British people that chose to continue their lives in India after Independence. Many saw no option but to remain. As Tusker (retired Colonel Smalley), in Paul Scott's 'Staying On', set in early 1972, explains why he remained in the only love letter he wrote to his wife Lucy: 'it seemed to me I'd invested in India, not money which I've never had, not talent (Ha!) which I've only had a limited amount of, nothing India needed or needs or has been one jot the better for, but was all I had to invest in anything. Me.' He knew no other way to live. He and his wife were heavily dependent on the affordable help at home. Ibrahim, their servant was an integral part of the household and much more than just a servant, and they had access to the hotel's *mali* (gardener) and a sweeper. Furthermore, they had low-cost accommodation in 'The Lodge' (an annexe of the 'tired' and crumbling Smith's Hotel) and the companionship with their neighbours, the Bhoolabhoys. At the same time, they enjoyed a quality of life and social standing that could not have been replicated at home in England. The thought of returning to post-war leafy Surrey with their limited resources was un-thinkable. Finances aside, they stayed because they loved India and so did many others who lived outside the realm of fiction.

John Masters started life as a professional soldier in India but went on to write historical fiction mainly set in India. In *Bhowani Junction* (1954) he deals with the dilemma facing British subjects who lived for many years, perhaps most of their lives, in India but who were faced with an uncertain future as India approached Independence. In *To the Coral Strand* (1962) his own personal future unravels in fiction as it describes the fate of an army officer who refuses to go quietly when expected to return home to Britain.

In her short story, *Miss Sahib*, part of a collection published as *A Stronger Climate* (1968), Ruth Prawer Jhabvala captures the tragic retirement years of an English school teacher, Miss Tuhy, who spent more than thirty years in India, found overwhelming love for her Indian pupils and the country, and after a very brief return to England, opted to live out her days in India where she was content but trapped, as 'she no longer had the fare home'. Jhabvala classifies those that stayed on as 'the sufferers'. In another story in the collection, *The Man with the Dog*, she describes a curious relationship between an elderly Dutchman, Boekelman, who had a dog named Susi and who had lived in India for many years, and an elderly, demure Indian lady (the narrator) in whose house he rents a room at a very modest rate. Trouble starts when Boekelman develops an interest in another woman and hatches a plan to move out; this utterly devastates his landlady. Yet another painful cross-cultural relationship superbly executed by Jhabvala.

She describes another group of Westerners as 'seekers'. *In Love with a Beautiful Girl* (1968) tells the story of Richard, who is working at the High Commission, and his relationship with Ruchira; 'she was beautiful, to him mysterious, and, he was sure – it could not be otherwise – passionate. He courted her assiduously and was well received. Fortunately, she came from a family that prided itself on being modern and forward-looking, so that no difficulties were put in the way of his meeting her.' I shall avoid spoiling the story and say no more.

Hostilities Between India and Pakistan

Following partition of India into the new Indian union and into West and East Pakistan, violent conflict has continued between the nations, mainly due to persistent territorial and underlying religious tensions. Before partition, it is often suggested that Hindus, Muslims and Sikhs had lived harmoniously together without conflict. At one level, this was certainly true with many examples of well-integrated mixed communities living peacefully together; Khushwant Singh's fictional village Mano Majra, in the Punjab would be one example but there are many others in real life. At the same time, we must acknowledge there have been numerous occasions over many centuries, notably in the eighth, tenth and twelfth centuries CE, when Muslim invaders have entered India from the north, visitations that were usually associated with monumental armed conflict. During the sixteenth and seventeenth centuries, a significant proportion of the Indian subcontinent was occupied and part of a great Mughal Empire, often under harsh leadership. Paradoxically, it was the British that brought closure to this period of 'imperial' Islamic Indian history in 1858 with the exile of the last emperor to Burma. Thus, the potential for inter-racial and inter-religious inspired violence was not new, either in the Calcutta riots of 1946 or at partition in 1947 or in the years that followed.

After the establishment of the two nations, India and Pakistan, war and sporadic lesser conflicts persisted. The first Indo-Pakistani War took place within three months of partition, prompted by concern

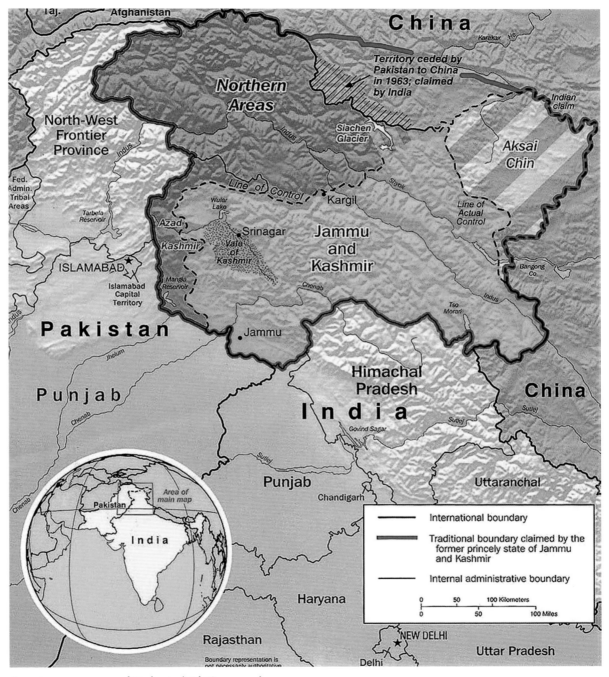

A contemporary map of Kashmir. (WikiCommons)

that the largely Muslim princely state of Jammu and Kashmir might accede to India. After three months of fighting, India had gained about two-thirds and Pakistan one-third of Jammu and Kashmir; following a UN resolution the conflict was ended. A second war in 1965 also concerned ownership of the Punjab; this lasted just seventeen days. It resulted in thousands of casualties and was finally resolved through diplomatic intervention by the USA and Soviet Union. 1971 saw the Bangladesh Liberation War, with the creation of the independent nation of Bangladesh and the demise of East Pakistan; at the same time Pakistan attacked India's western border during a period of about two weeks. Together, the human losses from these conflicts were the highest in the history of Indo-Pakistani aggression. In 1999 (the fourth Indo-Pakistani war), Pakistani forces crossed the *line of control* into Indian Punjab, again with many losses, but with US intervention they were persuaded to withdraw; it was widely agreed internationally that Pakistan had lost this war.

Tensions remain in this border area and regular minor skirmishes and 'terrorist acts' continue to this day. Again, we can look beyond the recent accounts of these struggles by journalists and historians and examine the subject in contemporary literature. Arundhati Roy's novel, *The Ministry of Utmost Happiness* (2017) graphically unveils the tragedy of the hostilities in Kashmir driven by those seeking independence and to separate from India.

Whatever the cases for and against separation, this does not make comfortable reading, largely because the narrative follows closely the lines of historical events but at the same time is enhanced by disturbing flashes of literary inspiration, tinged with magical realism.

There are also continuing disputes over entry into each other's territorial waters, usually on a small scale because local fishermen do not have the navigational aids to accurately identify their position at sea. Both India and Pakistan have a nuclear capability which they have threatened to use, although only Pakistan has a 'first strike' policy. Thus, although Jinnah and Nehru agreed a two-nation (now a three-nation) solution, and Mountbatten entrusted Radcliffe and his committee to draw the lines on the map, the immediate result was a disaster and it has not produced a long-term durable and peaceful outcome.

Inspirational India

Orientalism, a discourse which pitches East against West, and vice versa, politically, economically and culturally, framed skilfully by the powerful underlying theme of hegemony and empire, has in a formal sense probably had its day. That aside, we should not deny the past and fail to celebrate where what are now regarded as hostile acts have perhaps left traces of benefit, even if it might now be regarded as an unintended consequence. I have introduced already the notion of how Indian religions and philosophy, its classical music and visual arts and the more recent developments in science and technology have profoundly influenced Western thinking and creativity.

Jung was unquestionably influenced by Indian philosophy and religious thinking both before and after his first visit to India in 1938: 'by that time I had read a great deal about Indian philosophy and religious history and was deeply convinced of the value of oriental wisdom. But I had to travel to form my own conclusions and remained within myself like a homunculus in a retort. India affected me like

Swoboda's villagers by court painter, 1880s. (Author's collection)

a dream, for I was and remained in search of myself, of the truth peculiar to myself.' In his memoire he closes his reflections on India with, 'but India did not pass me by without a trace; it left tracks which lead from one infinity into another infinity'. Jung's experience went on to influence the writer Herman Hesse and probably many others.

Ravi Shankar and other classical Indian musicians have had a profound effect on Western musicians from Yehudi Menuhin to the Beatles. Many distinguished European artists have found inspiration in India – from Tilly Kettle and Henry Singleton in the eighteenth century exploring portraiture and heroic scenes of conflict, respectively, to William Daniell and his traditional landscapes. In the nineteenth century, Scottish watercolourist, William Simpson captured scenes of military conflict and pastoral landscapes in India and went on to paint more extensively in Asia and the Orient in Afghanistan, Crimea and China. Victoria's court artists, Winterhalter and Swoboda painted portraits of Indian royalty and villagers during visits to England and on field trips to India.

Nicholas Roerich, the Russian painter who focused predominantly on Himalayan landscapes, was recognised by Prime Minister Nehru after Independence as one of nine 'national treasure' artists. The Turner prize-winning Anish Kapoor RA, born in Bombay but living much of his professional life in England, returned to India in 1979 and said, 'I suddenly realised all those things I was making in art school and in my studio, had a relationship to what I saw in India.' His sculpture spans artistic traditions of both East and West without apology. Howard Hodgkin RA, who has created the largest body of work – mainly abstract paintings inspired by the subcontinent – of any contemporary British artist, was also an obsessive collector of Indian miniatures and contemporary paintings by Indian artists.

Stephen Cox RA, a sculptor who chose hard stone for his *métier* from early in his career, found inspiration for his work both in Britain and away from home in Italy, India and Egypt. Cox works on scale and has clearly taken from the art and culture of these international environments in which he has worked. Mark Tully, in *No Full Stops in India*, accuses Cox of being a neo-colonialist. In the 1980s Cox went to Mahabalipuram on a study grant from the British Council to work with traditional stone masons under the guidance of the Principal of the College of Architecture and Sculpture, Ganapati Sthapati. Tully relates a conversation with Sthapati during which he criticises Cox for his superficial approach to diorite and granite carving, his failure to acquire the necessary skills to work with this extraordinary hard stone and his dependence on local masons to carry out his work. Cox continued to work with local masons after the

Stephen Cox sculpture, Ganapathi and Devi, 1988. (Author's collection)

completion of the study grant and went on to buy a home in Mahabalipuram. I can see why Tully might use the term neo-colonialist but most modern sculpture on scale these days is produced by teams of workers; the contemporary works of Anish Kapoor RA and Damien Hirst being examples of this way of working. Nevertheless, Cox found inspiration in producing modern works in this ancient environment in South India.

Western dominance in the past over the Orient – the central theme of 'orientalism' – perhaps needs to be balanced against a global platform of tribal and national behaviours over the last three millennia. Almost every European country has had its borders crossed by a neighbour and many have been occupied and effectively colonised. The remnants of these excursions are still evident; there are too many examples to cite, although I was delighted to experience just a year or so ago the profound and enduring Arab and Islamic influence on the language, art, architecture, science and culture of southern Spain which followed occupation of the Iberian Peninsula by Arabs (Berber tribes) from the Maghreb, from 711 CE to the fall of Granada in 1491 CE, more than seven centuries. It was these Arab invaders that introduced 'Seville oranges' to Seville, together with a variety of other exotic plants such as date palms. They introduced Europe to the concept of 'Paradise gardens', a traditional form of garden in an arid climate, emanating originally from Persia. These gardens can be found in many places in Europe, notably in the Alhambra Palace in Granada, Spain and in the gardens of Versailles and in 'the Louvre' in France. Julius Caesar invaded but failed to occupy Britain during the first century BCE. His sortie was followed by Claudius' successful occupation about a century later, which put most of Britain under the rule of the Roman Empire for about four centuries. This was followed with invasions by the Angles, Saxons and Jutes (the so-called Anglo-Saxons) whose genes are now firmly embedded in British genomes. The Vikings made their presence felt in the eighth century CE (their activities can also be traced in contemporary English genomes), to be followed by a half-century of Norman rule in the eleventh century CE. The last invasion of Britain was in 1797 by the French after the Battle of Fishguard. Fortunately, this occupation lasted only a matter of days.

I believe the British now look back at these periods in history with some interest but rarely regret, and celebrate what remains, particularly of Roman and Norman colonisation. These incursions changed Britain, arguably for the better. The Romans – and to a lesser extent the Normans – had a profound effect on the development of the English language and the principles of Roman Law underpin today's English Law. The Romans also gave us a taste for viniculture and wine-making, which during the twentieth and twenty-first centuries have gone from strength to strength. There are endless excavated and conserved Roman sites and the residue of Roman roads which archaeologists continue to examine and many of us enjoy visiting. There is a long list of more than one hundred Norman churches and cathedrals (including Durham, Ely, Winchester, Norwich and Peterborough) which are meticulously maintained as part of our rich national heritage. The introduction of feudalism by the Normans may on reflection not be regarded as their greatest moment.

Despite the irritation and indeed anger that is still directed towards the British rule and exploitation of India, many of the architectural contributions, such as Lutyens' New Delhi, that were made during this period, remain in use and are conserved as heritage. Similarly, the grand buildings that were created during centuries of Mughal occupation and rule are celebrated and indeed promoted as important historic sites. Who would not want to see the Taj Mahal, the Red Fort of Jaipur and Fatehpur Sikri and the great mosques of Delhi? India has retained many of the government buildings, golf courses and traditional clubs that date back to British times, and for some years after Independence it was possible to travel across India on trains powered by steam engines from those former times.

I think what I am trying to say is that for more than 100,000 – possibly 200,000 years – man has had an insatiable appetite to wander around the globe searching for new opportunities, better climate and agricultural conditions, economic advancement and riches beyond what is available in their birthplace. The concept of territorial boundaries and ownership is a relatively recent development in the long history of homo sapiens. Sadly, conflict and other forms of aggression and exploitation have almost invariably been part of these transmigrations.

Authors in a Global Literary World

A relatively new debate has emerged in recent years namely the legitimacy of a writer from one culture to write fiction about another culture, so-called cultural or voice appropriation. Lionel Shriver was at the centre of a row which emerged during the Brisbane Writers Festival in 2016. Shriver strongly held the view the writer should not be restricted about the nature of the characters they create for their novels. Others were outraged by the idea that a writer could appropriate a character from another culture, without being part of that culture. I fear that the 'horse has bolted'. British writers have written about Indians and Indian writers about the British for more than a century, probably longer.

I recently re-read V.S. Naipaul's Booker Prize winning novel, *In a Free State* (1971). An innovative narrative, it is set in three locations, Washington, London and a fictional African country in which a major power upheaval is underway. Naipaul's characters include African Caribbeans, Indian Caribbeans, African Americans, white Americans, white British and Africans. In my humble, non-expert opinion, his characterisations are compelling and their varied voices utterly authentic. Unless we proceed with caution, we shall find ourselves criticising Arundhati Roy (also a former Booker Prize winner) in *The Ministry of Utmost Happiness* (2017) for writing inappropriately about transsexual individuals, Muslims, Sikhs and Hindus from different castes, none of whom I should guess would directly be closely aligned with her own current affiliations, but they are all Indian. It partly depends on how fine we interpret the grain of race and culture.

Increasing numbers of contemporary authors are from former colonised nations in Africa, India and the Caribbean, not forgetting of course the so-called 'white colonies' of Canada and Australia. Some of these authors work in their home territory while others have chosen to write abroad, such as in the UK and USA. Fortunately, they have felt free to write about themselves and their own nationals, about their diaspora in different parts of the world and about others, foreigners and former colonisers. Authors must be free to write about what they like, whether it be fact, fiction or fantasy. Surely we must all have the right to include each other in our fiction (and non-fiction), be judged on the veracity of the portrayal, but be willing to stand up to criticism if we are judged to get it wrong or do it badly?

Migrations of people from Britain to India and from India to Britain started on a small scale more than 400 years ago. In those early days this was not tourism – that is travel primarily for interest or entertainment – but like me, it was travel for work, enterprise or learning. Transmigrations began in both directions from the establishment of the East India Company, grew further as the British Empire developed and has continued after Independence until the present day.

Indians started to trickle into Britain in the seventeenth century, often returning with their employers as *ayahs* or domestic servants; in the eighteenth century some business travellers began to arrive but by the nineteenth century, professionals were coming too. There were further migrations in the 1930s, beautifully depicted in Dr Yasmin Khan's three-part BBC2 documentary, *A Passage to Britain* (2018). She obtained passenger lists for each of three sailings and followed the migrants and their relatives, many of whom were subsequently born in Britain. They mostly came for study or work, but a few left India to escape punishment for anti-British revolutionary activities. One of the most notable travellers on *The Viceroy of India* was Mulk Raj Anand, whose first novel *Untouchable* (1935) launched his career as a writer.

Since Independence, numbers resident in the UK have grown steadily to about 1.5m, which amounts to about 2.3 per cent of the population. Indians are probably the wealthiest minority in the UK. Some sons and daughters of these immigrants are now moving back to India with their partners, some of whom (about 12 per cent) will be in inter-racial relationships. With its healthy economic growth India is seen as a land of opportunity.

The British also travelled to India with their employer, initially the East India Company, when numbers grew over the years to between 150,000 and 200,000. Just before Independence in 1947, numbers are estimated to have risen still further.

Although colonisation of one nation by another has been a phenomenon that has spanned the globe, involving many empire builders across several millennia, today it is regarded with profound disdain. The process almost always involved violent conflict in varying degrees, oppression and loss of personal freedoms, including religious freedom and the pillaging of natural resources. Many peoples, tribes and nations have been participants in the acquisition of empire, including the Persians, Romans, Arabs, Mongols, Turks, Chinese, Russians, and some European nations, including the Spanish, Dutch, Portuguese, Italians, French, Germans and of course the British. Most nations do not speak easily of their imperial pasts and imperial history may be selectively under-represented in school curricula. At the same time there is now a loud call by students to 'decolonise' university teaching programmes to enable learning to be more representative of the modern post-imperial world.

The British took plenty during those years from the arrival of the East India Company in 1600 until Independence in 1947. It was an unbalanced trading relationship with huge net benefits leaking back to Britain. The importance of India as a major contributor to the creation of British wealth and global positioning as a world power should never be underestimated. The British also maintained a large standing army in India, much larger than was required to secure local borders, to have access to a trained high-quality militia whenever required. From the mid-nineteenth century the Indian Army (latterly known as the British Indian Army) fought alongside the British in Afghanistan, South Africa, Zanzibar, Turkey, Burma, Egypt and during both the world wars.

The case against the British has been made by many but never more brutally and decisively than by Shashi Tharoor, in his book *Inglorious Empire: What the British did to India* (2017). Tharoor was born in Britain, educated in India and the US, and went on to a distinguished career in the United Nations. He is currently a popular, respected and sometimes controversial member of the Indian Parliament and has held several ministerial positions. *Inglorious Empire* is an enthralling text, never dull, which reads as if he was putting the case for the prosecution in an Oxford Union debate – which is exactly what it is. Tharoor was invited in 2015 to speak in support of the motion 'Britain owes reparations to her former colonies'. He won the debate to great acclaim and went on to assemble his ideas into a book. In the Preface he protests that he has balanced the arguments in the book (possibly, and hopefully, more so than he had in the debate) but frankly the book still reads like one side of a debate. He systematically stacks up the evidence as to how the British 'looted India' ('loot' is a word of Sanskrit and Hindi origins). He refutes the assertion that the British had any role in the national unification of India, of promoting political unity, democracy and the parliamentary system, or in establishing the rule of law and the free press. In the days before the British arrived in India he asserts that caste was not an issue, suggesting that the British used caste as an element of its divide and rule strategy, and that large-scale conflict between Hindus and Muslims had not been a problem. I am not sure that these views have universal acceptance. Possible legacies, such as the railways, the tea industry and the English language, are discarded as selfish instruments of colonialism. Finally, he dismisses the positive spin of previous celebratory accounts of 'Empire' such as that written by the distinguished historian, Niall Ferguson (2003) and journalist and broadcaster, Jeremy Paxman (2011).

However, some still struggle to find redeeming features. It is even now debated as to whether the longstanding Mughal rule and then British rule in India were universally bad for the subcontinent. Some, but not all the Mughal dynasties brought economic improvement (although overall GDP flatlined during the eighteenth, nineteenth and twentieth centuries in parallel with the economies of China and the Middle East, and only really took off in the 1990s when the economy was liberated). Yes, the Mughals were tolerant of other religions, but their rule was rarely free of conflict; religious groups were engaging in armed conflict before the British arrived, although much of the time they lived peacefully and harmoniously as did Christians, Jews and Muslims in many other locations in the world outside the subcontinent. It must be acknowledged, however, that history shows that these relationships can be destabilised easily by relatively minor adverse fluctuations in the socio-political environment.

It has been argued that the British facilitated the unification of India through the process of the independence and 'abolition' of the multitude of princely states which began to emerge in the seventh century, but grew steadily between the fourteenth and the nineteenth centuries; no previous ruling regimes had sought to tackle this fragmentation. Their incorporation into an independent united India could be viewed as serious groundwork for the establishment of a modern Indian democracy. This arguably has benefited the nation by providing a sound base on which to develop a competitive manufacturing industry of some scale and a growing sustainable economy, attracting the respect and trust of other mature global economies and making it the strong trading partner that it is today. This cannot be said for many other former colonies of European nations which failed to establish independent democratic rule and have left national wealth in the hands of a political elite. There is some research evidence that suggests that the longer the period of colonisation, the more likely it is that there will be a durable, stable democracy after independence, although I am sure this position can be refuted by counter-argument.

A more positive view of British involvement in India is put forward by another British Indian, Kartar Lalvani, in *The Making of India: The Untold Story of British Enterprise* (2016). Lalvani was born in Karachi, came to London aged twenty-five to study pharmacy and went on to establish Vitabiotics, Britain's leading vitamin company. He looks at the British period in India through the eyes of a scientist, industrialist and entrepreneur. He aims to provide a balanced perspective but does not shy away from the exploitative aspects of British rule and the periods of violence and oppression.

He presents the case for some of the possible beneficial legacies, notably the establishment of a sound administrative infrastructure including the civil service, the judiciary and the codification of law, the police, banking and taxation, the army and secular democratic rule. However, his main focus is on the application of the benefits of the industrial revolutions beginning in the late eighteenth century and extending throughout the nineteenth and into the early twentieth century: the age of steam which brought rapid bi-directional sea travel to and from the subcontinent, ship building, the development of ports and harbours, the creation of canals and improved water supplies, the development of a road system and the rapid creation of an extensive rail network across a broad spectrum of terrains. The expansion of iron and steel production was essential for the railway enterprise and for a major programme of bridge construction. By the last quarter of the nineteenth century, electricity was being generated by hydroelectric and steam-based turbines. Lalvani also reflects that the British planned and created an impressive new capital city with its classic Anglo-Indian style municipal buildings; 'New Delhi was clearly built to last a thousand years.'

The British also began tea and rubber planting in India on a commercial scale, importing seeds for tea bushes from China and the seeds for rubber trees from Brazil; 70,000 seeds of *Hevea Brasiliensis* were smuggled to Kew Gardens by Henry Wickham in 1876 where they were used to produce rubber saplings for export to India, Ceylon and other locations in Southeast Asia in which the British had a commercial interest. The infrastructure was established for what remain important industries across India, both of which make sizable contributions to the economy.

However, the compelling counter-argument made by Tharoor and others is that Britain did not do this for India but selfishly for itself; and this must be true. I cannot find a single example where a colonising power has taken over another sovereign territory for altruistic reasons, although probably there are some unintended beneficial consequences. Perhaps 'benefits' do not always have to be gifts. The benefits of occupation may be unintended consequences that would not have occurred without the other painful effects. How should the British look back at the Roman and Norman invasions/occupations? They clearly did not come for our benefit and took control by force. How should the Spanish reflect on centuries of Islamic rule? These long-term occupations leave many residua, such as new architectural styles, the merging of cultural traditions and the blending of languages. Spanish is now peppered with words beginning in 'Al' such as *almohada* (pillow), *alfombra* (rug), *alcohol* (as in English), *almendra* (almond) and *algebra* (as in English).

How should the occupied countries of Europe during the two world wars regard their neighbours many years on, when almost everyone living has no personal recollection of these conflicts and the abuse that accompanied them? Simply, they have moved on and created the European Union, which, while facilitating economic advancement, has the intended consequence of securing peace in the continent.

However, the tables have now turned. Britain has become a favoured locus for Indian investment in the twenty-first century. The reasons investors give include the English language, familiarity with UK institutions, the 'ease of doing business' and facilitated entry into the EU market. The largest investors are Tata Motors, owners of Jaguar Land Rover, Tata Steel, and the Indian IT businesses, Infosys and Wipro. We should be quite clear that, like the British in India, these international Indian businesses are in the UK for their own material benefit; at the same time there are major gains for the UK economy.

How one finally sets up the score card of benefits and deficits of the relationship in colonial days is too difficult for me, but I think what counts today is how we use this long-standing relationship, which began well before the so-call special relationship with America, to our mutual advantage. We must never forget the past – and make sure that subsequent generations on both sides understand that this is a part of our joint history that must be acknowledged and remembered – while we forge ahead to optimise the mutual benefits that are awaiting exploitation.

In 2005 the man who had liberated the Indian economy in the early 1990s when he was Minister of Finance, received an honorary degree from his alma mater, the University of Oxford. Manmohan Singh was by then the President of India. His acceptance speech sensitively reviewed the relationship between India and the British over the past few centuries; he concluded generously that it was certainly not all bad and looked forward to a mutually productive collaborative, 'give and take' relationship in the future.

Towards the end of his speech he reminded his audience of the tribute paid to Britain by the poet and Nobel laureate, Rabindranath Tagore, in his poem *Bharat Tirtha* (The Pilgrimage that is India) written in 1911.

> *The West has today opened its door,*
> *There are treasures for us to take,*
> *We will take and we will also give,*
> *From the open shores of India's immense humanity.*

The Indian writer (and Man Booker prize winner for her 1997 *The God of Small Things*) and activist, Arundhati Roy wrote, 'isn't it true that there are times in the life of a people or a nation when the political climate demands that we – even the most sophisticated of us – overtly take sides? I believe that in the coming years, intellectuals and artists will be called upon to take sides, and this time, unlike the struggle for Independence, we won't have the luxury of fighting a "colonising enemy". We'll be fighting ourselves. We will be forced to ask ourselves some very uncomfortable questions about our values and traditions, our vision for the future, our responsibilities as citizens, the legitimacy of our "democratic institutions", the role of the state, the police, the army, the judiciary and the intellectual community.'

This surely is the future thinking that we must all embrace; examining *the now*, remembering but not necessarily blaming *the past*, but always *making the future*.

EPILOGUE

1. *There was neither non-existence nor existence then; there was neither the realm of space nor the sky which is beyond. What stirred? Where? In whose protection? Was there water, bottomlessly deep?*

2. *There was neither death nor immortality then. There was no distinguishing sign of night nor day. That one breathed, windless, by its own impulse. Other than that, there was nothing beyond.*

3. *Darkness was hidden by darkness in the beginning; with no distinguishing sign, all this was water. The life force that was covered with emptiness, that one arose through the power of heat.*

4. *Desire came upon that one in the beginning; that was the first seed of mind. Poets seeking in their heart with wisdom found the bond of existence in non-existence.*

5. *Their cord was extended across. Was there below? Was there above? There were seed-placers; there were powers. There was impulse beneath; there was giving-forth above.*

6. *Who really knows? Who will here proclaim it? Whence was it produced? Whence is this creation? The gods came afterwards, with the creation of this universe. Who then knows whence it has arisen?*

7. *Whence this creation has arisen – perhaps it formed itself, or perhaps it did not – the one who looks down on it, in the highest heaven, only he knows – or perhaps he does not know.*

The Rig Veda, Mandala 10, Hymn 129
The Creation Hymn, c. 1500 BCE
Translated by Wendy Doniger, 1981

So, as I prepare to sign off at the end of this journey, I realise that it has taken almost 'a lifetime'. It has been the opportunity of a lifetime to have tasted this nation so soon after it was liberated from centuries of occupation and imperialism and watch it re-emerge as an intellectual powerhouse, an incubator for emerging technologies, a hive of innovation and a generator of new intellectual and economic energy. At the same time, its wealth is polarised, migration from villages to cities has in many instances just moved poverty from one place to another, religion still divides the subcontinent both within and across national borders and conflict, along many of these fault lines, remains explosively close to the surface.

In these closing moments, I wonder whether it is possible to make sense of the inconsistencies, ambiguities and imponderables which have surfaced for me over the years. Throughout this discourse I have tried always to face up to the *facts*, while at the same time being open to the contribution that *fiction* and the other creative outputs have made to our understanding of history and contemporary culture. The greatest challenge has been to allow sufficient space for *fantasy*, for imagination, beliefs and for dreaming. Dreams are made by peoples' minds and it is people who can use their dreams to change our world.

FACT

Modern India is a synthesis of multiple influences, notably the genetic mixing from the early African (70 to 80,000 years ago) and central Asian migrations by the so-called Aryans who inhabited the Indus Valley creating the Harappan civilisation (3500–1500 BCE). India has a plethora of languages, a commendable array of architectural triumphs which span more than two millennia, and a unique religion, Hinduism (from which, it may be argued, other important, more recent religions have evolved such Jainism and Sikhism). Hinduism appeared at the same time as the other early, root monotheistic Abrahamic religions around 1500 BCE, but probably had its origins 'of thought' as early as 3000 BCE.

The early migrations were followed by the catalytic effects of more recent occupying forces, namely the Mughals between the sixth and nineteenth century and the numerous European colonisations by France, Portugal, The Netherlands and Britain, which began in the seventeenth century. The British presence in India, initially in the form of the East India Company and the early missionaries, and latterly as a colony of the British Empire, was probably the most significant in recent history and the one whose impact remains evident today. It would be wrong to suggest, however, that the centuries of Mughal presence have not had a lasting effect on India's development.

The move from dependency or domination to that of an independent state is rarely a smooth process, and for many now living in the subcontinent the consequences of separation into India, Pakistan and Bangladesh is still a cause of grief across the national borders. During 2017, the year of celebration of seventy years of independence, the question has been asked again and again as to whether it was the right solution and, if it was, could it have been done better? I have discussed this with Indians and Pakistanis (both those that remained and others who left to seek their fortunes in other parts of the world), particularly those whose families were disrupted by Radcliffe's precipitous drawing of lines on the map. I have the sense that a sizeable majority regret the division of the subcontinent, feeling that there are so many unresolved issues, notably the appropriate destiny of Muslim-dominated Kashmir (most of which was allocated to India), over which there is continuing conflict. Some Pakistanis (mainly expatriates) feel that while India has flourished, enjoying economic growth and increasingly respected as a global democracy with a voice, Pakistan has stagnated politically and economically. Some say that, 'nothing has changed in Pakistan since 1947'. Although Pakistan and Bangladesh are more than 90 per cent Muslim, arguably a success for 'partition', India still has a similar number of Muslims (approaching 180 million within its borders living as Indian citizens) as each of the other two countries; thus, not a total success in creating religious isolation.

So, what is the evidence? Since 1990 India has moved ahead of Pakistan with average economic growth rates of 7.5 per cent compared to 5 per cent. India eventually opened its economy and encouraged foreign investment whereas Pakistan followed the state-led economy paradigm of the former Soviet Union. India is ahead of Pakistan in other indices of development, including higher literacy rates, lower infant mortality, less obesity, less corruption, better life expectancy (although both countries have done well over the last seventy years, increasing life expectancy from about thirty-two years to greater than sixty years), higher manufacturing output (India is now sixth in the world), faster growth of international tourism, lower public debt and markedly lower dependency on the International Monetary Fund. However, both remain poor countries and India still faces the daunting task of pulling 200 million people out of poverty.

Independence did not solve the internal conflict over languages in India. Without doubt it fired up the debate as to what should be the 'national language' of India. Although there was heavy pressure applied from the north – sometimes called 'Hindi imperialism' – that Hindi should be the national language, the Indian constitution is silent on this issue but accepts that there are twenty-two so-called *scheduled* languages, and acknowledges the importance of English and two other European languages, French and Portuguese. More than 70 per cent of the *scheduled* languages are Indo-Aryan in origin and about 20 per cent are Dravidian, again reflecting the diversity of the Indian population which has developed over several millennia.

Because of economic growth, India has improved the accessibility to healthcare and made some impressive gains in literacy, accepting that these socio-economic improvements are not distributed equally across the nation. The pathway to this success has not always been smooth, as judged by the series of wars with Pakistan, the associated acts of terrorism and the politically driven, high-level political assassinations of Mahatma Gandhi (1948), Indira Gandhi (1984) and her son, Rajiv Gandhi (1991), and Benazir Bhutto, former Prime Minister of Pakistan who in 2007 died during an attack on her car with gunshots and a bomb. The exact cause of death is disputed.

Perhaps one of the most interesting facts of the post-Independence period is the insatiable appetite that the British appear to have to engage ever more closely with Indian history, its culture and religions, music and fine art and its cuisine; sometimes called 'popular orientalism'. I have explored many of these aspects earlier in this book, citing numerous examples of Booker Prize-winning novels set in India, an abundance of popular drama and documentary films that continue to fill our small and large screens, which now seems to be an unstoppable force. It might be argued that 2017 was a special year, and thus the spawning of a plethora of BBC TV offerings is easy to understand. To name but a few: *My family, Partition and Me: India 1947*, *The Ganges with Sue Perkins*, *Dangerous Borders: A Journey across India & Pakistan*. ITV also joined in with *Joanna Lumley's India* when she revived early memories of her birthplace. But this interest had started decades before. Important film contributions include *Sacred India* by Sangha Productions (2005), which follows the lives, pilgrimages and other activities of some of India's most holy

Muslim, Hindu, Sikh and Jain religious sects. During the last decade, the BBC ran several TV series about India such as, *India with Sanjeev Bhaskar* (2007), *The Story of India with Michael Wood* (2007), *Indian Hill Railways* (2010–12), *Caroline Quentin: A Passage through India* (2011), *The Real Marigold Hotel* (2016), *The World's Busiest Railway* (2015), *Sue Perkins in Kolkata* (2015), *Treasures of the Indus* (2015) and *Rick Stein's India: In Search of the Perfect Curry* (2013). Most recently we have had Channel 4's offering, *Indian Summer School* (2018) in which four unlikely British lads, who have for different reasons failed to engage with education at their local schools, are given the opportunity to study again for their GCSEs at the elite Doon School (attended by the Gandhi brothers and many distinguished Indians), set in the foothills of the Himalayas. 2018 also saw the BBC 4 TV documentary, *The Stolen Maharaja*, which charted the story of Duleep Singh, the last Maharaja of Lahore, focusing particularly on his relationship with Queen Victoria. In the same year we saw the frivolous but enjoyable BBC2 documentary, *Bollywood: The World's Biggest Film Industry*, which includes coverage of the story of a new wave of white British dancers leaving the UK to seek their fortune as 'film stars' in Mumbai. Finally, ITV has broadcast *Beecham House* (2019), a TV drama series created and directed by Gurinder Chadha, set in late 18th-century India, which plots the progress of fortune hunter, John Beecham. I would contest that this enduring fascination is not the norm for most former British colonies that gained independence at around the same time or a little later. It is the scale of this interest that I find remarkable and still wonder what draws so many of us to want to understand more about this nation. This profound interest, perhaps passion, for Indian history and culture, must be more than just a simple nostalgia for *things past*, as most of the individuals who have first-hand experience of imperial India are no longer with us.

Similarly, Asian UK immigrants and their progeny have been very successful in exploring the process of incorporation and adaptation into their new home and creating a genre of creative work that has been highly respected and that has attracted many distinguished awards. I would name just a few of the creators, such as Sanjeev Bhasker, Meera Syal, Gurinder Chadha, Monica Ali, Hanif Kureishi and Ayub Khan-Din. This work is devoured equally by all of us living in Britain and is not merely something that has been served up for the immigrant community. I accept totally that people from the Indian subcontinent are not the only diaspora to have written about colonial and postcolonial experiences, but for me it is just a question of scale.

FICTION

Fiction set in India has added to our understanding of some of the tricky issues of the times, such as inter-racial relationships, something that social historians might have found difficult. Some British people were attempting to discover the *real* India explored through the novel and historical fiction. It is not entirely clear as to what is meant by the *real* India, but I interpret this as a search for an authenticity which a cosseted colonial lifestyle could easily exclude. 'I want to see the *real* India,' says Mrs Moore in *A Passage to India*; 'I want to see it too, and only wish we could,' responds her travelling companion Miss Adela Quested. What is the real India? Forster leads us to believe that finding the real India involves meeting and talking to Indians. When Mrs Moore suggests to Dr Aziz that she might take him to the Club, he reminds her that 'Indians are not allowed into the Chandrapore Club, even as guests.' At the time, this was the convention of the day and it would be some decades before the old traditional clubs would open their membership to Indians. Although the English worked closely with Indian colleagues in the civil service and in the army, and an English elite would mix socially with Indian political leaders and the heads of princely states, close social interaction and true friendship would seem to have been relatively limited. Lucy Smalley of Scott's 'Staying On', during a visit to the fictional princely state of Mudpore, says 'this is the *real* India, the India that is of palaces, peacocks and gorgeous clothes'. This perhaps traditional, romanticised view differs from her next-door neighbour, Mrs Bhoolabhoy, the manager of Smith's Hotel, who has a more pragmatic view: 'there are many Western tourists in search of the real India as well as hippies who have found it and are having sex.'

Nevertheless, authors, particularly those writing in English, have been fascinated by inter-racial relationships notably, Forster (*A Passage to India*), Scott (*The Jewel in the Crown*), Jhabvala (*Heat and Dust*, *The Man with the Dog*, *In Love with a Beautiful Girl*), and Kaye (*Far Pavilions*). These stories describe relationships between Indian men and Englishwomen but not exclusively so. In *A Passage to India* Forster describes a close, but non-sexual relationship between Dr Aziz and the male college lecturer, Fielding, between whom there are several delicate moments of intimacy which span the entire narrative. We should remember that Forster's muse for Aziz was his adored friend of seventeen years, Masood, to whom he dedicates the novel and longed throughout their relationship to have achieved greater intimacy.

Scott's abrasive, dysfunctional character, Ronald Merrick, eventually reveals his homosexuality when he searches the bazaar for young boys; he is finally murdered by a young male servant in his own household.

At this point, we should not forget that for more than 200 years the British introduced the subcontinent to its own language, English. Arvind K. Mehrotra, Indian poet and literary critic, edited the scholarly volume, *A History of Indian Literature in English* (2003) which spans the last two centuries, seeking out the massive body of literary work, in this case written by largely Indian authors; for the rest, just Kipling, Forster and the nature writers Jim Corbett and Kenneth Anderson get a mention. In the first paragraph of his introduction to the book he discusses British domination of India; 'The introduction of English into the complex, hierarchical language system of India has proved the most enduring aspect of this domination.' He also reminds us of W.B. Yeats' often quoted view that 'no man can think or write with music and vigour except in his mother tongue'. True or untrue? He was referring to the writing of poetry, but Mehrotra's edited collection of essays would certainly not support this belief with respect to literary fiction.

FANTASY

At last I am free to speculate as to why things had or had not occurred in the way they did. A time to explore how dreams and fantasies found their way into the creation of modern India and in the telling of the stories that bring these moments into our lives today. The question that constantly turns in my mind is why Queen Victoria never made a visit to the 'jewel in her crown'. She sent the Prince of Wales to India in1877 for the Delhi Durbar after she assumed the title of Empress of India. This was a period when the journey by sea to India could be achieved in under two weeks and when Abdul, her *munshi*, was at the peak of his influence in her service and could have combined a royal visit with a family holiday in Agra. The conundrum seems to be rarely discussed, but I can only assume that her political advisers were concerned at least in part about security. Within three years of her coronation in 1838, Victoria survived eight attempts on her life by seven assailants, all of which took place in England. Furthermore, she did not have a 'Prince Regent' in whom she had confidence, so may have been reluctant to leave British shores for what could have been two or three months. Perhaps her commitment to recreate India in Osborne House was a substitute for experiencing the *real* India.

Following Victoria's death, there were clear indications that the British Raj and its wider empire were on borrowed time. While there were elements in the British Government after World War I which acknowledged that a planned orderly transfer of power was inevitable, there were others who could not countenance the loss of India and the wider consequences that this would have on the continuing stability of the British Empire. Gandhi's return to India in 1915 had a profound influence on the independence movement; he had a dream for a united India, with a 'small government' and a return to village values and self-determination. The dependency on British cotton cloth infuriated him. His peaceful civil disobedience movement was difficult if not impossible for the Government of India to manage.

The first major disaster that followed the rising tide of nationalism and the yearning for freedom was Brigadier Dyer's catastrophic decision to slaughter hundreds of innocent and unarmed protestors in the locale of the Sikh temple in Amritsar. O'Dwyer, the Lieutenant Governor of Punjab, was a hardliner and an arch imperialist; this would be the lesson that would finally quell any thoughts of independence and Dyer would seem to have agreed with him. It is a complete mystery, however, how having had many weeks to reflect on the outcome of his intervention Dyer calmly said to Parliament in answer to the specific question, that he would have used machine guns had he been able to gain access to the Bagh with his armoured vehicle. In *Midnight's Children*, Salman Rushdie chose to arm his soldiers with machine guns when all other accounts indicated that they were armed with rifles; perhaps a device of magical realism? Walter Reid, in his analysis, *Keeping the Jewel in the Crown: the British Betrayal of India* (2016), is clear that Britain only hung on to power by force, determined to maintain the provisions of the Government of India Act of 1919 in which 'India should remain an integral part the British Empire'. In the mid-1930s it became abundantly evident that this approach would not work in the long term, hence the evolution of the 1935 Government of India Act which assumed an all-India Federation which included the princely states. Rather than bringing the parties together, the Act heightened tensions between Hindus and Muslims concerned about the balance of power that the Act would dictate. This drove a wedge firmly between Hindus and Muslims, making the pathway to partition increasingly well defined.

Mahatma Gandhi had a dream for India: a free, independent nation peacefully integrated across its religious and regional divisions. A fractured India did not feature in this dream. At the end, when independence was in sight, he compromised, and with Nehru and Jinnah agreed that the nation should be divided. Following Independence and the freedom that followed, it is interesting to speculate as to why so many Indians and Pakistanis left the subcontinent in the 1950s and have continued to do so ever since. Indians constitute the largest diaspora worldwide with about thirty million living outside India, the largest gatherings in the Middle East (Gulf countries), the USA and the UK. The main driver appears to be economic enhancement. Indians now constitute about 2.3 per cent of the UK population, with 12 per cent of British doctors are of Indian origin. Immigrants from Pakistan and later from Bangladesh came in the 1970s and together now contribute about 1.9 million people (2.6 per cent) to the UK population. Although integration of Indians, Pakistanis and Bangladeshi's into the UK population is by no means perfect, representation in the British Parliament following the 2017 General Election is almost proportional to the number of people whose families originated from the subcontinent.

The relationship between Britain and India has changed substantially since I first visited fifty years ago. Now, both nations have dreams – new dreams – for the future. As Britain seeks greater independence from its European partners (Brexit) to find a new future which includes re-establishment of its sovereignty and laws, India has, for several decades, opened its doors seeking greater global engagement. Britain needs to reflect and be honest about its dependencies on other nations during the past four centuries and cherish the relationships that enabled its former success. The future is in partnerships, not 'splendid isolation'. As that Indian friend reminded me, some years ago, 'the future is brown, light brown'.

REFERENCES AND BIBLIOGRAPHY

Books (fact, fiction and fantasy), films and TV documentaries, fine art and other sources of inspiration that have made the writing of *Finding India* possible:

PREFACE

Hilary Mantel, Reith Lectures 2017

Howard Hodgkin interview, 1982 (YouTube) and *Howard Hodgkin: Painting India*, Hepworth Gallery, Wakefield, Yorkshire, 2017

Ronald Segal, *The Crisis of India*, 1965, Penguin Books

Ronald Segal, *Sanctions against South Africa*, 1964; International Conference on Economic Sanctions against South Africa, London, 14–17 April 1964

James Cameron, *An Indian Summer*, 1974, Macmillan

J.G. Farrell, *The Hill Station and Indian Diary*, 1981, Weidenfeld & Nicolson

George Orwell, *Why I Write*, 1946. Penguin Books, 2004

Walt Whitman, *Passage to India* (1872)

PART 1: IN THE BEGINNING

Juan Mascaro, *The Upanishads*, 1965, Penguin Books

Juan Mascaro, *The Bhagavad-Gita*, 1962, Penguin Books

V.S. Naipaul, *A Wounded Civilisation*, 1976, Random House

Paul Theroux, *The Great Railway Bazaar,* 1975, Hamish Hamilton

PART 2: OVER THE MOON

Those Magnificent Men in Their Flying Machines or How I Flew from London to Paris in 25 hours and 11 minutes (Film) 1965, Director Ken Annakin

Ramchandra Guha, *India After Gandhi*, 2007, Macmillan

PART 3: THE HOSPITAL IN THE VILLAGE BY THE SWAMP

The Thief of Baghdad (Film), 1969, Director Shriram Bohra

Satyam Shivam Sundaram (Film, Love *Sublime*), 1978, Director Raj Kapoor

Karma (Film), 1933, Director J.L. Freer Hunt

Cecil Cutting, *Hot Surgery*, 1962, London Missionary Society

Leonardo Mata, *The Children of Santa Maria Cauqué*, 1978, MIT

Charles Bitot, *Gazette Medicale de Paris*, 1863

The Casebooks of Dr John Snow (1813–1858), 1994, Wellcome Trust

PART 4: TEMPLES, TIGER COUNTRY AND TEA

Indian Hill Railways, BBC 4 TV, 2010

Edward Lear, *Indian Journal*, 1954, Coward-McCann

Mollie Panter Downes, *Ooty Preserved: A Victorian Hill Station*, 1967, Hamish Hamilton

E.M. Forster, *The Hill of Devi*, 1953, Edward Arnold

Dorothy Clarke Wilson, *Dr Ida: Passing on the Torch of Life*, 1959, Friendship Press

Denis Kincaid, *British Social Life in India, 1608-1947*, 1973 Routledge & Kegan Paul

E.M. Forster, *Passage to India*, 1924, Edward Arnold

36 Chowringhee Lane (Film), 1981, Director Arpana Sen

Cotton Mary (Film), 1999, Directors Ismail Merchant and Madhur Jaffrey

V.S. Naipaul, *An Area of Darkness*, 1964, André Deutsch

PART 5: A PERIOD OF ADJUSTMENT

Tennessee Williams, *Period of Adjustment* (Play), 1960

William Gooddy, *Time and the Central Nervous System*, 1988, Praeger

Nirad C. Chaudhuri, *The Continent of Circe*, 1965, Jaico Publishing House

PART 6: FILMING IN THE FOOTHILLS

Brief Encounter (Film), 1945, based on the one-act play by Noel Coward, Director David Lean

Paul Scott, *Staying On*, 1977, Heinemann

Staying On, Granada TV, 1980, Director Silvio Narizzano

Paul Scott, *The Raj Quartet* (The Jewel in the Crown, 1966; The Day of the Scorpion, 1968; The Towers of Silence, 1971; A Division of the Spils, 1975; G.K. Hall)

The Jewel in the Crown, Granada TV, 1984, Directors Christopher Morahan and Jim O'Brien

Gandhi (Film), 1982, Director Richard Attenborough

Far Pavilions, HBO and Goldcrest TV, 1984, Director Peter Duffell

Indian Summers, Channel 4 TV, 2015–16, Directors multiple

Irene Shubik, *Play For Today: The Evolution of Television Drama*, 2000, Manchester University Press

My Beautiful Launderette (Film), 1985, Director Stephen Frears

Budha of Suburbia, BBC2 TV, 1993, Director Roger Michell

East is East (Film), 1999, Director Damien O'Donnell

Bhaji on the Beach (Film), 1993, Director Gurinder Chadha

Viceroy's House (Film), 2017, Director Gurinder Chadha

Pamela Hicks, *Daughter of Empire: Life as a Mountbatten*, 2012, Weidenfeld & Nicolson

Walter Reid, *Keeping the Jewel in the Crown: The British Betrayal of India*, 2016, Berlinn

PART 7: MINGLING WITH MAHARAJAS

Rudyard Kipling, *Letters of Marque*, 1891, H.H. Wheeler

James Cameron, *An Indian Summer: A Personal Experience of India*, 1987, Penguin

E.M. Forster, *The Hill of Devi*, 1953, Edward Arnold

Wendy Moffat, *E.M. Forster: A New Life*, 2010, Bloomsbury

E.M. Forster, *A Passage to India*, 1924, Edward Arnold

Mulk Raj Anand, *Private Life of an Indian Prince*, 1953, Hutchinson

Maharaja (Film), 1998, Director Anil Sharma

Ruth Prawer Jhabvala, *Heat and Dust*, 1975, John Murray and Merchant-Ivory film, 1983

Nirad C. Chaudhuri, *The Autobiography of an Unknown Indian*, 1951, Macmillan
William M. Thackeray, *Vanity Fair*, 1848, Bradbury & Evans

PART 8: INTO MODERN INDIA

Yann Martel, *Life of Pi,* 2003, Random House. Film, 2012, Director Ang Lee
Lee Langley, *A House in Pondicherry*, 1995, Heinemann
David Walker, *Harry Black*, 1956, Collins
John Masters, *To the Coral Strand*, 1962, Collins
Louis de Bernières, *Birds Without Wings*, 2004, Harvill Secker
Satyajit Ray, *Apu Trilogy* (Films 1955–59) and *The Philosopher's Stone* (Film 1958)
Rudyard Kipling, *Kim*, 1901, Macmillan

PART 9: GAZING BACK AT THE HORIZON

L.P. Hartley, *The Go-Between*, 1953, Hamish Hamilton
Walter Scott, *Waverley*, 1814, Archibald Constable
Khushwant Singh, *Train to Pakistan*, 1956, Grove Press
Howard Brenton, *Drawing the Line* (Play), 2013, Nick Hern Books
Spike Milligan, *Puckoon*, 1963, Anthony Blond
Kurban Said, *Ali and Nino*, 1970, Hutchinson
Manohar Talegaonkar, *A Bend in the Ganges*, 1964, Hamish Hamilton
Chaman Nahal, *Azadi*, 1975, Houghton Mifflin
Salman Rushdie, *Midnight's Children*, 1980, Jonathon Cape
Anuk Arudpragasam, *The Story of a Brief Marriage*, 2016, Granta
R.K. Narayan, *Waiting for the Mahatma*, 1955, Methuen
Bali Rai, *City of Ghosts*, 2009, Doubleday
Downton Abbey, TV series (episode 8, season 5), 2014, written and produced by Julian Fellowes
Jallianwala Bagh (Film), 1977, Director Balraj Tah
The Legend of Bhagat Singh (Film), 2002, Director Rajkumar Santoshi
Phillauri (Film), 2017, Director Anshai Lal
Anita Anand, *The Patient Assassin: A True Tale of Massacre, Revenge and The Raj*, 2019, Simon & Schuster
William Dalrymple, Anita Anand, *Koh-i-Noor: The History of the World's Most Famous Diamond*, 2017, Bloomsbury
The Stolen Maharaja – Britain's Indian Royal, BBC 4 TV, 2018
Shrabani Basu, *Victoria and Abdul: The True Story of the Queen's Closest Confidant*, 2010, The History Press
Victoria and Abdul (Film), 2017, Director Stephen Frears
Queen Victoria's Last Love: Abdul Karim, Channel 4 TV documentary, 2012, Director, Rob Coldstream
Lytton Strachey, *Queen Victoria*, 1021, Chatto & Windus
John Masters, *Night Runners of Bengal*, 1951, Michael Joseph
M.M. Kaye, *Shadow of the Moon*, 1957, Longmans
Bhupal Singh, *Survey of Anglo-Indian Fiction*, 1975, Curzon
J.G. Farrell, *The Siege of Krishnapur*, 1973 Weidenfeld & Nicolson

PART 10: MEMORIES, DREAMS AND REFLECTIONS

C.G. Jung, A. Jaffe, *Memories, Dreams, Reflections*, 1963, Collins and Routledge & Kegan Paul

Herman Hesse, *Siddartha*, 1922, *Magister Ludi* (The Glass Bead Game), 1943, *Demian*, 1919, *Steppenwolf*, 1927

Passage to India (Film), 1984, writer and director David Lean

John Masters, *Bhowani Junction*, 1954, Michael Joseph

John Masters, *To the Coral Strand*, 1962, Michael Joseph

Ruth Prawer Jhabvala, *Miss Sahib, In Love with a Beautiful Girl*, and *The Man with the Dog*, published as a collection of short stories in *A Stronger Climate*, 1968, John Murray

Arundhati Roy, *Ministry of Utmost Happiness*, 2017, Hamish Hamilton

Mark Tully, *No Full Stops in India*, 1991, Viking

V.S. Naipaul, *In a Free State*, 1971, André Deutsch

A Passage to Britain, BBC2 TV, 2018, Yasmin Khan

Mulk Raj Anand, *Untouchable*, 1935, Wishart

Shashi Tharoor, *Inglorious Empire: What the British did to India*, 2017, Penguin Books

Niall Ferguson, *Empire: How Britain Made the Modern World*, 2002, Allen Lane

Jeremy Paxman, *Empire*, 2011, Viking

Kartar Lalvani, *The Making of India: The Untold Story of British Enterprise*, 2016, Bloomsbury

Brian Lapping, *End of Empire*, 1985, Granada

David Gilmour, *The British in India: Three Centuries of Ambition and Experience*, 2018, Allen Lane

Arundhati Roy, *God of Small Things*, 1997, IndiaInk

EPILOGUE

My Family, Partition and Me: India 1947, BBC1 TV, 2017

The Ganges with Sue Perkins, BBC1 TV, 2017

Dangerous Borders: A Journey Across India and Pakistan, BBC2 TV, 2017

Joanna Lumley's India, ITV, 2017

Sacred India, 2005, Sangha Productions, Directors F. Solton, D. Rabotteau

India with Sanjeev Bhaskar, BBC TV, 2007

The Story of India with Michael Wood, BBC2 TV, 2007

Indian Hill Railways, BBC4 TV, 2010–12

Caroline Quentin: A Passage Through India, ITV1, 2011

The Real Marigold Hotel, BBC1 TV, 2016

The World's Busiest Railway, BBC2 TV, 2015

Sue Perkins in Kolkata, BBC1 TV, 2015

Treasures of the Indus, BBC4 TV, 2015

Rick Stein's India: In Search of the Perfect Curry, BBC2 TV, 2013

Indian Summer School, Channel 4 TV, 2018

The Stolen Maharaja, BBC4 TV, 2018

Bollywood: The World's Biggest Film Industry, BBC2 TV, 2018

Beecham House, ITV, 2019

Arvid K. Mehrota, *A History of Indian Literature in English*, 2003, Hurst

Richard Cronin, *Imagining India*, 1989, St Martin's Press

Ralph J. Crane, *Inventing India: A History of India in English-Language Fiction*, 1992. Macmillan